Further praise for *What Is the Grass*

"[Mark] Doty puts on a clinic in how to read closely but expansively. . . . This is shining proof that criticism can make you want to hold it close."
—John Freeman, *LitHub*, Most Anticipated Books of 2020

"[A] masterful example [of the hybrid memoir]—weaving a close reading of Whitman's life and writings into Doty's own ruminations on art, queerness, humanism, and the American experience."
—Arianna Rebolini, *Buzzfeed*

"[A] dazzling and discursive meditation on Walt Whitman's poetry. . . . In this homage to a poet whose voice has become a 'permanent presence' in his head, [Doty] has written a masterpiece, one that is as rapturously fine as the book he so lovingly and intelligently elucidates."
—Phil Gambone, *Gay and Lesbian Review*

"Exuberant. . . . This is Doty at his best: In gorgeous, calibrated sentences, he evokes the flourishes and sprung rhythms that make Whitman so contemporary."
—Hamilton Cain, *San Francisco Chronicle*

"*What Is the Grass* is a deep dive into Walt Whitman's life, work, worldview, and something that feels like his cosmic theology. As if that weren't enough, we're also invited into Mark Doty's own candid self-seeking, in episodes of the author's life rendered in generous complexity. This beautiful, ingenious book affirms my belief in language as a living thing, and in the universe as a place overflowing with purpose and meaning. I wish all of the great poets could be reintroduced to me in such fashion!"
—Tracy K. Smith

"Quick-witted, slyly erotic, and sometimes ecstatic, this book explores Mark Doty's relationship with Walt Whitman, or with the idea of Walt Whitman. It is intimate in its reality and in all that it imagines, and it captures with splendid lyricism the author's generous obsession with his forebear. Mark Doty has written a literate and lovely volume."
—Andrew Solomon

also by MARK DOTY

WHAT IS
THE GRASS

WALT WHITMAN
IN MY LIFE

Mark Doty

W. W. NORTON & COMPANY
Independent Publishers Since 1923

Copyright © 2020 by Mark Doty

Pages 22–23: Frontispiece and title page for the first edition of
Leaves of Grass (Library of Congress). Courtesy GPA Photo Archive.
Page 34: Daguerreotype Portrait of Walt Whitman, 1853
from The New York Public Library.

For information about permission to reproduce selections from this book, write to
Permissions, W. W. Norton & Company, Inc., 500 Fifth Avenue, New York, NY 10110

For information about special discounts for bulk purchases, please contact
W. W. Norton Special Sales at specialsales@wwnorton.com or 800-233-4830

Manufacturing by Lake Book Manufacturing
Book design by Fearn Cutler de Vicq
Production manager: Lauren Abbate

Library of Congress Cataloging-in-Publication Data

Names: Doty, Mark, author.
Title: What is the grass : Walt Whitman in my life / Mark Doty.
Description: First edition. | New York : W. W. Norton & Company, [2020]
Identifiers: LCCN 2019044569 | ISBN 9780393070224 (hardcover) |
ISBN 9781324006053 (epub)
Subjects: LCSH: Doty, Mark. | Poets, American—20th century—Biography. |
Whitman, Walt, 1819–1892—Influence. | Whitman, Walt, 1819–1892—Appreciation.
Classification: LCC PS3554.O798 Z46 2020 | DDC 811/.54 [B]—dc23
LC record available at https://lccn.loc.gov/2019044569

ISBN 978-0-393-54141-0 pbk.

W. W. Norton & Company, Inc., 500 Fifth Avenue, New York, N.Y. 10110
www.wwnorton.com

W. W. Norton & Company Ltd., 15 Carlisle Street, London W1D 3BS

1 2 3 4 5 6 7 8 9 0

The best use of literature bends not toward the narrow and the absolute,
but toward the extravagant and the possible.

Mary Oliver, Upstream: Selected Essays

—•••—

Who knows but I am enjoying this?
Who knows but I am as good as looking at you now,
for all you cannot see me?

Walt Whitman, "Crossing Brooklyn Ferry"

CONTENTS

CONTENTS

WHAT IS
THE GRASS

APPARITION

Walt Whitman spent his final years in a two-story, wood-frame house on Mickle Street in Camden, New Jersey, less than half a mile's walk from the Delaware River, though in those days, after his debilitating stroke, he'd have been pushed there in his wheelchair by an attendant. Mickle Street long ago became Mickle Boulevard, then Dr. Martin Luther King Boulevard, a wide thoroughfare that funnels drivers through an inner city's battered edge toward attractions along the river, south of the Walt Whitman Bridge: a ferry dock, a bandshell for concerts, an aquarium with jellyfish and sharks.

The street was bristling with life the year of my first visit, 1996, though the towering Camden County Correctional Facility—windowless, anonymous brick—rose just across the street from the yellow clapboards of the poet's house. What message was intended, to the boys and young men diving after each other in mock battles, playing basketball on the edge of the street, hanging out on stoops or narrow porches outside the rowhouse doors? Whitman's place seemed set apart, as though it breathed the quieter air of another day, and the neighbors ignored it.

The house, now a museum operated by the state, keeps limited hours. You ring the bell and, if it's an open day, are admitted by a docent, pay an admission fee, and are offered a pamphlet about the poet and his history. I hear that the place has been polished a bit in the twenty years since my visit and has more of a professional sheen. But the way it looked then is indelible—in part because when I went back, not long ago, I'd forgotten to call ahead, and the place was closed. I had to content myself with looking around outside, and noticing how many of the neighboring houses were gone now, grassy lots in their place. The people were gone, too, though the jail façade had lost none of its faceless solidity.

No matter, really, that I'd found the doors locked; I could remember that first time. I loved the honey-colored light filtered through the shades, and his leather backpack, wonderfully crumpled. The old man's bed upstairs, heaps of books and papers on the floor around it just as he might have left them. Not, I'm a little embarrassed to report, unlike the floor of my own writing studio, where chaos can hold sway for some time before the rage to order coincides with the time to actually do something about it. The few rooms open to visitors were occupied by display cases filled with rather dutifully framed documents: letters from important persons, newspaper clippings, and invitations to banquets in the poet's honor, complete with menus.

Across the river that long-ago morning, in the American Literature Collection at the Rosenbach Museum and Library in Philadelphia, a helpful librarian cheered me on, pressing into my hands Isadora Duncan's copy of *Leaves of Grass*. The famous bohemian had danced these poems, as it were, found in them the pulse of her own freedom and nerve. She styled herself as a "Barefoot Classical Dancer," emulating poses on Grecian urns and the Parthenon friezes with an unrestrained physicality, an exuberant, "natural" sort of movement. Though she was detained on Ellis Island with her new husband, the Russian poet Sergei Yesenin, and denounced in Washington as a "Bolshevik hussy," she launched an American tour, and in 1922 danced barefoot in Cleveland in Attic costume, one breast bared. The young Hart Crane was in the audience that evening; the poet wrote to a friend that among all who attended, he was the sole spectator who had applauded.

Walt Whitman, Isadora Duncan, Hart Crane: could a list of artists be more American? Visionaries, outsiders and exiles, sexual pioneers, half-cracked, devoted wholeheartedly to unconventional notions of beauty, each longed for community and kindred spirits, and each stood mostly alone. They created the template of the American artist, who stands, as E. M. Forster wrote of the great Greek poet C. P. Cavafy, "at a slight angle to the universe." Ignored, often reviled in their own times, they've come now to embody them; their singular lights turn out to have been illuminating the way ahead all along. Add to their number Joseph Cornell, Marsden Hartley, Georgia O'Keefe, Gertrude Stein, Langston Hughes, Marianne Moore, Gwendolyn Brooks (a far more experimental poet than she's generally thought to be), Jack Spicer, Eileen Myles, and trace the sturdy vine of an American tradition. What can be seen from the margin—from Brooklyn Ferry or its inheritor the Bridge, from the unexpected vistas available from the Acropolis or Ghost Ranch, the florid modernism of a Paris salon or cheap East Village rooms in the 1970s—makes its way toward the center, opening pathways for a larger culture.

But it was hard, that afternoon in the cluttered house on Mickle Boulevard, to feel any sort of vitality transmitted forward. Whitman's family had left nearly all his possessions in the house. Too many mementos of the public life, stuff that might have gone into the scrapbook or attic of an elder poet wanting to be reminded who he once was. (Before you hear too much of a snarl in that comment, be aware that I have boxes of such material myself.)

I moved from one scrap of paper to another, feeling my interest drift. I heard the raucous banging from the street, the yawps of kids, the skittering pops of firecrackers. It was high summer, after all. Why linger in the archive, pages grown yellow in the warm amber leaking through the window shades? *If you want me again*, the poet had written, *look for me under your bootsoles.* What could be the point in wandering here, among these dry bits of evidence, looking for—what?

Then, on the topmost shelf in a glass display case, what I'd never have expected: a stuffed bird, a bit dilapidated, but poised and alert as taxidermy could manage. A deep, pleasing green. A conure maybe, a lorikeet, some sort of small parrot? He looked cheerfully and expectantly out at the world forever from a wooden box sealed with a pane of glass of its own, as though he were the occupant of a construction by Joseph Cornell. His eyes were glass, the liquid originals long lost to time. Firmly dead as he was, maybe all the more so for having been made immortal, he was nonetheless the first sign of the actual life lived here.

Intimate moment, breathing air.

I hear the little fellow's no longer on exhibit; a friend who'd gone especially to see him told me the bird had been moved to storage, or sent off for restoration. Moldering, perhaps, after all those years. I stared into his box. I thought of him climbing up a wool-sleeved arm toward Walt's shoulder, where he could sit there above the famous open collar. Then I did something I imagine we all do far more than is usually acknowledged: I slipped out of myself for a moment. I was looking through the eyes of that green friend when those eyes were still living gel. I saw the pinkish, wrinkled skin of a robust old man's neck, right before me, comforting, and suddenly I could smell his warm skin, dusted with talc from his bath.

•••

I DON'T MEAN that I saw Walt Whitman's ghost, not exactly; I have never quite made up my mind as to what of any individual self might go on after death. I've seen a man I loved die, and it seemed to me a pure liberation, neither an erasure nor something to fear, though it's difficult to hold on to that perception. But whatever becomes of us, surely every life creates echoes afterward, both in the physical world and in the intangible one. The dead reappear, in memory; I see something that reminds me of my mother (a silver bracelet embedded with a mosaic of turquoise, the kind of cracked or mossy flowerpots that appeared in her paintings) and some aspect of her affections, her interests, is with me now, forty years since she's been gone. We know that energy cannot be destroyed, but goes shape-shifting through the world. What was once in some portion that star is me now, and later I may be some strong supporting cells in the neck of an August lily, or the glint in the stem of a new-blown piece of glass. If our lot is mutability of form, then why be surprised that our energies might not be refracted and recurrent in the world: Walt Whitman looking back through light caught in a stuffed bird's convex, artificial eye?

The dead persist audibly in language. My parents' Southern figures of speech show up sometimes in my own: *She hopped on that like a hen on a june bug.* I don't, in fact, know what a june bug is, and am not sure I've ever seen one, but the phrase has lodged in me, in my lexicon, one of the places past and future are distinctly, inextricably interwoven.

Interwoven seems the right word for the way the language of poetry remains in the awareness of readers. Years of reading Whitman have led to the permanent presence of his voice in my physiology; dozens of phrases of his rise up in me, unbidden: *I sound my barbaric yawp over the rooftops of the world; it is not upon you alone the dark patches fell; I considered long and seriously of you before you were born; I might not tell anybody, but I will tell you.* I could go on—and reader, I will.

A poet is made, for us, of words, become so translated into the substance of speech as to dwell there, a presence caught in the prismatic, permanent life of lines and stanzas and memorable phrases, like the bubble of air captured in that most elegantly named of tools, the spirit level. What is it, then, when I see, as if looking right through that language I have internalized, the shoulder and arm of a man emerged, a hundred and fifty years ago, from his bath? *Time avails not,* Whitman wrote, *distance avails not.* Nothing too far away, nothing too long ago.

•••

DOES SEEING AN APPARITION come with a responsibility? Gift or summons, what might this echo of Walt Whitman want of me? There may be many answers to that question, but I'd begin with this one, the same thing he wanted from us when he was living: company.

I mean that seriously. What poet ever addressed his readers so often and so directly? A digital scan of his work reveals that the single word most used in his poetry is not the *I* we might have expected but *you.* The spiraling, edgeless "Song of Myself," his first great poem, ends *I stop somewhere waiting for you.* He waits for us because his poem requires us, because it is no ordinary poem, in the usual sense of an aesthetic object complete in itself. It *is* a poem, a remarkable one, but it's also a call to change our way of seeing self and other, a persuasive text that aims to revise our understandings of the most basic things. The poem wants to accompany us in the direction of awakening. If it were written by practically anyone else it could seem monumentally arrogant, the product of an ego without bounds, but Whitman instructs us that *I am not contained between my hat and my bootsoles;* this is the voice of a self without limit. And such a self must include, by nature, you.

You are included, from the beginning. Why be surprised, then, if a long-dead poet appears on an August afternoon, freshly bathed as he liked to be, and you catch a glimpse of his living body through the eyes of a companion bird he loved? If you, through some quirk of presence, are even allowed the scent of his warm, just-powdered skin?

——•••——

OF THE MANY POETS I LOVE, none has haunted me as Walt Whitman has. I want to keep company with him, in this book, want to account for his persistent presence in my life. And I want to try, at the same time, to seek out the wellsprings of the extraordinary flowering that seemed to appear out of nowhere in the middle of his life, in poems that look, sound, and think like nothing else before them. They have already reshaped American poetry, and the poetry of other countries and continents as well, but they have not yet finished their work of recasting our sense of what it means to be oneself, to be anyone at all.

THE
FIRST
SOURCE

ON THE
EXTREMEST VERGE

When Walt Whitman walked through Brooklyn Heights—
a sharp-aired morning, say, in the newly minted spring
of 1855—headed toward the printing office of his friend Andrew
Rome, did he know what he was carrying? I like imagining
him, a large, roughly handsome man who appears older than
his thirty-five years, the sense of purpose in his stride more pro-
nounced as he approaches the shop at the corner of Fulton and
Cranberry (an intersection that no longer exists, since the two
streets were reconfigured, in the twentieth century, with the
creation of Cadman Plaza). I picture a portfolio under his arm,
pasteboard sides covered in cloth like the green binding he'd
choose for his first edition, a ribbon closure tied to keep the pages
in place. Around him the traffic of shoppers and deliverymen,
errand boys, a few finer carriages, horse-carts clattery and pleas-
ingly fragrant, vendors' voices darting between the open spaces
in each other's repetitive declarations of what's for sale. Brooklyn
brisk with possibility, sky rinsed a powdery blue. Adventurous
little wind from the harbor, a chill still lingering on the shaded
sides of streets. Ordinary business: the world as it constructs itself
day after day streaming by.

Do his steps quicken or slow as he draws nearer the printer's
door? Some acquaintance greets him as he passes, but the poet

barely notices. His attention is fixed on the brink on which he's poised, the condition of about-to-become—himself. In a moment a wave of potential, the expansive dreaming overflow of his text, will crash against the marble threshold and begin to become a singular fact: his longed-for, dreamed-of book.

—•••—

WHEN I WAS TWENTY-FIVE, I went to a writers' conference, my first, on the California coast, on an Edenic Santa Cruz campus of yellow grassland pouring down the slopes to the sea. There were workshops and readings, and a good deal of staying up till one could drink no more, convivial nights of long talks—most often about our wish to become ourselves as writers, whatever that might mean, about longing, our deep desire to feel complete, real to ourselves. I made a raft of friends: a lean and intense fiction writer trying to find her way inside a novel that eluded her; the West Coast editor of *Playgirl,* a joyful, zaftig beauty who wore metallic caftans and shared with me her delicious, slender little cigars. It was 1978, I was still married, and secretive about my longing for men, but I had a mad crush on a warm, bearish man whose every gesture seemed to spread sweetness and good humor; like the *Playgirl* editor, he occupied space with notable delight in being a body. Toward the end of the gathering he told me, in an embrace flushed with wine and heat, that if he hadn't been having an affair with the woman across the hall from my room he'd have been with me. That would have been possible? I was dazed, and so happy with the idea that such a thing could have happened I honestly didn't mind so much that it hadn't.

There was another set of events, too, richer and stranger. The poet William Everson—the elder, animating spirit of the place, who had once been Brother Antoninus, a Dominican monk who renounced the order to pursue both art and pleasure—offered a series of meditative lectures, a loosely structured performance over several mornings called "The Birth of a Poet."

At an hour on the early side for apprentice writers, still groggy, we would troop down the hill toward a space deemed conducive to inwardness. Could it really have been called the Kiva, or have I invented that the way I have Walt Whitman's wide-awake stroll in that splendid Brooklyn spring? Everson himself was Whitmanic: streaming white hair, generous beard and eyebrows to match. He wore old jeans and a shearling vest over his white shirt, fleece turned inward against the coastal damp, the leather beaded and sketched in dark lines with animals and stars. It had been given to him, he said, by his friends among the Kiowa. In one of the two pockets in front resided a smallish bottle, a pint of the Jack Daniel's he would not be without.

Much of what he said I've forgotten. Certainly he described his spiritual vocation, how the calling to the monastic life and the calling to poetry were in fact the same thing, perhaps misheard at first, understood differently over time. He talked about his hero Robinson Jeffers, the great poet of that coastline, a fierce and lonely man with a touch of granite both in his profile and in the chill around his heart, who lashed out at his own species and wrote of beautiful "hurt hawks" because he could not bear the pain we inflict on one another, or the injury that must have been done to him. As great poets do, he found a way to transmute the personal wound into something larger. His rejection of human company became a way to love stone and wind and time, the grand elemental forces made visible on the bluff in Carmel where he built his own stone tower of a house. The surf and stones of Big Sur, if not larger than time or quite outside of it, were of a scale commensurate with the ages. I used to think I could never take pleasure in imagining the earth after the Anthropocene. But as the damage we've done grows clearer every day, I find myself in greater sympathy with Jeffers's position; his poems take comfort in the world going on without us, our petty scrawlings on the face of the planet all swept away. Even stone towers? Probably.

Like Whitman, Everson was also a printer. He told us about his printing press, the cold metal of it, the way setting type brought one closer to the body of the poem. How he'd made an edition of Jeffers's poems, each copy housed in a case of Monterey cypress; into the cover of each he'd inlaid a polished square of granite from Tor House itself. Many sips of whiskey between all this, pauses while Everson waited for the next thread to come clear. A little shuffling, circling dance, some coughs, some pacing, a sip of whiskey, and in a while a new direction emerging from the last.

Here is what he said that I've never forgotten. The movement of the soul is vertical, he claimed, descending into the world, and when we become incarnate, as Christ the model and exemplar of the human form did, then our vertical motion intersects with time, with the horizontality of the temporal world. When a book is made, then, the life of the maker is nailed, as it were, to the intersection of those two lines. *In the book*, he said, *the self is fixed, made concrete; the book is the intersection of the soul and time.*

•••

IN A QUIET ROOM for researchers at the Library of Congress, on a quiet August afternoon, I sit at a table alone while a helpful and solicitous librarian—glad, I think, for those thrilled by the proximity of great books, *the intersection of the soul and time*—brings me a copy of each of Whitman's first editions. I open the cardboard slipcover of the first, and hold in my own hands the oversized, thinnish, slightly unwieldy book, set it down into the foam cradle the librarian has provided, open the cover, and turn to the first page of the first poem. The hands of a man I love, dead so many years before I was ever born, have touched this page, and set these letters into type. In the blank space between stanzas, I can feel the forward motion of his thinking slowing, seeming to pool here, gather, until it spills over into the next stanza. In some places the type is "broken," a printer's term for when the ink does not fill the black form of the letter evenly; a hairline crack of white shines through, or a dapple of bare paper's left visible. Sometimes a little extra bit of ink pools at the top of a letter, or in a period. I know it's the mechanism of printing that has made these rough marks, making this page feel handmade, allowing me to touch the letters and feel their impress into the weave of the paper. (Don't be alarmed, the Library doesn't ask one to wear gloves. Gloves have been found to do more harm than good when handling archival material.) A poet, Whitman wrote, in the preface to this 1855 edition, *glows a moment on the extremest verge.* It seems to me that glow is pouring through this page, from behind it, even through the broken type, so bright the words seem nearly tattered and burned by it.

THE AUTHOR OF THOSE PAGES had a third-grade education, if the endless recitation of drills that comprised Brooklyn public schooling in the 1830s can be called that. At eleven, the age around which many boys of his era began to work and learn a trade, he apprenticed to a printer. In the years before the publication of his book he'd work as a printer and journalist (a common combination at the time), an itinerant schoolteacher in small Long Island towns, a bookseller, a carpenter, a builder of houses. Had he died before that curious, oversized first edition of *Leaves of Grass* was published, it's unlikely we'd ever have heard his name.

You'd think *something* in the early work of Walt Whitman would suggest the intelligence and scope, the sly wit and visionary luminosity of the pages stacked and wrapped in his ribboned portfolio. When he made his agreement with Andrew Rome he was thirty-five, and his publications consisted of a handful of forgettable poems and a larger quantity of windy prose: editorial pieces, melodramatic short stories, an urban mystery serialized in newspapers, and a clichéd temperance novel. But there's nothing at all to make us suspect that this man will write a decent poem, much less reinvent American poetry. He would pay to publish his book, write many of the reviews of it himself, sell precious few (if, in fact, any) copies, and then go right on to publish a second edition. Who'd have thought it would be a book that we have never finished reading? One that would be translated into every language in which poetry might be read, a book people scattered around the globe are holding at the moment you read this page. One he never finished writing, but simply revised and expanded until it was stretched, some thirty years later, into a lumpen thing, almost beyond recognition. A book of presumption and daring, expansiveness and wild ambition—one with a few antecedents, yes, but nonetheless startlingly original, unlike anything that had been written before.

Where on earth did it come from?

You can ask that question of any poem, and one inevitable answer is a simple one: work. No made thing springs up unbidden, even those that seem to. The poem that announced itself to the intoxicated Coleridge, before a knock at the door banished most of it from his memory, or the composition that sprung full blown into the head of Mozart, as he stepped down from a carriage after a satisfying dinner, *seemed* to pour from the artist's hand, so long schooled those hands had become. But years of labor inform those spontaneous productions. Though a poem over which one struggles may seem labored, it often prepares the way for new writing in which what's been learned emerges with an effortless grace.

In the end, though, work accounts for a poem of genius about as much as plumbing accounts for the fountains of Rome; it yields a necessary basis, the practical scaffolding that underlies the whole, but cannot in itself engender a sense of transport. To shift the figure from water to another element: labor may give a poem a ruddy glow, but no amount of it will set the page on fire.

The great poems of *Leaves of Grass* are spectacularly, uniquely on fire. There are, I admit, only a handful of them, although one is long enough that you can wander in it like a labyrinth, uncertain of where you're headed, but gradually, undeniably arriving someplace entirely new. The brilliant midcentury American poet and critic Randall Jarrell wrote that "a good poet is someone who manages, in a lifetime of standing out in thunderstorms, to be struck by lightning five or six times; a dozen or two dozen times and he is great." Who besides Shakespeare might have been struck by lightning two dozen times I cannot say; even in the life's work of many of our greatest poets, a few dazzling, electrical flashes are brighter than all the rest. We think no less of John Keats because he didn't write more of those odes, or of Elizabeth Bishop because her final collection, *Geography III*, wasn't longer.

And what daring, heat, and light Whitman's masterworks emit! They proceed with absolute confidence to make the wildest claims, inventing a cosmogony, a theology, a stance toward reality. They burn with evangelical urgency yet insist that no one requires a spiritual teacher. They find the basis for a social compact in the common bedrock of the desiring human body, and sing the inclusive, generous, common self in a mode so formally inventive that its first readers must have wondered if this was poetry at all. The combination of unbridled content and unfamiliar form seems to have left even readers of undeniable acumen in the dust. Emily Dickinson is said to have taken a peek inside and then firmly closed the book; Henry James noted, with devastating simplicity, "This will not do." I would like to think that writers of such genius, whatever they may have said, recognized as kin the astonishing outpouring of work that appeared from the hand of

a self-educated "rough" from Brooklyn, but there is no evidence
that they did. There is surely an uncomfortable sort of admiration
and kinship expressed in a letter from the great, tormented Jesuit
poet Gerard Manley Hopkins though: *I always knew in my heart
Walt Whitman's mind to be more like my own than any other man's living. As he is a very great scoundrel this is not a pleasant confession.*

•••

HOW COULD THIS STRANGE BOOK not have offered to its author
a hundred separate possibilities for uncertainty, even for doubt
of a particularly corrosive, self-lacerating kind? A book with no
author's name on the cover or title page, with a densely printed,
rather florid preface followed by twelve poems. *Were* they poems?
No consistent meter, no comfortable and familiar pattern of
rhyme. Not to mention the fact the book's opening salvo is a diz-
zying sixty-five-page text, the sheer rock-wall of it divided only
by stanza breaks. The sweeping lines, colloquial and Biblical at
once, seem meant to carry us from earth to—well, not heaven
exactly, but the earth seen in radical illumination. *I believe a leaf
of grass*, he writes, *is no less than the journey-work of the stars.* He
mocks religion while proclaiming the world holy. He loves being
incarnate, relishing sheer physicality—to walk, to feel the movement of atmosphere on one's skin—and the thrilling energies of
eros, the firefighter's fine muscles moving under their clothes. His
feints and silences are so transparent that they reveal at least as
much as they conceal.

Here's a quick example. The speaker, at the end of one stanza
in "Song of Myself," is thinking about the way he moves among
those who remember him:

*Picking out here one that shall be my amie,
Choosing to go with him on brotherly terms.*

Then we have a stanza break, and look where the poem goes:

> A *gigantic beauty of a stallion, fresh and responsive to my caresses,*
> *Head high in the forehead, wide between the ears,*
> *Limbs glossy and supple, tail dusting the ground,*
> *Eyes full of sparkling wickedness . . .*

That's a perfectly accurate description of a spirited horse, but it comes just a bit of white space after *brotherly terms*. It's useful to remember that "stanza" is Italian for "room," and that as we walk through the rooms of a poem, our experience of each space colors our perception of the next. *Responsive to my caresses, glossy and supple limbs, eyes full of sparkling wickedness:* surely the poet's sexy, playful description of this *gigantic beauty* is intended to make us read those *brotherly terms* in a new light.

What the poet is doing here doesn't quite qualify as hiding. A reader uninterested in—or unaware of?—same-sex desire could simply miss it. That simple stanza break allows us not to tie that animal body to a desiring human one if we don't want to. The poem plays on a sort of margin; I think it's fair to say that Whitman is enjoying this game, sporting in a mode of self-disclosure which will be read clearly by those who want and in fact need to read "between the lines." What scandalized readers in Whitman's time was his frankness about heterosexual bodies, and his portrayal of women as sexual beings. Only those alert to same-sex desire seemed capable of reading a deeper level of scandal in the poems, a "secret"— shared in broad daylight but largely unreadable—that was for them more nourishing than any other text of their time.

This peculiar, daring book, not even finished that morning when Whitman carried his manuscript into the printer's office, still to be added to, and quickly revised, and at odds in form and content with essentially everything in print in its day—how could it not have racked its author with uncertainty?

I am not sure if, during the trance of composition in which Whitman wrote the greatest of his poems, he entertained a doubt at all. "Song of Myself" offers no evidence that he held a single reservation, or feared that he could not say what he needed to. (He does at one point doubt the capacity of *language* to say what he means, but that is not the same thing as mistrusting one's own ability to use it.) In the 1855 edition, the poem doesn't yet bear the title the poet would later settle on; it's not clear that it has a title at all. It swells, drifts, eddies and circles back; its pages are divided into stanzas, but no section breaks divide the reading experience into manageable units. The reader's tossed headlong into a cascading, seemingly edgeless text in which it's nearly impossible to find one's bearings.

Mornings over the first few months Whitman would appear at the printer's office, read the paper, talk, assist, and in between commercial jobs, set at least some of his own pages in type. Andrew Rome's brother and business partner James had died just months before, and the aggrieved printer must have welcomed the company. His shop mostly printed legal forms of one kind and another, and when in July he issued the company's first book, oversized, its pages resembled the paper they must have also used for wills, contracts, and promissory notes. Two hundred copies, and then eventually some seven hundred in all, would be carried to a nearby bindery, a few bound in paper, the rest stitched, glued, and bound in green cloth, with the letters of the title stamped in gold: *Leaves of Grass*.

———•••———

THE THIN, OVERSIZED BOOK WAS, to put it plainly, weird. It was bound in green cloth, and stamped in gold with roots, branches, and grain woven together to form the letters of the title, in imitation of a popular book, *Fern Leaves from Fanny's Portfolio,* by Whitman's friend Sara Willis. Under the name Fanny Fern, Willis published newspaper columns widely read by and circulated among women at mid-century. So widely, in fact, that her first book had sold some seventy thousand copies, from which she earned a dime apiece—enough to land her financial independence and a townhouse in Brooklyn. Whitman admired her, not the least for her success.

Open Whitman's book, and after the obligatory white page (a visible moment of silence) is the engraved image of a man, not one a poetry reader of the time would have expected to meet. No gentleman in serious clothes, authority backed by laden bookcases, maybe a classical bust looming behind. No romantic in a loose cravat looking dreamily toward the empyrean, tethers to earth loosened by fevers or opiates.

The engraving was based on a photograph of Whitman now lost, which is unusual in that he was photographed often, and carefully saved these images. Here he's a slouch-hatted workman, outfit and demeanor radically informal; his undershirt shows behind his open collar. It isn't easy to name the attitude his facial expression and posture convey. Certainly there's a relaxed quality in the tilt of the pelvis, the easy way his shoulders fall, and the slouch of the hat. But the angle of the face, the narrowed eyes and slightly raised eyebrows have a quality of assessment about them. Is he taking our measure? You could take that hand on the hip as a cocky gesture, as if he's looking us up and down and saying, Well, who are you? *Affectionate, haughty, electrical,* he writes, *I and this mystery here we stand.*

Haughty and *electrical* I can see, but *affectionate?* Not a quality this image suggests, but what I'm reading as an evaluative gaze may in fact be a not altogether successful representation of something else—the look of one still dreaming, the way new infants sometimes seem still to gaze upon something they've not yet fully left behind?

Leaves

of

Grass.

————◆————

Brooklyn, New York:
1855.

No author's name is given, on the cover, spine, or opening pages, save for, in the tiniest of italic fonts in the center of an Antarctic page, these words: *Entered according to Act of Congress in the year 1855, by WALTER WHITMAN, in the Clerk's office of the District Court of the United State for the Southern District of New York.* You have to reach page 29 to find Walter Whitman's new name, the name of the man he became to write these poems: *Walt Whitman, an American, one of the roughs, a kosmos.* Imagine self-publishing your first book and not putting your name on it! Asked about this oddity years later by his worshipful young secretary Horace Traubel, the elderly poet replied, I suspect quite sincerely, "It would have been like putting a name on the universe." In other words, he is not, in the usual sense, the author, or not entirely so; *Leaves of Grass* is a kind of collaboration with totality, and Whitman believed wholeheartedly that it was given to him. Although disguised as a volume of parlor verse in its decorous binding, the book was from its inception a provocation, an assault, an outcry, a gospel. I like to imagine those pages, before they were set into type, the energy not yet released from them compressed until it would explode, in a movement that continues unabated as I write, one hundred and sixty-four years later.

NOTHING THAT
HAS CEASED TO ARRIVE

The fountaining outpouring of *Leaves of Grass* was fed by five sources, five streams. These currents, which can't entirely be separated from one another, give the book its remarkable freshness; its best pages breathe an air perennially new. They fired Whitman's confidence and his daring; they were the fuel that allowed his work to rocket forward, and enabled him to reinvent himself as something the world had not yet seen: a truly American poet.

The first of these—and here I mean "first" in terms of primacy, not of sequence—was an experience, or more likely a set of them, of transforming character, loosening *the doors from their jambs* and demanding that the poet approach what it was to be "myself" in an entirely new light. We don't have a good vocabulary for these experiences. They come in variations and degrees, from a slight apprehension of the strangeness of being to the ravishing dissolution of boundaries called enlightenment. A mystical experience, a peak experience, a blurring or merge between self and other, a liberation from the limits of space and time. When Whitman wrote of the poet working on that *extremest verge,* surely this is what he meant.

I make a claim no historian can validate; how could we prove anyone's experience of heightened consciousness? Inferring from the work back to the life is suspect; it underestimates the power of artifice, suggesting that only someone who had this particular sort of experience could write about it. As Philip Levine once said, Shakespeare was neither a king nor a Roman, but somehow he got it right.

But what makes those kings and Romans matter to us is neither their crowns nor their empires; they touch and captivate because they are, in different costume, *us*. What you can know about Shakespeare from those plays is that he had a rich subjective understanding of the will to power, of ambition and its consequences, and of the thirst for justice. Walt Whitman's great poems embody two essential human experiences as fully as any poems I know: the joyous and burning fact of being a desiring body among other bodies, and the sense that, at its core, the self is without boundary. *I am not contained between by hat and my bootsoles*, he tells us. If this is so, then where *am* I contained?

There are radiant moments in Blake, Rilke, Proust, and Flaubert in which the division between subject and object dissolves away, resulting in a barely communicable joy. You can find luminous traces of this state in the ecstatic poetry of many traditions, but who ever held this light up as long and as steadily as Whitman did, or made it seem so ordinary and human? He left no account of the sort of experiences I suggest, no letters or prose journal, and needless to say no one observed them. The evidence lies in the way the poems radiate an experience of the unbounded. In Section 5 of "Song of Myself," he offers this narration:

> *I believe in you my soul, the other I am must not abase itself to you,*
> *And you must not be abased to the other.*

> *Loafe with me on the grass, loose the stop from your throat,*
> *Not words, not music or rhyme I want, not custom or lecture,*
> *   not even the best.*
> *Only the lull I like, the hum of your valved voice.*

You can feel the hand of Whitman the printer here; his lines proceed in a calm, measured fashion, and he places his stanza breaks with clear purpose: in those white spaces or moments of silence he is thinking, allowing subtle shifts in time, in placement in the physical world, in the pitch and tone of his voice, even in his choice of addressee.

That first stanza, with its direct address to the soul, is of a piece with much of what's come before in the poem so far— effusive, and not grounded in any particular moment or place. We've been listening to a rhetorical performance, more oration than narrative. But *Loafe with me on the grass* begins to shift things; whose voice does the speaker want to hear? As the next stanza begins, "you" now seems to be someone in particular, a lover:

> *I mind how we lay in June, such a transparent summer morning,*
> *How you settled your head athwart my hips and gently turned over*
>   *upon me,*
> *And parted the shirt from my bosom-bone, and plunged your*
>   *tongue to my bare-stript heart,*
> *And reached till you felt my beard, and reached till you held my*
>   *feet.*

This is the first story told in "Song of Myself," the seed from which all the rest springs. What was an invitation has shifted to a memory; *we lay in June, such a transparent summer morning* complicates the pronouns considerably: is that *we* the speaker and his soul still? Or is "my soul" suddenly revealed to be an endearment, a term of love for a beloved other? Or a term of identification? Any time a poet uses the pronoun *you*, the word to some degree attaches itself to the reader, and certainly Whitman addresses his readers directly over and over again in "Song of Myself." Does he really mean to say that once he lay beside whoever holds this book now, that he has been beside us, in some warm transparent morning? *Transparent* is such a perfect adjective here I'm almost convinced.

You and *I* will blur into one another so many times in the pages to come that the question of just who lay on the grass beside whom will become entirely moot. *You* is no phantom but firmly embodied, and positioned, in a startlingly direct passage, to kiss the speaker's bare chest. If one hand holds the feet and the other the beard, it's pretty clear where the head must be— right in the middle of the body, positioned nicely for oral sex. Which lends a whole new dimension to *Loose the stop from your throat;* the valves of the voice will open, it may be, in more ways than one.

Now comes another stanza break loaded with event. What happens in that silent white space? Tender sex, presumably, and the bliss that ushers the speaker into a remarkable experience of elevation and identification with all things.

> *Swiftly arose and spread around me the peace and knowledge that*
> *pass all the argument of the earth,*
> *And I know that the hand of God is the elderhand of my own,*
> *And I know that the spirit of God is the eldest brother of my own,*
> *And that all the men ever born are also my brothers, and women*
> *my sisters and lovers,*
> *And that a kelson of the creation is love,*
> *And limitless are leaves stiff or drooping in the fields,*
> *And brown ants in the little wells beneath them,*
> *And mossy scabs of the worm fence, and heaped stones, and elder*
> *and mullen and pokeweed.*

That is one of the most beautiful sentences in American poetry, and one of the most confident sentences in any poem in English. The mere fact that it *is* a single sentence conveys author-ity: it never hesitates. Whitman begins in the past tense (*Swiftly*

arose and spread around me . . .) but the knowledge this experience conveys resides firmly in the now, continuing and ongoing.
He includes the phrase "I know" twice, and every single thing
named is an instance of something the speaker knows, with certainty, from the heightened perspective that has been granted
him. He moves swiftly from sex to knowledge to a kinship with
God, and from there to all men and women, and from there to all
of creation. *Elderhand*, a compounding of Whitman's invention
with a note of awe in it, might be the loveliest neologism I know.
A *kelson* is the long central beam in a wooden ship, holding the
ribs in place; the image suggests not only that the creation is
ordered and unified by love, but that, like a ship, it's going somewhere, and carries us all forward in a common direction.

Had this passage ended grandly, I wouldn't be half as inclined
to believe it. But after Whitman's announcement that love is a
structural element of the universe comes an unlikely diminu-
endo, as he turns from that height to the tiniest things: drooping
leaves and ants and mossy scabs. These too are illuminated by the
compassionate knowledge that has flooded the poet's body, as he
arrives at a kinship not only with the divine, and with other people; *heaped stones and elder and mullen and pokeweed* are all swept up
in that same love.

———•••———

IN SOME WAYS, the gender of the lovers in this glorious passage
truly doesn't matter; out of this tender coupling, out of this bodily
pleasure arises an experience out of the body, a profound felt connection to all of creation, which seems to shine with an orderly
coherence, to possess the deep strength of a vessel structured by
love. In that light the speaker can understand that his own hand
is an embodiment of the divine, a co-instrument of creation, and
that even the least of the world's elements is to be seen in the full
measure of its reality, understood as limitless.

But suppose this visionary, undeniably Edenic state arose from a sexual experience one had been taught was at best unmentionable, perhaps nonexistent, at worst reviled, condemned as sick or evil, a twisted expression of wounded souls which was by its nature offensive to God? How same-sex desire was understood in Whitman's day, and how that understanding shifted in Whitman's lifetime, is a complex, sometimes vexing subject I'll come to later on. Here I simply want to suggest that the most profound sense of peace, of compassion and of affirmation, has appeared in a place where one did not expect to find it, and this surprise must be an aspect of the speaker's unmistakable joy.

———•••———

MY CLASSES CENTER ON POETRY, but since poems show us again and again that form and content can't really be separated, we find ourselves talking about language and technique *and* about every kind of experience a poem may represent. Poetry exists to find words for what resists easy naming; we are most often driven to write it or read it when any other sort of language seems incapable of the work required.

When I mention experiences of boundlessness, or a sense that "I" is not the singular me cordoned off from the world by my own edges, I find that my students tend to nod appreciatively. They often express degrees of recognition, as opposed to the sort of silence likely to indicate that they think I've lost my mind. Such experiences appear in or flicker around the edges of every life; we are mysterious to ourselves, and often sense that there are depths we can't easily sound, or that the origins or destiny of the human reside somewhere in a silence we carry within us. Wallace Stevens honored no deity but the human imagination, but he asserts at the end of "The Idea of Order at Key West" that it is in poetry we might find

Words of the fragrant portals, dimly-starred,
And of ourselves and of our origins . . .

Visions are not as far from ordinary life as we sometimes think, and artists need to live as if revelation is never finished.

I have sometimes slipped the familiar bonds of myself. Or, to say it differently, I've felt myself a participant in the limitless, as though I'd set down, for a little while, the bound-in-his-skin biographical self I think I am. The most powerful of these experiences happened in 1970, when I was seventeen. I'd been trying on various kinds of spiritual practice, both because I had a hunger for them and because such interests were in the cultural air I breathed. I was eager, too, to escape from a difficult family scene, and some stubborn part of me was refusing to be held down or diminished by the grief and damage that marked the household where I sometimes lived. But I can't see the experience I had in the mountains above Tucson that year in psychological terms; it wasn't a symptom of anything. I'm as certain as Walt Whitman in the three stanzas above that what I experienced came from what Gerard Manley Hopkins called "the dearest freshness deep down things."

Ruth and I had driven up into the Santa Catalinas, the mountains north of Tucson, to escape the heat. We'd stopped maybe two-thirds of the way up, at a picnic site by the roadside, high enough up the mountain that manzanita and dry thickets had given way to cooler air and evergreens. There were picnic tables among the firs, and open areas where one might spread a blanket and lie down under branches and glimpses of open sky with a few big shining clouds, and not a soul there but us. We were easy in our relationship at that moment; I was trying on heterosexuality, and doing better at it than I'd thought I could; and she was liking having a young boyfriend, we enjoyed each other's company. (Of course I knew she was older than me, but she was always vague as to how much, and in those days I understood her vagueness to be an aspect of her charm.) We'd brought a cooler with sandwiches and a jug of ice tea or lemonade, maybe we had a beer; I think I remember an embroidered Mexican blouse she wore, in a sort of peasant style. She was reading, as always in those days, for her graduate exams, and perhaps she read something to me. After eating and talking, and maybe making out a little, she went back to reading silently, and I lay on my back on the blanket, resting, my eyes half open.

In a little while I became aware of a young tree, a shapely fir a few yards from the edge of the blanket, perhaps my height or a bit taller. As I took it in I began to sense it had a kind of substantiality about it; it was *there,* a being in the world, if that makes any sense. I mean that in myself I felt its presence, and in some interior fashion that involved a gesture of consciousness, I acknowledged its presence.

Then the tree acknowledged me back. How could I have ever expected that? It felt precisely as if the wave of interest and regard I had sent to the tree was returned to me, easily, simply. I was more delighted than startled. We were alive in the world together, the young tree and I; I was young too; we were kin; we were centers of energetic awareness in an energetic field . . . the sense of it begins to slip away as I try to say what happened and the words multiply. Well, not the sense, the sensation.

I felt simply that we two were alive at once, and that we took pleasure in being aware of one another.

Part of that pleasure was a kind of delighted laughter, on my part. Because what I had taken to be not alive, or at least not conscious, and not a part of myself, was in fact intently awake, and looking at me as I did at it, in friendship, in greeting. Then I realized that every tree I could see in the pine grove was equally alive, and equally not inert to me or apart from me as I had believed. We were here together, as were the clouds overhead, and the late sunlight slanting through the rims of them, and the pitchy cones resting on the pine-scented floor of shed needles . . . *mullen and pokeweed.*

And then a roaring began, in the treetops, as of wind, as if everything were stirring in a mounting storm that wasn't there, and a great energy was stirring in me, an opening out, and I must have moved or made some sound, because Ruth said something then, and I began to come back down into myself. Though not without a sense of shine to all things—a feeling that persisted for hours—and a fresh, inexplicable happiness.

I feel no embarrassment or discomfort in telling you this, save for this last part. Back in the car, driving down the mountain, Ruth said, *I keep smelling incense.* And I knew what she meant, because for me the air was perfumed with it too, the lovely ancient scent of sandalwood. Why should that detail embarrass me? I suppose because it seems to claim some external validation— we *both* smelled it—as though that were the point, to offer some proof of my joyous hour of grace. There's no proving such things; they reside in subjective awareness, part of the way we know for a few minutes or an hour, whatever length of time some door seems to stand open. I have no idea how long that experience and its afterglow lasted. I don't want the gift of sandalwood to seem like some special claim. I believe such experiences are available and not uncommon, though we pave over the way to them with so much distraction and tension and desire. It was something that happened to me; it came out of nowhere, and never returned in just that way again. For all I know the odor of sandalwood may be latent everywhere, waiting to be noticed.

•••

IN EVIDENCE, THIS PHOTOGRAPH. It was taken by a Brooklyn photographer, probably Gabriel Harrison. It's a daguerreotype,

which means that the subject would have needed to hold this position for two minutes, in order to avoid blurring. Look at this face, and imagine that length of holding still, holding this expression. Or imagine, perhaps, this expression on your own face at all. We know instinctively how to convey all sorts of emotion through facial expression, but this one—what can it mean, how do you read it?

I would say first of all that this gaze is not directed toward the photographer, nor contained within its moment of exposure. This face looks far beyond the minutes in which the picture was taken; it arrives in the present from a considerable distance. Its power to hold our attention rests in the eyes, which are clear and magnetic and look through us to something beyond the viewer. As I look from the eyes to the slight smile and then back to the eyes again, it seems the distance between this face and the world is lit up by love. It's a look that pours out compassion, and if it betrays a certain weariness or impatience, that quality is softened by tenderness. Often nineteenth-century portrait photographs have a feeling of absence about them, the subject sealed off from us, entombed by the image, a captive of time lost. Not this one. There is nothing *over* about this face, nothing that has ceased to arrive in the present.

EVERY ATOM

At the beginning of the astonishing sixty-five-page sprawl he'd later call "Song of Myself," Whitman swept aside anything he'd written before, as if with one powerful gesture he pushed off his desk everything no longer useful to him. What went crashing to the floor? His own tentative early poems, and the expected forms and decorum of American poetry. Where does a poet find such courage, the will and stamina to make a radical beginning? It must lie in an internal imperative to give form to the inchoate: something that hasn't been spoken, not yet articulated in a way that resonates with the felt texture of experience. The unsaid can be the source of an enormous pressure, a nearly physical need to say what living is like. If the poetic vocabulary of one's day, the stances and forms of the hour, don't seem capable of incorporating the way the world feels—well then, the pressure is intensified. Perhaps that's why the three opening lines of Whitman's poem, and of his book, seem to geyser out of the depths; he has waited so long to find them, for these words to emerge as if from nowhere:

> *I celebrate myself,*
> *And what I shall assume you shall assume,*
> *For every atom belonging to me as good belongs to you.*

Thus Whitman introduces the man he has become or invented to the world. A useful edition of Whitman edited by Robert Hass, *Song of Myself and Other Poems*, includes a lexicon that defines unfamiliar words in the title poem and explains what ones that *seem* familiar meant in Whitman's day. Hass notes that in 1855 *celebrate* meant more an act of religious observance—"the priest celebrated the Eucharist," for instance, or "the family celebrated Passover"—than it suggested either happy affirmation or throwing a party.

The poet's first action here is to praise, affirming and elevating his own body and soul, but from his second line it's plain that the notion of self here will not go uncomplicated.

And what I assume you shall assume is an act of performative speech, the kind of bold assertion (like "I now pronounce you man and wife") in which something becomes true because a person in authority says it is. The source of this authority, at this very early point in the poem, is perhaps only the speaker's confidence. *Assume* can mean to suppose, taking some premise as a given, or it can mean to take something on, as in to assume power, or you might take responsibility for something not originally yours, as in assuming a debt. Thus the line could be taken as supremely arrogant; why should we think or feel or take on the responsibilities the speaker in this poem does? How would he have any way of knowing? His assertion doesn't make sense until the line that follows: *For every atom belonging to me as good belongs to you.*

Poetic imagination isn't usually directed by the will. Some other part of the self seems to go forward on its own as—beginning in image or metaphor or music, a phrase that floats up and sticks in the mind—a poem begins. Stanley Kunitz used to say his poems began in sound, and sense had to fight its way in. Whitman's poems, in his great early heyday, seem to have begun in voice. I'd guess this new and commanding speaker and his headlong assertions simply rose up in Whitman. He'd have had to figure out who it belonged to; this tone and manner seemed to bear no relation to anything else he'd written. This speaker has two boots planted firmly on the ground, and stands at his full height. The sweeping confidence in these opening lines sets the tone for the entire outpouring to follow.

Who is it this voice addresses? It seems too big and public to be directed toward a lover or a friend, and yet there's an intimacy about it, too. You wouldn't say *every atom belonging to me as good belongs to you* to just anyone. It feels too personal for that, a claim of radical proximity—though it's also a sly reminder that atoms don't belong to anyone. They don't hold still, so what's a part of you today may not be tomorrow. On that level of reality what would ownership mean, anyway?

If all atoms are held in common, then differences between us are immaterial: the color of your skin, your gender, your material wealth, the degree of privilege any of these grant you—as immaterial, on the atomic level, as whether you were born in Gdańsk or Havana. Whitman says that our assumptions—what we understand, what we take into ourselves as we read his poem—can be the same *because* we are constituted in the same way. Is this true? The poem declares that this is a foundational truth for the pages to follow, that the poem operates under this law.

These three lines also establish the poem in the present tense. Whitman's not telling us about something that already happened; his poem operates in the now, and seems to report on thinking, feeling, and perception. Along the way we'll hear short narratives of remembered experience, family stories, even the tale of a sea battle the speaker's heard about. But the body of the poem seems spoken in the moment of its composition, which lends the voice a living edge, and helps to account for the poem's aura of timelessness. Because the text acknowledges the present tense of its own making, the reader seems to receive it in that same present tense, or at least a contiguous present. This is an aspect of Whitman's modernity, anticipating what readers find in the poems of Frank O'Hara and James Schuyler, who likewise trace the motion of awareness, out to say how it feels to be alive from moment to moment.

Who talks this way, or has such an easy relationship to certainty? Who is this man to celebrate himself? From its very beginning, the poem asks us to take up the question of who this *I* might be. That first sentence is so direct and authoritative as to make it seem an article of faith, a proclamation nailed to the poem's door. A thesis statement is a risky place to start anything other than a brief essay for English 1, a poem most of all, but Whitman emblazons one of the poem's guiding principles right at the start. He wants us to know this is no ordinary poem. Not a lyrical evocation of feeling, not an account of an experience leading to an epiphany, not a moral lesson nor a hymn of praise—though it will contain all those things. The model of "Song of Myself" is rhetorical, and oratorical: a principle has been stated, and thus the poem has set up the work ahead of it to convince us that this axiom is true.

Which is more off-putting, praising yourself in the first poem in your first book, or beginning it with a one-sentence distillation of your theme? *What I shall assume you shall assume* seems almost peremptory at first; who dares to dismiss our difference, and say we'll play along, accepting—even if just for the duration of the poem—his notions? This is the first instance of Whitman's most seductive gesture. He asserts that the speaker knows something we do not, although this realization is available to us, and he will lead us toward it. He likes giving us a glimpse of our future: *I will be even with you, and you shall be even with me*, he writes a few lines later, and then, a page later, this remarkable promise: *Stop this day and night with me and you shall possess the origin of all poems.*

There are readers who don't want to be told what will happen to them, who resist being included in this way or dislike the idea of being subsumed in a larger, collective self for which this voice seems to speak. For many others these claims are both tantalizing and compelling; the writer seems to know we are here, not as a collective gaze but as *I* and *I*, or *you* and *you*; the poem feels spoken to each of us in particular, and has a quality of inevitability about it: *Stop this day and night with me* is an invitation to respond now, at the moment you read that phrase, and it continues with promise and prediction: and *you shall possess the origin of all poems*.

The poem, speaking from its continuous present into our moment of attention, seems always to know that you, its reader, are there. You will not go unseen.

THE ELDERHAND

At Crane Beach, north of Boston, near Ipswich, I walk miles on a spit of dunes not much changed from the way I'd guess it must have looked for centuries: marsh and beach grass, hummocks of bayberry and beach plum, groves of scrubby juniper and oaks. I have a long walk back, after the rain begins, and duck into the changing shed to shower and get dry and warm a little while.

But once I push open the metal door marked MEN and enter the room in which I'd imagined—what? A few lockers, wooden benches—I seem to step out of the daily world. It's the same thing poetry does, opening within the ordinary a space where time pools or stills, and something blazes up out of the familiar.

The steaming room smells of warm water, wet flip-flops, bathing suits—everything rubbery and damp, so much moisture that light through the fogged glass in the roof glows through swathes of steam. Scents of lotion, talc, sneakers. Skin.

And so much of it: men sit on benches, stand to change, lean against walls, wait for the showers, wait for the rain to stop. Old men sit on the bench, ropy arms and curving bellies, shoulders bent forward, arms resting between their knees. Boys too small to be still, wriggling bodies brown from the sun. Pale men, shoulders dusted with freckles, cheeks and foreheads pinked by the day; black men so dark their bodies shine blue. Every solid or mottled shade, every girth and height, naked or nearly so, united by their sudden proximity as they wait out the heavy rain drumming the roof.

It feels like a box of pulsing, masculine life. Overwhelming physicality, so much of the flesh in one place it seems to be of the soul. Not erotic exactly, unless it is an aspect of eros to be made aware that you are a quantity of skin in a larger field of skin, as if a brushstroke in a painting might be made aware of itself as one of the uncountable strokes that comprise the whole. A plethora of strokes. The word I want to use here is *pleroma,* a Gnostic term for the fullness of all that is divine; it means the totality of God, who is darkness and silence, and only knowable through the aspects of divinity that come into the light out of that fecund absence, a "space" that is not a space.

TOWARD THE END of his impossible, magnificent signature poem, Walt Whitman seems to be dissolving into the song of himself, sinking into the ground beneath our feet, becoming part of vapor and dusk, even part of the bodies of his readers: he will *filter and fibre your blood,* he writes,

> *I depart as air, I shake my white locks at the runaway sun,*
> *I effuse my flesh in eddies and drift it in lacy jags.*

Of all the things one might do with one's own body, to "effuse" seems among the most unlikely. What can he mean? So much flesh, in that steamy crowded room, that somehow the bodies seem more physical, more palpably made of matter— how could one drift one's flesh there, *in lacy jags?* Among so much skin that it somehow doesn't seem individual any more, but a kind of collectivity of skin?

This is crucial to Whitman's poem—not just the swirling, circular outpouring of "Song of Myself," but the great structure he seems to be building, his best work all facets of a single whole—this claim for the fluidity and instability of the body and the self.

Do you feel it, your self as a tenuous construct, your body a temporary and unstable outpost of consciousness? I do, without being able to name this perception in a way that feels quite right—or not able to say it easily, anyway. English grammar supposes a stable object, a stable subject to be acted upon: *I throw the ball to Ned.* At that moment my dog Ned and I are doing something together, engaged in throwing and catching, so my sentence is an attempt to describe a collaborative process, but the structure of my attempt ignores the connection of the two involved, and makes the subject, me, most important, implying that it's my will, my action that matters most.

If in fact I focus on the "I" that's doing the throwing, I'm not likely to throw the ball very well. Immersion in the moment puts the verb in the foreground, something more like *Throwing/catching ball we.* The more engaged you are, the less aware you are of yourself. This is why one sometimes sits down to write, sidling up to the work at hand, and then in a while looks up at the clock to find that hours have passed. Self-consciousness fades as we become completely engaged in the present, in the way that children lose themselves in the boundless materials of sand, water, or clay. *Playing* is a pale verb for what they are actually doing, which is more like what Elizabeth Bishop called "a perfectly useless, self-forgetful concentration." It would not be unlikely to find that a child playing alone in beach sand *effuses* or that her awareness drifts *in lacy jags.*

I AM NOT CONTAINED between my hat and my bootsoles.

Begin with the body: water, vapor, air. You're the shore on which an ocean of air is constantly breaking, in waves of breath.

"Inside" and "outside" of lungs, permeable boundary of skin, eyes, ears, nose, holes in the body for substance passing in and out, no stable and fixed entity that is you, but a moving set of points through which pass water, air, light, food, parts of the bodies of others: their breath, tongues, genitals, hands.

The summer spinach I bought today at the Iyengar Yoga Market on West Thirteenth Street came from Milford, New York, where it expanded itself from tight dry coded seed with water and light and solar heat, grew and rustled in darkness, responded to the rhythm of day-length and moon, and now, uprooted, has ridden in a truck to New York City, and this evening will become part of the salad that I'll make for dinner, along with lettuce and arugula from a farm stand in Bridgehampton, and cheese made from almond milk. All this was not part of me and now will be part of me, and so is in some fashion the history and culture of spinach: the long-held knowledge of growth, the history of seed-saving, variety, breeding and naming. The world enters us and departs, just as language and image and idea are imprinted upon our consciousness, considered, forgotten, passed on, released. I make this book out of thinking, feeling, experience, light on my computer screen; as I write the light from the screen enters my body through my eyes, the impulses of my brain move my fingers to push against these keys (a little too firmly, I am told, from my years of working on typewriters). There is no place in the world where that which is "I" firmly, clearly ends, no line of demarcation. The body of a jellyfish is somewhere between 94 and 98 percent water, which means that a body of water is moving in the water. A jellyfish lacks much in the way of separation from its milieu, and might reasonably be said to be something more like a process the water is performing, an activity taking place in water, than a separate being.

This is how the architect Christopher Alexander suggests we learn to think about structure. He uses the example of a whirlpool, which is not a not a thing in itself capable of being separated from its surround but an action in the field, a way the continuous body of the water is behaving. If you try to talk about a whirlpool or a tornado or a waterfall as an object you inevitably distort it; it demands to be understood as a process. Alexander believes we need to apply this same thinking to a house: it's a part of a field of perception and action, and only able to be whole, pleasing, and beautiful if held in its context instead of treated as something extricable from its surroundings and its use.

This line of thinking accounts for the astonishing beauty of jellyfish, when you're able to see their unerring grace in photographs or their remarkable fluidity in an aquarium: they are entirely at home in their element, because they mostly *are* their element. I have never been able to trace the name of the Japanese philosopher who is supposed to have said, "A fish never makes an aesthetic mistake."

•••

OR BEGIN WITH PHYSICS. The world's a field of energy; matter and energy are not separate "things" but ways of behaving; the world isn't substance but motion. In a field of being, I am an intensification of that field; I'm a point where the world opens a pair of eyes to look at itself.

Every atom belonging to me as good belongs to you. Atoms, of course, belong to no one. (Though now that water has been so successfully marketed, some brazen capitalist seems bound to try.) Our atoms came from the furnaces of long-gone stars, and swirled in galactic clouds; they crashed through the limbs of enormous reptiles and fountained up the vascular systems of huge trees, were Xerxes and Catullus, Nefertiti and Mother Ann Lee. Neither is stability to be found in the short run: breathe in, breathe out, drink, sweat, eat, excrete; we're porous, and, as in the instance of my Iyengar spinach, the boundary lines our preconceptions teach us are real are, with a modest shift of perception, hard to discern.

Whitman's aim, in his greatest and most characteristic work, is the restructuring of reality. He intends to rewrite our sense of what subjectivity is—or at least wants us to acknowledge that the reality we already experience doesn't conform to the traditional separation of subject and object, but to something more like the flux of being his poems portray. He is out to rewrite ontology; his assault is a friendly one, but frontal nonetheless.

———•••———

To be in any form, he asks, *what is that?*

Whitman's questions are one of the continuingly startling things about him. Some of my students resist this aspect of his work, and suspect him of posing as a wonderer, asking questions to which he already has a firm answer in mind. True, sometimes he uses a question, as opposed to a statement, in order to disarm us and draw us further into the argument of his poem. When he asks,

> *What do you think has become of the young and old men?*
> *And what do you think has become of the women and children?*

he certainly does have an answer. But Whitman's greatest questions are provocations of another order. Take *What is the grass?* What sort of question is that? It's aflame with implication: that the common word doesn't help to settle the matter, that there is something fundamentally peculiar or difficult about the phenomenon at hand that requires our attention. Change the noun and you'll see my point. What is a maple tree, what is a horse? Those are questions we do not ask.

To be in any form, what is that? is this sort of question, and becomes a different one depending on which words are stressed:

To BE in any form
To be IN any form
To be in ANY form.

Maybe it's the inevitable result of realizing that one isn't contained between one's hat and one's boots. I am not this form, or rather I don't stop at this form's apparent limits. But I am *in* a form, or so the structure of language would posit; that self which is larger than limit is somehow inside a limit.

———

SUNDAY MORNING IN MENDOCINO, driving rain coming in off the Pacific, scouring the bluffs all night and cascading over the band of moorland before the dreamy little town begins. We're in a coffee shop reading e-mail when a homeless man enters— or I assume he's homeless, a late-middle-aged man, with a sun-tightened face, shoulder bags, backpack, and rolled and belted blanket, leading a slow-walking, serious black Lab. He chooses a corner, kneels down, unhitches and unrolls the blanket, spreads it on the floor for her, talks softly to the dog, saying something like, *We'll get warm in here, we'll dry out in here.* He gets her settled, then goes for a cup of coffee and comes back. He goes outside for a minute; she watches the door with a fixed gaze, unwavering eyes the color of wet bark, muzzle lifted. Suddenly I so do not want to be left; I have one companion whom I require; what if he doesn't come back this time? He's always come back though sometimes it's a long wait, and you can't ever be certain, and who besides me would take care of him if he didn't come back?

Then I shake my head and there's a beautiful nervous dog on the floor and I'm sitting on a stool in front of my laptop screen reading my mail.

———

IF YOU'RE ALREADY EVERYTHING, already complete, then what need could there be to speak, to write a poem?

But "Song of Myself" is in fact suffused with longing, a fervor for the only thing that isn't me: you. This is why *you* is the most often repeated word in Whitman's work. It's you who must be won over, you the reader whom the writer and his book desire, you the lover whom the soul seeks. The poem wishes to free you from the illusion that you're separate; it wants you to remember what you know, already, on some level: that you are me. Or, more precisely, we are it.

There's no real difference between us, seen from the position of heightened, benevolent distance at which the singer of "Song of Myself" stands. But he understands that it's human not to be in that state, so the poem's characteristic gesture is one of reaching toward us—the poet's arm around our shoulders, the poet's hand in ours, the poet whispering in our ear. *I was chilled with the cold type and cylinder and wet paper between us*, he writes, wanting not the intermediary of print but the warm congress of voice with ear, skin with skin.

The result is oddly twofold. On the one hand, we're reminded that we are reading a poem, a made version of a human voice, printed on a page in our hands; books are bound (forgive me) in time and by their physical borders. Poems reside on the page.

Whitman calls this poem "Song of Myself," and a song after all lives not so much in sheet music as it does when it is performed. Voices are unbound, free-floating, arising when you *loose the stop from your throat*. The moments when Whitman wants us to be aware that we are "hearing" his voice on a page are often those when he becomes uncannily present. Then it seems his body is behind the words, leaning into the page from the other side, pressurizing his language so we feel the intensity of his longing for us, his huge will to bring us into the company of his poem.

Or perhaps to tell us that we are already of that company, though we may not have known it. There is no address to the reader quite like this elsewhere; it is a performance of astonishing intimacy,

> *This hour I tell things in confidence,*
> *I might not tell everybody, but I will tell you.*

And:

> *I . . . would fetch you whoever you are flush with myself.*

And:

> *Shoulder your duds, and I will mine, and let us hasten forth;*
> *Wonderful cities and free nations we shall fetch as we go.*

And, of course, the poem's unforgettable, ineluctable close: *I stop somewhere waiting for you.* If this is an incarnation of the voice of Being itself, surely it's the friendliest incarnation ever. Compare it to the cold, magnificent Thunderer speaking out of the whirlwind in Job and you hear immediately the difference between the sublime indifference of the universe and an avatar of human warmth. Whitman is no disembodied spirit, but a man with a whirlwind within him:

> *I rise extatic through all, and sweep with the true gravitation,*
> *The whirling and whirling is elemental within me.*

A FRIENDLY INCARNATION. There's a central figure in the Buddhist pantheon, a character so beloved you can find his or her name in a dozen forms; Avalokiteśvara or Chenresik or Guan Yin seems to cross lines of culture, language, and gender effortlessly. Whitman read Vedanta, and was aware of the influx of translated religious texts from Asia in the spiritual and cultural hotbed of new ideas that was the Northeast in 1850, but who knows what he knew of Buddhism? What matters, to my mind, is imaginative sympathy, and Whitman would have seen in Avalokiteśvara a kindred inclination. The name means *he who looks down on the world*, or *he who looks down upon sound*, hearing the cries of all beings. Perhaps Whitman has something like this archetypal listener in mind when he writes,

> I think I will do nothing for a long time but listen,
> And accrue what I hear unto myself . . . and let sounds contribute
> toward me

And accrue the sounds of the world do, in Whitman's poem, from *the bravura of birds* to *the angry base of disjointed friendship* to *a tenor large and fresh as the creation.*

Who was Avalokiteśvara? A monk on the edge of complete enlightenment, the legend goes, who vowed not to enter into that state until all sentient beings had gone before him. Therefore he became a figure of limitless compassion, looking down from his position of understanding onto the struggles of all creatures who have not yet arrived there. Imagine a Buddha who turns to us and says, *Shoulder your duds!* Walt Whitman in "Song of Myself" is a homespun American Avalokiteśvara; he finds with immeasurable joy his own realization of unity, and that vision leads to a tenderness toward all things: *And I know that the hand of God is the elderhand of my own . . . And that a kelson of the creation is love.* Surely Avalokiteśvara is the "elderhand" of Walt Whitman; this passage overflows with a universal, swelling tenderness. The material world of the poem is lit up with this sense of splendor, the radiant worth of each element of earth:

I believe a leaf of grass is no less than the journey-work of the stars,
And the pismire is equally perfect, and a grain of sand,
    and the egg of the wren,
And the tree-toad is a chef-d'ouvre for the highest,
And the running blackberry would adorn the parlors of heaven,
And the narrowest hinge in my hand puts to scorn all machinery.

Radiant, and endless: I am all and all never ceases,

And I know I am deathless,
I know this orbit of mine cannot be swept by a carpenter's compass,
I know I shall not pass like a child's carlacue cut with a burnt stick
    at night.

When I was a kid I used to love the July evening pleasure of drawing in the air with "sparklers," wooden sticks dipped in something incendiary. Once lit, they hissed a little fountain of sparks an inch or two from the tip till they burned down to a black stub. You could make a *carlacue* that would seem to linger in the air for seconds after the source of the light was gone. This is a stunning image for the fleeting nature of the self: a passing figure scribbled on the dark. Stand at a little distance in time, and the individual really *is* as fleeting as that track of light. But seen from the vantage of the whole, from the larger life that seems, impossibly, to speak to us from this strange poem, we do not pass.

———•••———

BOTH HUMAN AND SOMEHOW above the human at once, the speaker of "Song of Myself" is poised at a level where individuality is an entertaining spectacle. This is the source of the intricate variety of the world Whitman sets out to chronicle in his famous catalogs. Every part of the world, even an occasion of suffering or scene of degradation, is notable, worthy of attention. But since the self speaking is the great multifarious life of the whole, the loss of any individual doesn't really matter: *there is really no death, and if ever there was it led forward life . . .*

Maybe Avalokiteśvara, who became a god after all, lives at that height, but Walt Whitman could experience *the peace and joy and knowledge that pass all the art and argument of the earth* and then return to a crowded house in Brooklyn, his unpaid bills, his drunken mother, the unemptied chamber pot under the bed he shared with his developmentally disabled younger brother. The gift of an encompassing vision so radical as to crack the foundations of the self does not change entirely the life that goes on after the veil's been parted. The self that slipped out of the limits of individuality, time, and place dwelled beside a self still bound by limit. The god in him may have seen everything as *flashing sparks from the wheel*, but the man struggled with ambition, attachment, and desire, a profound longing for connection to comfort body and soul, and understood that the particular is always perishing, and therefore all the more to be cherished.

If I can stand somewhere near the level of "Song of Myself," I understand that my dog Ned is a glorious incarnation of energy, one of the endless flashing bright points of the universe unfolding itself. Energy takes pleasure in the disguise of matter, in the long adventure of incarnation, disappearing and then discovering him/her/itself again. If I look at the same creature from my more familiar, limited vantage point, he's purely himself, a set of endearing gestures and characteristics that will never come again. Thus his disappearance is tragic— in the way that all the world is, all its parts forever going away. *Time avails not, distance avails not.* But without the limits of perceived separateness, without the agency of time, how could the adventure of living have poignance, how could individuality really matter?

Thus Whitman dwells in duality. He knows the vision of the

higher self to be real, but he can't feel it all the time. He was, in the great early poems, working on a verge that was extreme indeed. But years later he would say to his friend John Burroughs that his early poems had been written in a kind of trance, to which he could not will himself to return. So a discrepancy between selves haunts a number of poems:

> *Trippers and askers surround me*
> *People I meet. . . . . the effect upon me of my early life. . . .*
> *of the ward and city I live in. . . . of the nation,*
> *The latest news. . . . discoveries, inventions, societies. . . .*
> *authors old and new,*
> *My dinner, dress, associates, looks, business, compliments, dues,*
> *The real or fancied indifference of some man or woman I love,*
> *The sickness of one of my folks . . . or depressions or exaltations,*
> *They come to me days and nights and go from me again,*
> *But they are not the Me myself.*
>
> *Apart from the pulling and hauling stands what I am . . .*

The Me myself. Is that who was sitting in the steamy changing shed?

---•••---

THE CHILD WRITES with a burnt stick on the night. Whitman writes in pencil and in ink, in his small green notebooks. Then he begins, in Brooklyn Heights, to set his words in type, arranging the stanzas and the lineation on the printing plate, choosing where to "wrap" a line so that the words move continuously on the page, arranging the white space between stanzas so as to reflect the motion of thought. He will not pass like the child's illuminated scrawl because he has made his poem solid; he has, as the poet Frank Bidart puts it, "fastened" his voice to the page.

———•••———

ANOTHER WAY TO UNDERSTAND IT: the emanation of all that skin is language; out of our collective physical being comes a voice, and the genius of Whitman's poem is to incarnate that voice. That is why every line of the poem can be read as spoken by that which is all of us, the collective, pervasive presence that is speech, that is language experiencing us. Language the living thing, living through us.

———•••———

WHAT I ACTUALLY THOUGHT at the time, in the dim humid light of all those bodies—what I thought, though I can't say why: *This is what it was like before we were born.*

LUCKIER

Years ago, in Lincoln, Nebraska—far from home in more ways than one—I realized I'd forgotten my copy of *Leaves of Grass*. I was teaching a poetry workshop in fifteen minutes. I walked into the nearest used bookstore, pulled a copy off the shelf (there is a copy of the *Leaves* in every used bookstore, everywhere in the nation, count on it), and bought the book without opening it. The passage I wanted was the sixth section of "Song of Myself," which begins with these famous lines:

> *A child said, What is the grass? fetching it to me with full hands;*
> *How could I answer the child?. . . . I do not know what it*
>   *is any more than he.*

Ten minutes later, standing over a whirring little copy machine, I turned to the page I'd sought. It was inked in the margins with notes, inscribed in the looping, markedly undergraduate hand of a student, a young woman, I assumed, the dots on her *i*'s surrounded with little rings of flower petals. She had written, beside the poet's initial question, "Isn't it grass?"

I was exasperated, then amused, and later my class laughed about it when I told the story. But as we talked, I was surprised to discover I felt grateful to the young note-taker for providing a clear illustration of a mindset I recognize. She seems content with the knowledge she already has. Once the grass has been identified, a defining label conferred, she won't need to consider it again.

But the child has not asked, after all, "What is this green stuff?" and is not in search of a word; she or he wants something else. What, exactly? The question is deeper and stranger than it first seems, on the order of Marianne Moore's question, "What are years?" or the query of King David in the Psalms: "What is man that Thou art mindful of him?" These questions don't seek labels, classifications, or technical answers; they are after something more essential, and in that quest the question of what being *is* inevitably resides. *To be in any form, what is that?*

Those questions seem unlikely to trouble the student decorating her letters in the poem's margin. I'm making an example of her, I know, based on a single comment; in all likelihood she's a far more complex person than her marginal note would suggest. But here she expresses—or perhaps records the way her literature teacher expressed—the opposite of the artistic temperament, answering the poet's question with a pragmatic one.

This presents a sweet, provocative paradox. The poet, the one you'd expect to have faith in language, knows that naming alone does nothing to dispel mystery. For him a word is a gesture in the direction of reality, and does not limit or circumscribe; the poet knows that nothing at all is settled by the word. On the contrary, perhaps what words do is propel us further into the uncertain nature of the real. They pry open possibilities, and suddenly the plain grass seems to be rustling with meanings.

———•••———

MY EAST TENNESSEE GRANDMOTHER, who was born around twenty years after Whitman published his first edition, believed this world to be in its final days. The songs she sang and verses she read aloud pictured what surrounds us as a veil to be seen through, a text of instruction. Like Emerson—whose riveting lecture in New York in the 1840s on the need for a truly American poet set one member of his audience, Walt Whitman, ablaze before nearly a word of *Leaves of Grass* had been written—she thought the world a scrutable book of signs.

She liked to read aloud to me from Revelations. Biblical authorities had thoroughly explicated the New Testament, making its meanings fixed and clear, but this book remained rewardingly mysterious. I was four, and I enjoyed her readings thoroughly: here were winged horsemen, and the earth cracking open, and dripping beasts rising from the sea.

Whitman insisted that one needed no spiritual teacher, no intermediaries between oneself and the divine, and no holy scriptures—except, perhaps, his own! This probably makes him more of a Protestant than my Presbyterian grandmother, who loved the radio preacher Oral Roberts and relied on his voice for strength and guidance. The poet's allegiance was to the pleasure and instruction to be gained in reading the signs for oneself.

Thus Section 6 begins with an engaging series of metaphors, offered in an attempt to say what the grass is. They are presented as speculations, or hunches, and most begin with some variation of the phrase "I guess." No "I guess" is to be found in the Bible; no prophet proposes varying ways to read the same emblem, and no knowledge seems tentative, or under construction. The poet's answers are exploratory, and the multiplicity of them suggests no single answer will suffice. One figure does not cancel out the others; the grass is a flag, a handkerchief, a hieroglyphic text, a host of living tongues. These images comprise a thought experiment, an inquiry into the nature of grass, into the nature of nature—even, really, into thinking itself, how the words and images we use to frame the world themselves define what we're able to see.

I loved to sit on my grandmother's lap while she read me those apocalyptic verses, in the green rocking chair I'd known forever as hers. I felt enthroned, in a wonderful way, and my realm consisted of her lap and the book. She'd hold the black leatherette cover between her two intricately aged hands, spotted and veined, so that both of us could see it. Each page was printed in two columns, with numbers beside each verse, and I liked how the words of Jesus appeared in red ink the color of licorice or cherries. I'd ridden on my uncle's lap, on his roan mare, and he'd lifted me up to touch cherries on a tree in his orchard, still green, though reddened on one side, sweetness on the way.

This was reading: in the warm space where you are held, you listen to the words and let yourself go wherever they want to take you. You can follow the movement of her finger along the line of print and learn to tell where words start and stop. The spaces that open between sentences, those you fill up yourself, with the images that rise up in you as you listen: cherries, sweet chariot, red ink.

"HAVING BEEN A PRINTER MYSELF," Whitman told Horace Traubel, "I have what may be called an anticipatory eye—know pretty well as I write how a thing will turn up in the type—appear—take form." Whitman set the first dozen pages or so of his first edition in type himself, and this section was among those pages. You can feel the hand of the printer in them: the physical arrangement of the words on the page mirrors the movement of thought. Each proffered possibility gets its own stanza: a single image is presented, considered, set down. In the white space of silence between stanzas the poet seems to be gathering himself, feeling his way toward his next assertion. The mind pauses, dwells, prepares to speak.

It's a little hard to imagine, from the vantage of our time, just how radical an innovation this was. How odd it seemed to Whitman's early readers, who were accustomed to those evenly patterned stanzas—lines in groups of two or three or four, most often, but then in longer clusters too—that would remain standard poetic custom for another fifty years. Stanza breaks like these mostly serve to create a pattern. They are intervals of measurement, not a space for making meaning.

But every time Whitman ends a stanza in "Song of Myself," a thought or line of thinking comes to rest, and it seems as if the speaker waits, as we do, for the next idea, the poem's next gesture, to well up and then spill onto the page. The poem breaks into a new modernity by turning silence into an active force, charging absence with an alert, considering presence. In Whitman's hands—literally so, in these pages where he's set the type himself—the blank space between stanzas seems athrum with possibility; we pause and watch thought loom up out of silence.

These stanzas suggest that the poet is coming to knowledge *as the poem is being spoken*, not simply offering an orderly recitation of an insight already attained. Thus we're allowed a remarkably intimate relation with the interiority of another—or at least with an active, dynamic representation of a mind at work. The poem intends, in its very structure, its stops and starts, guesses and hesitations, to build a model of consciousness, a dramatic presentation of the self engaged in experience. These poems seem to come into being before our eyes. This is why Whitman so often writes in the present tense, why he turns to us with his questions and invitations; he understands that his voice exists in a continuously occurring moment, speaking directly to *men and women of a generation* and *many generations hence*.

—•••—

"I GUESS," THE PHRASE THAT LAUNCHES many of these stanzas, is the language of the fellow depicted on the frontispiece of the book, slouch hat and hand on hip, open shirt and open stance. His casually spoken surmises allow us to relax into each stanza's

premise and entertain the ones to come. These aren't firm assertions, but something more like possibilities for contemplation.

> *I guess it must be the flag of my disposition, out of hopeful*
> *green stuff woven.*

> *Or I guess it is the handkerchief of the Lord,*
> *A scented gift and remembrancer designedly dropped,*
> *Bearing the owner's name someway in the corners, that we*
> *may see and remark, and say Whose?*

It's a good thing this friendly, offhand voice disarms us, since
the poem moves swiftly into peculiar territory. *A scented gift and
remembrancer designedly dropped* has a playful rhythmic flourish to
it, and sounds innocently Victorian. Until, that is, one pictures
Jehovah daintily letting drop a perfumed, monogramed token in
order to catch our attention. Such seductive behavior is at odds,
to put it mildly, with traditionally masculine images of the
Almighty. Could the Voice that spoke from the burning bush be
a feminine flirt?

> *Or I guess the grass is itself a child. . . . the produced babe*
> *of the vegetation.*

> *Or I guess it is a uniform hieroglyphic,*
> *And it means, Sprouting alike in broad zones and narrow zones,*
> *Growing among black folks as among white,*
> *Kanuck, Tuckahoe, Congressman, Cuff, I give them the*
> *same, I receive them the same.*

The grass is mirror of the child who asked the question, and
perhaps by extension a double of the poet, who relinquishes adult
knowledge and practical certainty for a childlike, questioning

openness that restores to things their original strangeness. After the beat of a stanza break comes a new proposition: the grass itself is writing, like the poem spread before us, and its intent is to signify the vegetative world's perfect democracy, the equality of all in the eyes of nature.

Whitman knew hieroglyphics from a private Egyptological museum upstairs at 659 Broadway, in the neighborhood now known as SoHo. The museum housed the collection of Dr. Henry Abbott, a British physician who'd lived for decades in Cairo. The poet wrote in the museum's guest book that he had visited twenty times—drawn by splendid sculptures, or the mummified bull and cats on display, or the complex and elusive script on long strips of papyrus? He was often the sole visitor; Abbott's museum closed in just seven years, never having achieved popular success.

The collection would later find its way into the Brooklyn Museum, where it continues to grant viewers something it must also have evoked for Whitman: a sense of the immensity of time, the vastness that lies beneath or behind the present moment. He must have been struck by the poignance of something as fragile as writing reaching across the space of five thousand years; perhaps witnessing such persistence makes the work of a poet seem less embattled, less private or futile. If, five thousand years after you struggle to capture on the page the character of some passing moment, an instance of grief or delight, someone in a city that did not exist in your lifetime translated your words . . . The life of the poem might be extended in ways you cannot know, and continue in a world so far from yours as to be nearly unimaginable. The circle that is the outer edge of your life extends, and goes on extending.

The words the grass spells out are written in an ancient language, but they are clearly legible. It sprouts alike in expansive countryside and urban plots, and is indifferent to political or cultural forces, be they liberal or restrictive. *Growing among black folks as among white* is a clear and direct refutation of white supremacy, an assertion of equality framed by using the testimony of earth. Nature does not care about race, the poet asserts, writing at a time when ideas of what is "natural" were often used to justify slavery, the elimination of native peoples, and the subjugation of women. This is the first venture into overtly political territory in a poem we might view, up to this point, as a spiritual text. Whitman was not a poet who could hold the spiritual and the social apart, and his poem becomes larger and more distinctly American by acknowledging here what Wallace Stevens would later call "the pressure of reality." Democracy, ethics, how we are to form a social compact that honors and allows the dignity and beauty of all our bodies—these elements are now on stage in "Song of Myself."

Spoken aloud, the short list of persons the grass treats equally is a lively example of Whitman's often acute ear. *Kanuck, Tuckahoe, Congressman, Cuff*: the sequence of *k*'s and hard *c*'s puts the lips, jaws, and tongue through a quick workout. The political wind that's just blown into the poem leads Whitman to make a very American list. *Kanuck* is slang for Canadian, *Tuckahoe* a tribe from the Northeast. *Congressman* needs no gloss, though it's worth noting that Whitman didn't hold much respect for them. *Cuff* is a now-archaic slang term for African American. It's startling, halfway through this line, to discover that now the grass is speaking, ventriloquized by the poet: *I give them the same, I receive them the same.*

Because the written word is silent, it seems natural to imagine the grass as quietly covering the earth with its alphabet. But now the speaker not only hears the grass, he slips into its voice. What the grass says here is equally true of Whitman: His poem is uttered to the world, freely available, offered: *I give them the same, I receive them the same.*

Receive is the pivotal word here. It's easy to see how the poem receives us, its doors equally open to all. In what way does the grass receive us? Now the trapdoor in Whitman's meditation opens and sends him tumbling down beneath the soil, into the earth itself, the underworld the poem's been feeling its way toward.

The next line is an anarchist's bomb tossed into the house of nineteenth-century verse. I suspect it's the first one-line stanza in American poetry. Isolated as it is by white space above and below, it seems to stop us in our tracks, as what's been an associative, unhurried meditation suddenly accumulates solidity and urgency, its weight made apparent in these twelve words, with their calm, reverent ferocity:

And now it seems to me the beautiful uncut hair of graves.

I have read that line hundreds of times, in many contexts, and inevitably I still respond with a quick, internal gasp. It comes winging into the poem as if from nowhere—yet absolutely, inevitably belongs here as well, the poem's center of gravity, its linchpin.

With an unshakeable confidence conveyed by directness and brevity, Whitman asserts that something we're not accustomed to considering beautiful is so. Take away that one adjective of praise and the line loses much of its power, partly because the *uncut hair of graves* carries some of the creepy commonplace that the hair of the dead goes on growing in the grave. But put *beautiful*— usually a rather flat, unenlightening adjective—back in place, and the line feels electric. This isn't the mown and tended grass of the cemeteries of thriving churches, or of the well-to-do. The poet prefers the unkempt graves, the wild ones, the unmarked ones, and how would we know where they are? The answer is simple: everywhere.

Larry Levis, an American poet of the later twentieth century and a far sadder, shattered heir of Whitman, described the earth as "a limitless ossuary of horses." Given all the horses who've ever lived on earth, isn't the soil a great repository of their remains?

Just as it is the ossuary of us, from the beginning of human time; those who drew wry, elegant forms on the walls of caves, who invented syntax, who dragged the first city's stones into place, those who baked the kings' cakes and those who dragged the aristocrats to their deaths, the slave traders and the unthinkably miserable packed into their holds, farmers and readers and those who made hats: all held in the vast treasury of flecks of what once were and sometimes still are bones. A sad chain of Soviet dogs, as far as I know, are the only creatures born on earth whose remains did not return to it.

Did you doubt, a sly Whitman seems to ask in the background, *that this was leading somewhere? Trust me.* In this line the locked doors of matter have swung open, and reality has revealed itself to the poet's gaze. Until this process of questioning had been undertaken, bringing the speaker to this moment, it was not possible for him to see the true nature of the grass: That it is a visible, reanimated, breathing form of the dead.

I WAS FIVE, the night my grandmother died. That year we lived on the edge of Nashville, in a large rented farmhouse. The horses that roamed in the pastures around the house and the ramshackle outbuildings behind it weren't ours. In the largest of the pastures they looked tiny, when they were farthest away.

A commotion wakes me in the night, red light turning in a circle in the driveway—are the horses scared? I'm on the couch, wrapped in a quilt, maybe one she made. Everyone's too busy to attend to me. I think it's my mother who tells me what's happened, how my grandmother woke in the night gasping for air, and threw the window in her room open wide, and still couldn't breathe. I understand that a minister is coming, a fact that seems odd and important, and that I should stay here, out of the way, and let my parents tend to whatever it is they need to do.

This story now moves out of time, into dream time, so I don't know if my dream came then and there, on the couch, where I'd been placed in an out-of-the-way spot, to spare me something, or because they needed my room, my bed. Logic would say the dream came then, but it seems sure to me that in fact it came sooner, and this is why I wasn't crying or afraid. This was what the boy I was saw: my room was entirely dark, except at the foot of my bed there was a circle of light, the way a lamp will sometimes cast a perfect circle on the floor. In the circle was an old cane chair, with a round seat and curved back, and my grandmother stood behind it. She'd come to see me, and to tell me things she wanted me to hear. Of what she said I remember nothing at all, and I doubt that I remembered any word of hers a day later, or even an hour. What I recall is a sense of absolute and unconditional love, of protection and warmth; whatever awaited me in this life, she was a guardian, a steady presence, and not gone.

———•••———

TENDERLY WILL I USE YOU, the poet says to the *curling grass*, because his insight into the nature of matter brings him into a new kinship to things. If everything we see is composed of reconstituted, returning bodies, then aren't we called to regard the least thing in the world carefully?

> *It may be you transpire from the breasts of young men,*
> *It may be if I had known them I would have loved them;*
> *It may be you are from old people and from women, and*
> *   from offspring taken soon out of their mothers' laps,*
> *And here you are the mothers' laps.*

As the grass formed a flag, a handkerchief, a child and a hieroglyphic, the poem concerned itself with composition. Now it must attend to decomposition, how the elements of the world break apart and come together again in new forms. The grass has sprouted from these various bodies, and though the separation of a child taken young from the mother is an occasion of grief, look—suddenly you are the thing you've lost! What sort of strange gift and continuance is that?

This is as good a place as any to talk about another meaning flickering through these stanzas. Printers like Whitman set wooden type into frames, using blanks between words, and spacer bars and screw-in bolts to hold the text in place from either side, above and below. Such work made for a complex craft, requiring practice to create printed pages that were centered, orderly, and well designed. It was common for printers to make up dummy pages, setting any text of their own devising, then ink the type to check the results. Such pages—bits of nonsense, trial runs, nothing to be taken too seriously—were, in printers' slang, called "grass."

The suggestion then—already nascent in the stanza about grass as hieroglyphic—is that, like flesh itself, words are in circulation, springing into being everywhere, falling away. Just as our bodies cycle through the world of materiality, so the poem of the world inscribes and speaks itself.

> *This grass is very dark to be from the white heads of old mothers,*
> *Darker than the colorless beards of old men,*
> *Dark to come from under the faint red roofs of mouths.*
>
> *O I perceive after all so many uttering tongues!*
> *And I perceive they do not come from the roofs of mouths*
>   *for nothing.*

Whitman's associative movement in this passage is marvelously available, from beards to mouths, from mouths to tongues, from tongues to utterance. Now that hieroglyphic is not merely a field of letters waiting to be read, but an active congress of tongues. The title of Whitman's endlessly evolving book doesn't point to the usual "blades" or "spears" of grass, but leaves, pages in one book, not separate beings but part of one organism, one tree. The poem itself is made of grass. The poem composes itself out of what decomposes. The words of the dead, the words of the old books, emerge here into new pattern and new life.

> *I wish I could translate the hints about the dead young men*
> *and women,*
> *And the hints about old men and mothers, and the offspring*
> *taken soon out of their laps.*

The poet longs for the power to translate the speech of things, the language of all those uttering tongues. It's as if he is somehow invoking this power, calling upon whatever reserves of interiority, whatever energies residing in language and in the grass itself that might allow such a radical transmission. He turns to a question as if drawing in his breath. It's a gesture of humility. Just as he said "I do not know what it is" when the child posed the question that launched the poem, he asks twice now "What do you think . . ." as if he wants understanding to be held communally, to be constructed together.

But this rhetorical maneuver—a device he might have gleaned from orators he admired—also prepares us to accept the sweeping statements of the final stanza in their blazing certainty. By making the question ours as well as his, he gains authority to assert the poem's ultimate, daring claim.

> *What do you think has become of the young and old men?*
> *What do you think has become of the women and*
> *children?*

They are alive and well somewhere;
The smallest sprout shows there is really no death,
And if ever there was it led forward life, and does not wait
    at the end to arrest it,
And ceased the moment life appeared.

Imagine that last stanza ending after the second line, and you can see what a careful work of persuasive rhetoric this passage performs. It is difficult to say "there really is no death." We counter that claim instinctively; of course we die. But Whitman goes on, and that little "if" allows the initial negation of death to be less baldly declarative, made more complex by its surroundings. Looking back from this vantage point, it suddenly becomes clear that the poem could have ended at many points along the way; many of these stanza-ends have the feel of some kind of psychic arrival, a claim placed upon meaning. Had the poet's energies faltered sooner, we'd be reading the poem still, but it's the astonishing extension of its reach that makes it the towering thing it is, with an ending that nothing could have entirely prepared us for. After his gesture of qualification, Whitman seems again to draw energy, to summon whatever powers will move him forward, and leaps to his final stanza.

All goes onward and outward . . . . and nothing collapses,
And to die is different from what any one supposed, and
    luckier.

As Whitman wrestled with this unruly scrawl of a poem over time, one of the nods he made toward convention was to make all his ellipses consistent, using the standard three dots. But in his first edition, he uses these dots in a more expressive way, ranging between three and eight dots in a row as if to indicate either how much has been left out or how long he might like us to pause. Here the four dots create a silence contained inside the penultimate line that seems to make it vibrate with contained energy, an expanding space held in place by the opposition of the two phrases on either side of it, as if it were indeed a bit of that "onward and outward." Just as the grass cannot be contained within any single metaphor, its meanings inexhaustible, so death likewise cannot be adequately named. It is, permanently, "different." That is a nearly hollow word, almost an empty signifier, like "beautiful" above, but Whitman again charges an essentially null term with unaccountable life.

The poem could stop, after "what any one supposed," and we'd be left with a completed arc, a fulfilled text. But he has one more gesture to make, in the breathtaking addition of his final two words. *Luckier* is a slangy, streetwise term, decidedly American, one that would no-wise appear in, say, Wordsworth. It has a conversational immediacy, and it asks us, in a single word, to reconsider all we've just read, to revisit these images of grass leaping from the mouths of the dead, from the dead mothers' laps, curling from the chests of young men like dark green hair, and to understand that those are images of good fortune, and of joy.

The dead are not lost, but in circulation; they are involved in the present, in active participation. Bits of them are streaming through your hand and mine, just as language is circulating through us. Lexicon and materiality forever move onward and outward in the continuous wheeling expansion this world is. This is no mere philosophical proposition on Whitman's part, not an intellectual understanding but a felt actuality. We are alive forever in the endless circulation of matter. Nothing luckier, stranger, or more beautiful could ever happen. There is no better place.

THE
SECOND
SOURCE

—••—

SIX

THE UNWRITEABLE

At Gregori's, once you've paid your twenty dollars and checked your clothes and shoes with the friendly men in the antechamber to the left, you are given a mask—the small black kind, like Zorro's. Stretch the elastic a little, you're told, then slip the mask on carefully; there are only enough to go around and they break easily. Once it's on, you hear your own breathing. The almond-shaped openings restrict the field of vision a little: you look straight ahead, the periphery of your gaze softens in an oval of darkness. Now you're ready to enter the party.

Gregori has parties every Friday night, with a carefully culti-vated guest list of men he's met online or in clubs, or guys who've approached him because they've heard about his gatherings. You have to be invited, and the invitation, presumably, is important to the legality of the party—it underscores the fact that this is a private event, held in a private apartment, so this isn't a business subject to regulation, but simply a gathering. Gregori wants at least to see a photo of you or get a recommendation from someone he knows, but in truth the parties are attended by a wide vari-ety of men: young and lean guys who look like they take yoga classes many times a week, musclemen with their rubbery, steroi-dal curves, older guys into leather or with a kind of military style, and plenty of men who haven't seen the inside of a gym lately.

The men are predominately white or Latin, a few Asians; the only black guy around is one of Gregori's beautiful helpers, a six-foot chiseled tower in red briefs who mans—there could be no other verb!—the door.

But the masked party happens once a month only. The masks don't hide much; were there an acquaintance or a co-worker behind them you wouldn't have trouble recognizing him. But sometimes a gesture in the direction of anonymity is all that's required. Gregori says the party draws married and bisexual men, actors, guys on the down-low, who feel, between the dim lighting and the slight veil, free. They pose or rest or couple in the soft light washing down from a video screen hung high up on the walls of the two-story room. (They triple, I want to say, or otherwise multiply, but I need to wash "couple" and "multiply" free of the weight of their heterosexual imagery. Little is limited here to two, and nothing will be conceived but possibility.) The men clothed only in the black fabric framing their eyes look strangely Venetian, as though Tiepolo had made secret frescoes of an eighteenth-century sex party.

How has Gregori found these men? A bisexual pal of his goes to clubs in Manhattan patronized by swinging straight couples, and when one of the guys is clearly attracted to him, he gives him Gregori's card. Gregori cruises online sites to find the guys who'd be pleased by the prospect of a veil. If the masks, in a few hours, are worn loosely around the neck like collars, or strewn on the floor beside the sofa, left on a tabletop—well, their work is done. They have opened the doors of the evening, have announced an intent, and now they are no longer necessary.

I DREAM, AS I'M SETTING OUT to write this, that I'm walking in a weedy and tangled area in the back of my garden, a part I've never really attended to much, when I discover that there's a neglected path that goes on, opening out farther than I knew, and there are daffodils already sprouting, though it's still late in the winter, and the rough beds lead right down to the bay. I didn't know we bordered open water! But I can go farther: up an easy slope out of the garden, where you can see across a valley where sheep are sporting and then the path runs on behind the field to a town I think I recognize, but once I'm there I realize it's a town I've never seen. It's clear that home is so much larger and more unfamiliar than I knew.

———•••———

I HAVE BEEN A MASKED MAN—not for a long time, now, but there was a period in my life, in my twenties, when I—how to say it?—lived in hiding, lived a double life, was sexually duplicitous? All problematic terms. I was married to Ruth and having sex with a man. I imagine that I would have been terrified of Gregori's party, had there been such a thing in Des Moines; I can't imagine myself then being able to move to that level of unself-consciousness, that degree of abandon. Would that even have been what I wanted? I imagined that one man, one incendiary, generous, open-spirited man, would entrance me, one broad chest would give me a place to lay my head. And, for a time, he did.

Then why on earth was I married?

———•••———

WHEN I WAS SEVENTEEN, a freshman in college living in my parents' house, I met Ruth at a poetry reading. She was short, blonde, her body rounded like her vowels; her voice had been forged in central Louisiana and revised in Houston. She was one of a group of grad students reading their work in some anonymous lounge in the student center; her poems were imagistic, fragmented, and to my ear compellingly weird, as if they emerged from some interior cave still wet with the stuff of dream life. I liked Blake and García Lorca, André Breton and Charles Simic, so of course I liked her, and I went up to her after to tell her so, and she exclaimed, "Mark, I'm so glad to see you!" though we'd never met, and I took that as a sign.

A week later I saw her again, at a party at my poetry professor's beautiful house in the desert. We got drunk on scotch, talked for hours in a state of increasing enrapturement, and made out in my car. "Made out" is deceptively casual. I think it must have felt momentous to me; I must have felt I was doing something I was supposed to do. These statements are speculative because I feel, in some sense, I wasn't there. I was giving myself up to a current, I wasn't making a decision; I was being carried in the direction the world intended—did I think then it was the world that meant this life for me? She said, "I feel like an Easter egg." I loved that. I was seventeen, and to be touched or kissed by anyone was thrilling. I'd had sex exactly twice, in the men's room in the basement of the Liberal Arts building. My art history class—where we studied slide after slide of classical nudes, and my teacher duly appraised their proportions and poses—was right down the hall, and so I'd go from those perfected marble boys to the intricate graffiti of the stalls, their walls pierced by gloryholes, and the hungry mouths and eyes on the other side. You could see just a single eye, or if the man on the other side sat back and you put your eye to the hole, you might see him stroking an erect cock, the startling trembling fact of it exposed for you there in a public place. I was powerless in the face of my lust, but I was terrified too. Was this the life opening in front of me? My father had warned me about queers, to be wary of men who asked me to go home with them, and this was as much of a conversation as we'd had on the subject. My mother had given vent to her disgust at homosexual intercourse (though it couldn't really be distinguished from the rage and distaste she seemed to feel for the heterosexual variety, too).

In a month or two I told Ruth I was bisexual, which I may have believed. I was, in fact, "bisexual," since I was having sex with her and thinking about men, but I don't think that's quite what the term is meant to connote. She seemed to experience this information as something absurd, and told me I was mistaken, and then we didn't talk about it again for years. We were living together by summer, and one day she said, rather petulantly, *My friends all want to know when we're going to get married.* I said, *October?* And that was that. There were maybe thirty guests in our apartment, at the wedding—including my parents and our poetry teacher—and we had champagne and cake on the terrace, popping the corks toward Arizona Mortuary across the street and watching as the bats flew out from the roof at twilight.

•••

JUDITH BUTLER SAYS HETEROSEXUALITY is an inevitable comedy because no one can really fulfill the absurd expectations for the categories defined as "man" and "woman." Perhaps more accurate to say that all sexuality is a comedy, since we are bound to codes that forever fail to describe quite who we are, and though these externals constitute a portion of our subjectivity (how can I not, to some degree, be the gay man I'm told I am?), they're never entire, thank goodness, never circumscribe us completely.

It was clear from the beginning that our marriage would be a painful comedy. I drove Ruth to school one day to her afternoon class, and pulled into a gated parking lot so I could take her right up to the steps of the building, and before I could even ask, the attendant said, *Oh, do you just want to drop your mother off?* I hadn't understood that's how we'd be seen. One night I came home late from some place or another, and there was a guy hanging out under a streetlight in front of a bar down the block, a place called the Graduate. I knew it was a gay bar, but just seeing this boy—a hundred yards away perhaps—nobody would have had to tell me: even this far away his school-letter jacket was glowing with desire; he was facing in my direction, we were sending some beam to one another entirely undetectable by any means other than the human body, his white-sleeved jacket a sweet hungry icon. I turned and went into the house. I was eighteen and alive with longing, and I turned and went into the house and lay down beside my sleeping wife.

Which makes me want to say that I was a stupid boy. Smart when it came to reading, to talking about books and films and especially poems, those spells and chants and passageways into the underlife I loved, but about how to live or how to honor my own heart or my own loins I knew nothing at all.

The comedy deepened. Ruth told me she had a son, by her previous marriage, of whom she'd lost custody, and this was the great loss of her life. Where was he? I wanted to know. Living with his grandparents now, in Arkansas. She waited until we were married to tell me she had a son? Because we were moving to Iowa, where she'd gotten a teaching job, we could stop along the way, and I could meet him, which meant that she had to tell me how old he was. I was eighteen, and so was my stepson.

•••

YOU WILL PERHAPS SEE WHY a writer who's had a good deal to say about other periods of his life has considered this material unwriteable: it seems gothic, ridiculous. To narrate these years seems inevitably to accuse Ruth, and to invite me to offer justifications for my own foolishness in marrying her. We did what we did. It amazes me, it makes me think of Milosz's unforgettable line about the weight of history: "I ask not out of sorrow, but in wonder." It is indeed wonder that I feel, that this absurd life took place, and yet it's true that I can't return to it without a certain degree of rage, too, and a memory of that ferocious, self-enclosed longing. There was a clock, downtown, on the top of a skyscraper, that flashed its numbers all night long; you could see it from the bedroom of our apartment. 1:27, 1:33 . . . How many nights did I watch those numbers, during the hours when there were only three of them?

⁕

WHY WRITE THIS NOW? Because Hank is dead, just this week, of cancer. My wife is years gone, and now him, and thus of the three of us I live to tell the untold tale, what I promised, at least tacitly, I wouldn't say. And Hank's wife, maybe she has a story too?

But I get ahead of myself. I met my stepson, on his grandparents' farm in the Arkansas backcountry. He was exactly the boy I was not: six feet two like me, but while I'd been reading Kenneth Patchen and smoking dope, he'd been playing football and digging potatoes. We played like two big dogs who've just met: we swam in the Arkansas, in our cut-off jeans, we wrestled and chased after one another on the bank. With him I was the boy I'd never been, and if what passed between us had nothing of sex in it, it was surely suffused with eros: all body, and entirely apart from his mother. Then Ruth and I drove to Des Moines, where another life commenced.

The elements of this new existence seemed barely to touch one another at all: I worked in a day-care center, and became passionately interested in the education of young children; I wrote poetry, at night and on weekends; in the late hours, privately, I burned for the company of men; I attended English Department functions with my wife. It was at one of these, in the impeccably comfortable apartment of a senior English professor of considerable authority named Dr. Maurice La Belle, that I met a hairdresser from Iowa City—handsome, ten years older than me, sporting the unmistakable new gay look of the day: tightly curled short hair, a dark moustache, a tan, a lean and well-managed form in tightish clothes. We walked onto a terrace together. He kissed me on the mouth. I was instantly erect—he felt my crotch and pushed

79

his tongue farther into my mouth—but I pulled back and said, *For God's sake my wife is in the next room.* He insisted on giving me his phone number—well, I guess he didn't exactly have to talk me into accepting it. He had no card, and I had nothing handy to write it on, so he inscribed it neatly on the back of my Social Security card. Which means I still have it, forty years later. Oh, Jim from Iowa City, what are the chances you're still alive, or still at that number?

•••

I WAS FLEEING FROM A DOOR that was tumbling open in front of me and, in my less-than-direct way, trying to tug the door open myself. I developed a series of crushes on men who were almost but not quite available: Richard, Hans, guys with a certain vibe of openness or ambiguity who'd become my friends and turn out to be attracted only to women, though they might flirt with me or allow an embrace, even a dry kiss. I'd be spun into dizziness by this, somehow, I thought, satisfied. I had leaned my weight against the door; it hadn't opened but I could feel some fresh and bracing wind blowing in from the other side.

Then I met the man I'm calling Hank. I need, for reasons that will become clear later on, to becloud some of the circumstances of our encounter. Say we sang in a choir together, lobbied for better funding for social services, sat a few easels away from one another in a drawing class. I remember the pleasure of a long conversation, outdoors, on a cool spring afternoon. We'd started to chat a little, and one joke or story led to another, and soon it became evident, the pleasure we were taking in one another's company. If you'd stood back and watched us, you'd have seen two men in their twenties, both tall, one more lanky and the other a bit thicker, swaying a little as they spoke, hands in their pockets, heads leaning in toward one another, then stepping back to laugh, the conversation going on into the afternoon, one mak-

80

ing as though to leave but then stopping again, talking on, the unmistakable physical language of a connection being formed.

We took to going out for beers, playing pinball, listening to bands. This did not fit into the narrative of my marriage, where I seemed expected to live like a married man, not like a boy in my early twenties; I think Ruth must have seen my nights out as an annoyance but also a kind of safety valve, or a male zone not unlike my Huck Finn and Tom Sawyer wrestling with her son. In between batting the beautiful chrome balls around their playing fields beneath the glass we were talking and talking about common acquaintances, politics, work, drawing closer. Then Hank went somewhere or other, on a longish trip, and came back with slides, and to see them I went to his house one evening, a little rented place on the other side of town.

The best place to view the slides was the bedroom; there was a largish bare wall for a screen, and we could put the carousel projector on the bed, and sprawl on either side of it with a beer while he narrated the images of his journey, and as the pictures progressed our arms and shoulders came closer to one another, and I could feel my own heartbeat, and I was aware, beneath the worn cotton of the tie-dyed T-shirt he wore, of his.

⁕

ALL MY LIFE I HAVE LOOKED and looked at the mystery of desire, and I feel no closer to understanding it. Nothing else has so shaped my decisions, my way of life; were one to inventory the costs of sexual difference the total would be enormous, yet I know that I would have paid any price. But what is it that compels us, what is it we want? Touch? Entrance behind the barrier of the skin, to penetrate the boundaries of another body, or be penetrated ourselves, as a remedy for our extreme loneliness, the awful sensation of the singular self in the singular skin? Some narcotic form of forgetfulness, an opiate dispensed by the hands of another? Not orgasm, finally, and only partly pleasure: there are many sorts of pleasure, many forms of satisfaction, but what other has the deep lodestone pull that sex has? And I don't believe it's simply biology, the imperative to reproduce—since for me, obviously, there will be no issue from the unions I can't seem to live without. I want; that is the *prima facie* thing, the ground of being. But what is it, in a man's body, in the heat and touch and warm interior, the rush and delay of contact, what is it that I want? Shouldn't I be able, after a life's worth of practice, to name that?

So I return to Whitman:

> *Blind loving wrestling touch! Sheathed hooded*
> *   sharptoothed touch!*
> *Did it make you ache so, leaving me?*

> *Parting tracked by arriving . . . . perpetual payment*
> *   of the perpetual loan,*
> *Rich showering rain, and recompense richer*
> *   afterward.*

What is *recompense richer*? I know that it exists, and I know it resides outside of language, and I know it is not to be denied. We refuse what is originary in ourselves to our peril; what wells up is to be attended to. Blake says, *It is better to murder an infant in its cradle than to nurse desires unacted upon.* This sounds horrifying until you realize that the infant you're killing, if you do not allow your desire to emerge into the daylight, is yourself, the person you might become if you move in the direction of fulfillment. (Not *to* fulfillment, mind you; I no longer believe in that, except as a temporary state, but we need to proceed in satisfaction's direction.)

I WAS TWENTY-ONE YEARS OLD, and now my real life had started, though I wouldn't have said it that way then. The next morning I was in the bathroom at home, getting ready for work, and Ruth pointed out to me that I was certainly in a good mood, because I was singing. And it was true; I wanted nothing more than to open my mouth and sing.

Once or twice a week, Hank and I would meet, at his place, for sex. In a while he moved to an old apartment building in a neighborhood nearer to mine, the kind with a rattling cage elevator that cast complicated shadows down the hall, and that's where I always remember him: the candlelit bedroom, a long horizontal mirror beside the bed he kept curtained until it was needed, a bottle of lotion warming in a tub of hot water, music he liked. His song for me was Phoebe Snow, "Poetry Man," and that kind of jazz-inflected R & B, or the energetic but plaintive Emmylou Harris, that's the sort of soundtrack to those nights. Ardent, inquisitive, exploratory nights. I was the first man he'd had sex with; my own sexual encounters with men before him were merely functional; we had no actual knowledge, and there was joy in creating some. How is it that you could take a long cock into your mouth without gagging, and what were the motions of lips or tongue that would create pleasure? And fucking, that wild taboo mystery of penetration? Hank went first, and almost immediately found that discomfort gave way to radical pleasure. I thought I'd never be able to take anything up my ass; I imagined I just wasn't built that way. But Hank said, *Oh no, if I'm going to do this, you're doing it, too.* And after the initial panic and tension— oh, stars! That same kind of involuntary intake of breath when suddenly you see winter stars spread across a black sky in the country—that scale, that sharp air of possibility.

How can these things ever be inscribed, do they forever belong to the realm of the unwriteable? I have the language of pornography, I have the language of anatomy or medicine, I have the language of euphemism, and I'm happy with none of them.

In Nick Flynn's memoir *Another Bullshit Night in Suck City* there's a list, maybe two or three hundred terms, for being drunk. I could make a list like that for fucking and come absolutely no closer to what I want to say; it is as if the transformative bodily experience lives on one side of the veil and language on the other. What can I say? I fucked him, he fucked me, and then we'd go out and get something to eat and then go back and pick up where we left off. Wild nights, wild nights!—pressurized to diamond-light by secrecy for nearly three years. We never spoke of them to anyone, not a single word.

•••

WHEN I DESCRIBED GREGORI'S PARTY, I focused on the experience of the man wearing the mask, the one looking out through those restricting apertures. But something happens, too, to the one who is looking at the man in the mask. Anything veiled is granted the mysterious capacity to hold more than the uncovered; that which we cannot entirely see becomes the repository of the inarticulate need of the viewer, of inchoate desire. In his book *Stealing the Mona Lisa*, Darian Leader describes how that now-exhausted image became iconic, a pinnacle of Western painting, only after it was stolen from the Louvre, early in the twentieth century; people used to come to view the absence of the picture, gazing into the space where it had hung.

There was a way in which Hank and I partook of this dynamic. I was not, at this point, ready to leave Ruth: a complex web of guilt and shame and misplaced loyalties held me, and Hank shook his head in disbelief at the whole thing but also accepted the situation. And in fact, he did not want to set up housekeeping together: he liked women, too, and began a new relationship while we were still burning up the hours together in our hidden weeknight encampments. He said that he couldn't live a gay life, didn't want that stigma; he was from a little Dakota town, and he'd been a freak there all his life, and he'd had judgment enough. How could I judge that, I who'd been wearing my married-man mask for years?

But how open our bodies were to one another! This combination of utter availability and of closed doors—what was his life like when I wasn't around, or mine without him?—was incendiary; it fueled our passion, it allowed us to love and to want and to need everything we believed might lie behind the mask.

And it meant, too, that when circumstances changed, so did we. My marriage finally foundered. Ruth's drinking escalated; I'd cover her classes when she was too sick to go, haul the empty bottles back to the state liquor store with increasing horror at their number, watch as she made out with a student on the couch at a party whose theme was the work of Alain Robbe-Grillet. Each guest had been told to arrive at a certain hour—8:16, 9:27—and to dress the part, so Ruth and I had gone in formal wear and small black masks, and I'd carried in one hand a toy silver revolver. I pushed us into therapy; I talked and talked—though never about Hank and our affair, not once—until I could name more of what held me in that house where she raged and wept and passed out nightly. We split apart in a firestorm of rage and recrimination; I went to Kenya for a month, to the great game preserves at Amboseli and Maasai Mara, she to the psych ward, and when I came back I told her it was over and found a cheap little apartment a few blocks away, closer to the university—a dim little place where I cried mightily, and where I soon found I very much liked living.

But Hank? We saw each other a few more times, but it was clear all the terms had shifted. I was too available; he was too interested in the woman he was seeing. I liked him as much as I always had, a sweet thread of friendship stitched us together, but everything felt wrong.

———•••———

ONCE, BEFORE I WAS A NEWLY FREE MAN, Hank had an accident, on his motor scooter. Nothing was broken but he was bruised and scraped, the skin of his arms and legs and torso battered and scabbed with surface wounds. I went to visit him. He was recovering at a relative's place—though we were alone that afternoon—and he was lying in a big lounge chair, wearing just a pair of gym shorts, probably a little hazed on painkillers, and so happy to see me. We talked for a while, him narrating the tale of the accident with a grave face, eyes growing wider as he told me how he had been knocked off into the gravel, and how he'd been unconscious for a while, and what he'd woken to. Then I knelt beside him to kiss him, first his mouth and then each of his dark nipples, and a bit of unbroken skin on his belly. Then we eased his gym shorts down, and I took his heavy cock in my mouth until it was hard, and sucked it till he came. He was so grateful for these ministrations, he rested his hand on my head and cried.

Now I understand that his body—beautiful though no gym body of a later decade, a broad chest with a rich swath of hair, the beard pointing downward as though to point to the symmetry of him, the warm total embrace—was one of the doors through which I entered my actual life.

I left town, moving on for job and adventure and to distance myself, once I was ready, from the wreckage of my marriage. He married; I saw him and the sweet and funny and open-hearted woman he married later on, and though we talked about much in the past, we never talked about our nights together, and to this day I have no idea what she knew or knows.

Those involved would probably guess anyway, but out of respect for her I want to leave the externals vague. There's no one else to protect. Hank died, just this last week; I learned from a mutual friend I hear from now and then. Ruth died a few years ago; how she survived as long as she did is beyond me. Though she spent much of her life professing her weakness and need, she was one of those substance abusers with a constitution of pure tempered metal. If the truth be told, she was something of a pit bull, and we arrived, in time, at the uneasy friendship of people who were married twenty or thirty years ago.

Oh my dears. What would you think, if you saw me at Gregori's, where I've taken on a volunteer job, for one evening, in the clothes-check room, just for the sheer pleasure of helping the desiring, beautiful men out of their street identities and into their nakedness and then into their masks? It gives me so much pleasure, to have this odd social role, to set the men at ease, to usher them into the deeper hours of the night. How would you ever understand the places to which I've traveled?

SEVEN

(IS IT NIGHT?
ARE WE HERE ALONE?)

Whatever the dead did or did not do in bed is largely irrecoverable. Evidence— if there ever *was* evidence—has long vanished. Unless someone still living can serve as reliable witness, our knowledge is inferred and provisional, supposition or educated guess. Try to trace the histories of sexualities outside the mainstream and this is even more the case; queer sex leaves no marriage records or genealogies inscribed in family Bibles. Police records and court documents light up a few dark corners, usually in sadly blunt and glancing ways. Letters and diaries help to suggest the contours of a private life, but much remains veiled, the curtains closed. Whoever may have held, touched, or trembled with desire for the poet's body, and whoever he himself desired, Walt Whitman is language now: millions of books, pixels on computer screens, poems copied out in notebooks, incised in concrete on pavement and piers in New York City, committed to memory or tattooed on skin. His body of work is his only body now, gorgeous, revelatory, daring, contradictory, both radically honest and carefully veiled. Its meanings reside in us, in the ways we readers use these poems as signposts, maps, temporary inhabitations—even, sometimes, dwelling places.

Still, I can't say that I don't care, or don't want to know. Had we a technology for reading whatever subtle energetic impressions the past inscribes, I'd be eager to calibrate the dials to a day in 1855, position the impossible camera above and behind Walt Whitman's shoulder, and follow him through the course of his day and night. I'd enjoy such an exercise with other poets I love, but at some points, honoring their privacy and our distance, I'd switch off the lens. My need to know Whitman, to track the rambling or purposeful wanderings of his hours, springs from a desire of another order. Granted this impossible act of surveillance, I confess I'd leave the camera on. I *need* to know.

Why? Let me try to unpack my reasons. In a distinctive way, Whitman's work begins in the body, in his insistence on his physical presence. *I too*, he writes in "Crossing Brooklyn Ferry," *received identity of my body.* Selfhood begins in the facts of being flesh. Whitman's work is so much the song of the self that he says of his own book, in a poem of 1860 called "So long!," *Who touches this, touches a man.* It's an odd, compelling notion, that the book is a published and distributed extension of its author's presence; holding his book, are you touching the poet's skin? In the line that follows the poet's voice slips into a more intimate register, a private aside to the reader sheltered in the privacy of parentheses: *(Is it night? Are we here alone?)* He wants, clearly, to touch us back.

If a book is the voice made permanent—the intersection of the soul and time, as William Everson said, sipping Jack Daniel's from the pint bottle tucked in his Kiowa vest—then Whitman, in order to be himself, must carry his physicality with him, into the book, into the present moment. A signature characteristic of his voice is the way it seems to inhabit the present, the reader's moment. *I am with you,* he writes, *and know how it is.* How what is? To be present in this moment, to long for the object of desire, and hunger to lose for a while one's separateness. He understands the terrible poignance of the human voice in time, of the long, steady life of words beside the quick-burning life of the body. *I am with you, and know how it is.* If ever there was a poet whose work required readers to trust him, to know that he believes what he says, it's this one. We can't grant this speaker the intimacy he seeks if we don't think he means it.

He's sly, often playful, but no one would describe him as insincere. When he is ironic it's because he understands the disparity between his homespun diction and casual tone and the gravity of his intent. He can rant now and then, or crack a joke, but his humor is in the service of forging trust:

> *This hour I tell things in confidence.*
> *I might not tell everybody, but I will tell you.*

He wants us to know he doesn't take himself too seriously, does not possess some wisdom that we can't also possess. He can speak from extraordinary heights (*the hand of God is the elderhand of my own*) but he is *not stuck-up.* He wants nothing as much as that we might *shoulder our duds* and join him, carry his book (nicely pocket-sized, in the 1856 edition) around in our work jackets, and follow the earnest instructions he delivers in his preface:

> *This is what you shall do: Love the earth and sun*
> *and the animals, despise riches, give alms to every one*
> *that asks, stand up for the stupid and crazy, devote your*
> *income and labor to others, hate tyrants, argue not con-*
> *cerning God, have patience and indulgence toward the*
> *people, take off your hat to nothing known or unknown*
> *or to any man or number of men, go freely with pow-*
> *erful uneducated persons and with the young and with*
> *the mothers of families, read these leaves in the open air*

every season of every year of your life, re-examine all
you have been told at school or church or in any book,
dismiss whatever insults your own soul, and your very
flesh shall be a great poem . . .

———•••———

WHITMAN KNOWS *how it is* to love another body, one like his, and how the startling rush of intimacy when we find ourselves skin to skin can dissolve otherness. His evocations of eros toward and between men have a rightness about them, a felt accuracy. They make me realize the aptness of the phrase "the ring of truth," as if words chimed when they drew closest to the real.

The second source of Whitman's poetry is queer sexuality then, and it pervades his work in unprecedented, remarkable ways. He is a citizen of modernity, and his book speaks from subject positions and perspectives that had not yet been inscribed in our literature. He seems to stand near the heart of things, in the heat of an erotic merge, a radiant sense of connection to the bodies of others, but also to be a perpetual outsider. Sexual life carries him beneath the social surfaces, reveals the flesh beneath the uniforms, and calls appearances into question, disrupting what's assumed to be true.

I don't mean just physical acts, pleasure, or the force of desire, but rather the way a proscribed sexuality gives access to the sort of perceptions and understandings that the twentieth-century critic Herbert Marcuse called "extra-societal insights." Writing about marijuana, Marcuse suggested that the drug would only allow its users to see into their culture and its assumptions from the outer edge, as it were, while it was illegal. A joint you bought at a state-licensed dispensary, then, would most likely teach you as much about your country and your times as drinking a beer might. But an illegal one's another matter; stepping outside the bounds of the acceptable sets us apart, and sets us thinking. What is criminal about what I am doing, and why is it prohibited? Do I feel different when the law says I am? Who gains, who loses from this law? How is it enforced? What is it supposed to accomplish, and what does it actually do? What are its unintended effects, and are they truly unintended?

If visionary experience had led Whitman to a boundless identification with all of life, then his desires both deepened that identification and set him apart. They inked within him a profound faith in the possibilities of communion, and a seemingly unquenchable loneliness that his poems attempted to heal. Eros is, after all, one of the gates to what Mary Oliver has called "the furnace of meaning in the human story."

WHAT IT MEANT, to be a man who loved and desired men in Whitman's day, isn't an easy question to answer. Psychology was fairly early on in its project of medicalizing personality; the binary division of human yearnings established by the world-splitting words *homosexual* and *heterosexual* hadn't happened, and wouldn't till the 1880s and '90s. (The term *homosexual* proceeded *heterosexual* in print, a sure sign of the discipline's interest in establishing what was abnormal.) This is not to say that human beings discovered a whole new range of sexual practices near the end of the nineteenth century—imagine!—but rather that they began to think of what they were doing differently, and to categorize themselves in new ways.

A well-known dance hall in lower Manhattan offered, for example, the opportunity for men to dance with other men—specifically with men in drag, who were referred to as "fairies." To dance with a fairy did not make you a fairy, and presumably when the fairies took off their dresses and washed their faces they were, once again, men. Both roles, "man" and "fairy," were a behavior, and did not constitute an identity. It seems likely that nineteenth-century American life provided many opportunities for such "behaviors." Passionate friendships (like the one between Whitman's hero Abraham Lincoln and the yet-to-be president's roommate of four years, and lifetime friend, Joshua Speed) were widely accepted and idealized, between women and between men. Cities like New York were packed with young men who'd left the farm behind for jobs; they lived in rooming houses, sharing beds in close quarters. Whatever sexual play went on in these circumstances seems to have gone on without being named. What caused Whitman's poems to scandalize his audience, and eventually cost him his clerical job working for the Secretary of the Interior, were his portrayals of heterosexual coupling, then-shocking depictions of women who felt, and enjoyed, sexual desire. Readers in our time may have to work to find these passages in Whitman's poems; his women are far more concerned with producing strong babies and nourishing milk than they are with enjoying themselves. Victorian readers—who idolized and sentimentalized mothers—were so alarmed by Whitman's strapping and fertile Amazons that they mostly missed the far more erotic passages about male lovers. Perhaps because for them what we'd call "homosexuality" had not been named, and thus remained largely unreadable.

———•••———

WHITMAN CAME OF AGE IN THE 1840S. Either his character was shaped by the decade or happened to be a perfect fit; the expansive, optimistic curiosity of the times was superbly suited to his own. New York and Boston in particular were seedbeds for new movements centered on human betterment. Among the poet's friends and acquaintances were feminists, advocates of free love, champions of nude sunbathing and communal living, advocates of high-fiber diets and of what we'd now call "health food," independent publishers, students of the newly translated Bhagavad Gita and the Upanishads, and activists committed to a host of progressive social causes. These disparate projects had in common a belief in human perfectability. Even phrenology, a pseudoscience that fascinated Whitman, bent in this direction. Phrenologists proposed that the physiognomy of the human head revealed everything about us; whether particular points on the scalp were raised, flat, or depressed indicated the strength or weakness of intellect, intelligence, sexual desire, the capacity for friendship, and so on. This sounds woefully deterministic until one learns that phrenologists believed it possible, through effort, to *change* the contours of the head. Practice exercising your courage, discover bravery within yourself, and the concomitant spot on the head would reflect the transformation within.

Whitman thrived in this bohemian milieu, and "Song of Myself" in particular is threaded through with bits of reference to what he gleaned from his reading, from lectures and conversations concerning the new thinking, the intellectual fashions of the day. His work as a journalist brought him into contact with what was new in New York life, with the shows and performances, the fashions and styles that held the limelight of the hour, and his first great poem seems a synthesis of all this, the work of a representative soul of a new world ordering, filtering, and celebrating the vital stuff of his moment.

For all his exuberance, and despite the remarkable forthrightness of his poems, there remains a sense of the veiled, of the necessity of indirection. Slippage between stanzas so we're not quite sure who a pronoun refers to, resonant metaphoric details in which things seem eroticized without clear referents—these gestures seem to cloud the direction of desire just enough to create uncertainty. Or to allow only those "in the know" to read the homoeroticism of the poems.

Since homosexuality didn't exist as a defined concept, in 1855, it wasn't illegal. But it was inadmissible; there was no lexicon for it. The poet's notion of *the love of comrades,* understandable to his times as "passionate friendship," became inscrutable as soon as eros was introduced. That "men" danced with "fairies" might be tolerated if not accepted or embraced, but the notion of two men as loving, sexual equals wasn't even figured in the classical models of same-sex relations that the nineteenth century largely regarded as antique error. To write a poetry any more direct than Whitman's would have been an anomaly of such proportions that it probably never would have been published, even self-published, but simply would have fallen out of sight. How far can a poem depart from its times, when there is no intellectual, cultural, or social framework for it, and thus no means for it to be received? "Song of Myself" strides far ahead of its times, but it cannot leave its moment behind entirely.

But Whitman isn't only protecting himself with his veils and feints. He wants the Walt Whitman who speaks in this poem to be a representative man, a New World everyman.

> *These are the thoughts of all men in all ages and lands,*
> *   they are not original with me,*
> *If they are not yours as much as mine they are nothing, or next*
> *   to nothing . . .*

Therefore the speaker must be inclusive, responsive both to women and to men; he must be able to slip into all sorts of identities, finding himself in each. If the core of aliveness in each of us, what Whitman calls *the Me myself,* could speak, then this would be that energy's voice. It's the oddly impersonal core of the self, looking out through any of the infinite eyes that Being opens to look at itself.

And there's another problem, too. Whitman wants to be both a sexual radical and a sage. In the former role he wants to tear the doors from their jambs and celebrate the dawn:

Something I cannot see puts upward libidinous prongs,
Seas of bright juice suffuse heaven.

He also wanted to be widely admired, publicly celebrated, and most of all loved, as the title that came to rest upon his shoulders, the Good Gray Poet, came to suggest. "Good Gray Poets" do not describe the dawn as a wash of illuminated semen shot across the atmosphere. I'm not at all sure these two positions are compatible, or reconcilable, and their contradictory pull must have been a lifetime's source of conflict, and sometimes of compromise.

The years between the beautiful, eccentric first edition of *Leaves of Grass* and Whitman's death in 1892 saw a sea change in the ways human behavior, sexual and otherwise, was understood. Psychology was out to cure human ills, or at least categorize them, through a process of medicalizing personality. Identifying the abnormal was a means of defining health, and increasingly medicine defined for us all the ways we might be wrong. The phrenologists' cheering (if rather nutty) notion of the malleability of the skull gave way to a biological determinism, in which the slope of the forehead or the distance between the eyes might be indicators of permanent weakness or deviance from the norm, and racial characteristics were read as indicators of intelligence or moral character. It isn't much of a step, really, from there to sterilization, euthanasia, and some of the twentieth century's greater crimes.

At the same time, a growing subculture found in Whitman's work a mirror of their own lives, a compatriot and a prophet. Hadn't he asked to be a leader, and called for his *camerados* to join him? He must have felt pressured from both sides, so to speak— from those readers who loved the most popular of his poems, the rhyming and sentimental elegy for Lincoln, "Oh Captain! My Captain!," the most popular of Whitman's poems in his own lifetime, and from those who also walked or wanted to walk *on paths untrodden* and find "Calamus lovers" of their own in the open air. This would have been a difficult contradiction to negotiate, nearly intolerable.

This perhaps explains why he claimed, absurdly, to have fathered six children with a mistress in his twenties in Louisiana. Or why he changed the pronouns in many of his drafts, and why he vehemently denied, to the British theorist of sexuality John Addington Symonds, who put the question directly, that he was attracted to men. Whitman died in 1892, three years before the trials of Oscar Wilde put the crime of "gross indecency" on the international stage, when Wilde's impassioned defense of same-sex passion rang out to generations to come but fell on the deaf ears of magistrates. It was a nightmarish fate; Wilde lost everything, home, marriage, career, his reprehensible boyfriend Lord Alfred Douglas, and served two years in prison, condemned to hard labor that destroyed his health. He died, destitute, two years later in Paris. Whitman, of course, could not have known any of this was coming, but I'd guess the chill in the air had already begun to coalesce, as those cultural forces anxious about matters of decency, fearful of change, sought out a new enemy.

⁃••⁃

IN SUMMER 2017, in London, I saw an exhibition at the Tate Britain called Queer British Art, 1861–1967, a brilliantly curated show that ranged from fey pre-Raphaelite paintings of androgynous boys to splendidly modernist portraits of stylish women with severe haircuts, to Francis Bacon's tortured lovers, their bodies and spirits broken on invisible racks. I was energized by the show, thrilled by its intelligence, but there was one object there that oppressed me from the moment I saw it, and whose memory will not leave me alone.

It was not a work of art at all, but a narrow wooden door, with a small square opening at eye level divided by a grid of interwoven metal bars. It took me a moment, even after I read the informational panel, to register what it was: the door of Wilde's cell, taken from Reading Gaol when that hellhole was demolished. It was awful in part because it was so narrow. Everyone who met Wilde remarked first on his charm and his size; though the delicacy of his manner and his prose might lead one to expect otherwise, he was a big man, over six feet and amply proportioned. They must have squeezed him, again and again, through this tiny door, and how big could that cell have been? The nightmare of the large body in that tiny space, those years of confinement . . . It was an unredeemable, inescapable emblem. Though this was surely not what the curator had intended, its terrible gravity tried to cancel the affirmation, the wit and beauty or shameless glamour or camp of everything else in those gallery rooms. It did not succeed, not entirely. But it held its own, hell portal, nowhere gate, the sign of everything that wants to erase us.

•••

ON HIS AMERICAN TOUR IN 1882, Oscar Wilde was twenty-seven years old. He sought out Whitman, then sixty-two, because the British edition of *Leaves of Grass,* a selected version edited by William Michael Rossetti that omitted some of the more overtly sexual poems, had become a sensation among readers of poetry, freethinkers, and members of an emergent subculture of gay men who saw their newly named sexuality (Urnings, inverts, Uranians?) celebrated in the poet's work. Whitman, presumably expecting a dull appointment with an admirer or perhaps a light-weight, merely clever writer, privately asked his assistant Horace to leave them, then return in half an hour and show Mr. Wilde to the door.

But when Horace appeared, Whitman told him to take the afternoon off, as his services would not be needed, and Walt and Oscar proceeded upstairs to continue their private visit over several hours. "He is a fine large handsome youngster," the poet wrote, in a letter to a friend, and "he had the *good* sense to take a great fancy to *me*." Though Horace preserved some notes that must have been dictated by Whitman later, of what the poet and his visitor actually said we know, of course, nothing.

EIGHT

BUDS FOLDED
BENEATH SPEECH

The world may be one unfenced field of being, but the delineation of parts makes art possible. Whitman came to realize that readers of what one astute reader called his "epic of self-making" needed a little scaffolding, some help in moving through the disorienting experience of his sixty-five-page poem. He numbered the stanzas in the edition of 1860, and then broke the poem into numbered sections in 1867. These rests provide the tonic of silence between bouts of speech. Silence creates emphasis, throwing into high relief the words that fall before or after it.

Of the fifty-two sections the poet devised, the briefest are two six-line units utterly different from one another. Here is Section 17:

> *These are the thoughts of all men in all ages and lands,*
> *they are not original with me,*
> *If they are not yours as much as mine they are nothing or next*
> *to nothing,*
> *If they do not enclose everything they are next to nothing,*
> *If they are not the riddle and the untying of the riddle they are*
> *nothing,*

If they are not just as close as they are distant they are nothing.

This is the grass that grows wherever the land is and the water
        is,
This is the common air that bathes the globe.

This is Whitman in his most transparent mode; he says what he means, and means what he says, and resorts to imagery only in the most generic of ways: grass, land, and water are common as the last stanza's air; the terms refer to *any* grass, land, or water. His music, in that beautiful first stanza, arises from anaphora, as he begins lines with *if they are not* three times in a row. His elegantly legalistic, argumentative syntax makes the passage sing. Stanzaic form seems to have been dictated by this parallelism; the chain of "if they are . . ." phrases suggests a symmetrical lining-up on the page, and the metaphoric leap—that these thoughts are in fact the psychic equivalent of grass and water and air, as plain and necessary as those ordinary things are—necessitates the second stanza.

Section 29 of "Song of Myself," though also only six lines long, is a production of quite a different order:

Blind loving wrestling touch! Sheathed hooded sharptoothed
        touch!
Did it make you ache so, leaving me?

Parting tracked by arriving . . . . perpetual payment of the perpetual
        loan,
Rich showering rain, and recompense richer afterward.

Sprouts take and accumulate . . . . stand by the curb prolific and
        vital,
Landscapes projected masculine, full-sized and golden.

Why does the poet now speak in a way that makes Section 17 seem entirely straightforward by contrast? Why the couplets? And what on earth is going on in these lines?

In this part of his poem, Whitman's been thinking about the power of touch. One section concludes: *To touch my person to someone else's skin is almost more than I can stand,* and the next one elaborates the idea that touch is disruptive and powerful: *My flesh and blood playing out lightning to strike what is hardly different from myself.* The skin of another arouses such a feeling of excess that the poet directly address touch itself: *Unclench your floodgates, you are too much for me.* That is a charming demurral, reminiscent of the lover who cries out "Stop, stop!" with absolutely no interest in being obeyed. It's also self-contradictory; wouldn't it be *clenching* that would stop the tide?

By the time we get to Section 29 the floodgates are wide open. Drenched in eros, Whitman's lines enact the ecstatic. Their potency lies in the way they traffic in terms that seem to pull against one another; this touch is blind, loving, and wrestling all at once. These adjectives, in the first half of the opening line, are mirrored by the three in the remaining half. The two halves of the line are elegantly symmetrical, but the result is an overload—six modifiers for a single noun in one line!—that makes the kind of touch being described here seem far less clear. It's simply not possible to conceptualize this touch in a logical way, yet the over-all sense created by this collision of terms is unmistakable: an evocation of sexual activity that is loving and rough, combative and piercing. It's a challenge to try to unpack its terms:

blind   —takes place in darkness
                           —anonymous
                           —indifferent to its object
                           —desperate
                           —out of control

loving	—tender
	—erotic
	—affectionate
wrestling	—combative
	—playful, sporting
	—masculine
sheathed	—protected, like a sword
	(and thus potentially dangerous,
	though not about to wound)
	—hidden
	—like a foreskin
hooded	—hidden, clothed
	—anonymous
	—unknowable
	—like a foreskin
	—like a snake
sharptoothed	—dangerous
	—venomous
	—animalistic
	—like a snake
	—phallic

This first line—*Blind loving wrestling touch! Sheathed hooded sharptoothed touch!*—has no specific actors, but in the second line the players appear: *your* departure has caused *you* to ache, leaving *me*; is the pain of this departure something like the wildly complex experience of touch described in the first line? Should we re-read that first line, now, as an evocation of the experience of not-touching, the pain of withdrawal?

And who is *you*? Poetic tradition encourages us to read any speaker and addressee not otherwise identified as lovers, specifically heterosexual ones. Whitman doesn't attempt to resist this tradition, exactly, but the description of touch here is so rough and fractious, not to mention so phallic, that it's very hard to read it as a description of heterosexual coupling. Still, using the genderless second person pronoun allows Whitman a bit of free space, a theater of operations—though it's plain that this section is deeply engaged in an evocation of masculinity.

I is consistently male in "Song of Myself"—though now and then the speaker slips briefly into a female body, and for a few words ventriloquizes grass. But *you* is a far more slippery proposition. At times, *you* clearly addresses the reader, whom the speaker wishes to befriend, counsel, win over, or seduce; at times the addressee is the speaker's own soul; at times, as in *Did it make you ache so, leaving me,* the poem seems spoken to a specific other who is already in relation to the speaker. The structural politics of the poem are such that the boundaries between these three roles are called into question, blurring into a complex erotic relation that proposes a new platform for the description of reality. We can't always be certain if Whitman's *you* is singular or plural, and that indeed is part of the point.

The sort of parting the poem considers is complicated by the next two couplets, whose lines echo the internal mirroring of line one, the first with its parade of *p* sounds (*parting, perpetual, payment*), the second with its recurrent *r*'s (*rich, rain, recompense, richer*). From here on out, there is no agency in the section, no identifiable actors; the exchange taking place is the operative force. This exchange is characterized in multiple ways: it is arrival and parting, paying and lending, rain and recompense. It suggests a notion of sexual exchange as part of complex cycles—of presence and absence, of economics, and of the natural world. To wrestle with the emotional multivalence of touch, the known and unknown lover, to come and go, to plant seed and harvest, to borrow and repay—this free-floating exchange leads Whitman to a fiercely sexy vision of the natural world, in which both specific sprout and entire landscape are prolific, vital, *masculine, full-sized and golden.*

This is about as far from the tradition of "Mother Nature" as a reader is likely to be carried! And thus an instructive point of contrast with Whitman's later, recurrent, generally disastrous attempts to celebrate heterosexual fecundity and instruct women in the birthing of "superbest" offspring. D. H. Lawrence was on the money when he wrote that, for Whitman, women are always "a function." Despite the poet's radicalism in asserting the fact of female sexual desire, and despite his call for women's equality, he can't seem to place a woman in any sort of sexual context without thinking about reproduction; it's all spurting milk and swelling belly.

But when it comes to the lusty free-floating exchange figured in this section, Whitman is neither hygienic nor dutiful. Section 29 is marked, instead, by sheer participatory pleasure.

But what to make of "projected"? Whitman touches on this notion in Section 25:

Dazzling and tremendous how quick the sun-rise would
    kill me,
If I could not now and always send sun-rise out of me.

We are, it seems, co-creators; the outer world is not alien to consciousness but overlapping. Is to "send" the same as to project? Whitman, lover of theater and opera, would have known the power of scenic projections. Magic lanterns had been in use since the seventeenth century, and by the mid-nineteenth the powerful lamps called "limelights" (which burned the eponymous substance, and give us our term for the spotlight of public attention) shone brilliant projections onto the stage. In this light (forgive me), the notion of the projected landscape takes on another dimension. Or perhaps it's more accurate to say it has *less* dimension, but becomes a phantom, a phenomenon of appearances, no more solid than images cast upon a wall or a stage curtain. This sense of ephemerality suggests that landscapes, the things of this world, arise out of the exchange, a process in which we participate. They are born, as we are, in eros; we make them; we participate in the work of generating reality. No wonder Mother Nature is not the appropriate figure here, for in Whitman's wild revisioning, it's a pair—a multiplicity?—of male lovers who generate the sprouts. The stanza hides behind its innocent-looking couplets a vision of homoerotic creation.

And this leads to the *why* of the form. Whitman delivers this passage in couplets, a much more regular pattern than marks the bulk of his poem. He usually arranges stanzas like verse paragraphs, starting a new one as time or focus changes, or when he introduces a new rhetorical movement. There's no mystery to that kind of stanza, a naked one, if you will, for a poet who often professes his love of nakedness. His form conceals nothing, its workings and rationale on open display.

But these couplets behave differently; their symmetry comes not from sense but from mathematics: three couplets, the first of two sentences, the second and third each a single sentence. The couplets could easily be seen as "arbitrary," in the way that all regular forms are; they impose an order on the free movement of sentences. They are a form of "clothing" experience, and to clothe is always both to cloak and to emphasize what is covered. Style, said Jean Cocteau, is a simple way of saying complicated things, and Whitman's formal choice seems a superb example of the point.

Two-line stanzas feel apt here because there are two lovers in the poem, two partners in the exchange, and dual aspects in the cyclical processes: parting and arriving, loan and payment, rain and recompense

But these couplets are more than mimetic. They underscore what isn't said, pointing to the silence generated by the white space between. In his *Summa Lyrica*, the poet and critic Allen Grossman has argued that short lines point toward the absence of what is excluded; they indicate the pressure created by what is missing. Whitman's use of the couplet works the same way, I think, as if he wishes to underscore the discontinuities of the passage, to point to the veil that falls between the reader and the text, unlike those famous declarative moments in "Song of Myself" when Whitman seems determined to rip veils (and even whole doorways) away. In contrast, what he is saying here cannot be taken at face value, because there isn't any "face"—instead we're presented with a swirl of terms of exchange, and images of fertility, tension, and release held inside the framing devices of the couplets, which invite us to read, literally, between the lines.

TO READ BETWEEN THE LINES.

I keep thinking about *recompense richer afterward*: something seductive in that promise, the lure of fulfillment, of physical satisfaction, made more alluring because it is so mysteriously named.

Something similar occurs in a famously weird bit Whitman excised from his beautiful poem "The Sleepers" after the 1855 edition. If "Song of Myself" is the poet's great solar oratorio, "The Sleepers" is a hymn to night, a dreamy, shadowed nocturne. The poem imagines those who sleep, across all of the earth, joined together in their rest and their unguarded beauty. A phantom presence moving from bed to bed, the poet seems to become each sleeper, *to dream in my dream all the dreams*. The poem speeds up, partway through, and though the narrative is blurred, it seems the speaker becomes a woman, becomes a celebrant of night, is in love, is cast out, and is naked in the dark under a bridge when this stanza appears:

The cloth laps a first sweet eating and drinking,
Laps life-swelling yolks . . . . laps ear of rose-corn, milky
      and just ripened;
The white teeth stay, and the boss-tooth advances in
      darkness,
And liquor is spilled on lips and bosoms by touching
      glasses, and the best liquor afterward.

We couldn't say what cloth, or what yolks, or whose teeth, or toward whom the "boss-tooth" is advancing; action is floating or swirling, unattached to agency. It's interesting to place this beside one of the other truly sexy American poems of the nineteenth century, Emily Dickinson's poem 249 (or 269, depending upon which editor's edition you consult. Dickinson's work has been a contested territory since her sister Vinnie opened Emily's desk after her death and found some 1,700 poems neatly stored there.) "Wild Nights," as it is often called, although Dickinson refused titles for her work, imagines a night of lovemaking as "rowing in Eden." The poem deals in metaphor every bit as much as Whitman's, but it's beautifully clear, and saturated in pleasure, while the anxiety in Whitman's lines seems to scramble narrative in a way reminiscent of the account of touch offered in Section 29.

Whitman's syntax here is also very close to the structure of his fierce hymn to touch: *the best liquor afterward* and *richer recompense afterward* both fall at the end of sentences, so similar as to suggest that he wanted us to hear the echo, to underscore his joy in what is richer than rain and better than any liquor.

•••

TO READ BETWEEN THE LINES.
    In Section 25, Whitman considers the limits of speaking: *Do you not know O speech how the buds beneath you are folded?* (There, by the way, is another wrinkle in the poet's thrilling uses of the

second person.) The couplets of Section 29 seem arranged to *show* these folded buds—the desire, pleasure, and intensity folded inside of language, which remain unspeakable.

•••

"UNSPEAKABLE"—UNSPEAKABILITY?—comes in three varieties.

First, that which cannot be said because one does not know it, and therefore cannot say it.

Second, that which cannot be spoken because it is culturally impermissible to do so.

And third, that which cannot be named because it is impossible, since the language provides no terms, no words to enable articulation.

I do not think that the unsayable, in Whitman, partakes much of the first quality, though critics have argued that only a complex internal mechanism of repression could allow a poet to both proclaim a radical philosophy of sexual fellowship, especially same-sex coupling, as a basis for political change *and* expect that he would be *absorbed by his country* . . . This is indeed a shattering contradiction, but Whitman seems to have been acutely self-aware, and he surely knew that in America we cannot reconcile horniness and wisdom. (That this is still the case is richly demonstrated in the debacle of the last years of the Clinton administration, when the president famously gave a young White House intern a copy of *Leaves of Grass* as part of a process of seducing her, and the nation knew far more about the stain on her blue dress than most would have wished to know.)

Perhaps this irreconcilability lies behind the formal tensions between "verse paragraphing" and the tight construct of the couplet; the transparence of one sits beside the opacity of the other, and the contradiction cannot be resolved, but instead must simply be accommodated. A great poem of self-doubt of the later 1850s, "As I Ebb'd with the Ocean of Life," shows us a speaker ferociously disappointed in the reception of his own vision, acutely aware of the strangeness of what he's said. Whitman's best poems demonstrate an almost unimaginable prescience; he and Dickinson, among nineteenth-century American poets, possess a nearly chilling self-consciousness, an acute self-analysis. Edward Carpenter, the British anarchist, writer, and champion of the Arts and Crafts movement whose life and romance were the model for E. M. Forster's novel *Maurice,* wrote this elegant description of a visit with Whitman in 1877; the emphases are Carpenter's own:

> *If I had thought before (and I do not know that I had) that Whitman was eccentric, unbalanced, violent, my first interview certainly produced quite a contrary effect. No one could be more considerate, I may almost say courteous; no one could have more simplicity of manner and freedom from egotistic wrigglings; and I never met any one who gave me more the impression of* knowing what he was doing *more than he did.*

But the second and third forms of the unsayable are central to a reading of the poems. In the realm of the impermissible, Whitman astonishes over and over with his forthrightness. From 1855 until the final edition of the *Leaves* in 1892, he persisted in importing the unnamed into the public world of the sayable. Of course he made choices that seem, to the contemporary reader, ill-advised; surely the funniest of these is his revision of a line in "Native Moments" which shifts from 1860's "I take for my love some prostitute . . ." to 1876's "I pick out some low person for my dearest friend . . ." If he sometimes changed his pronouns, or shifted the order of poems in order to blur the nature of a particular allegiance, and if he betrayed his own sexuality when con-

fronted head-on, it would nonetheless be absurd to expect him to
have been any *more* radical than he actually managed to be.

In Section 24 of "Song of Myself" alone, there are passages so
odd and nervy that they have lost little of their power to startle.
Here Whitman discusses the voices that move through him:

> *Through me many long dumb voices,*
> *Voices of the interminable generations of slaves,*
> *Voices of prostitutes and of deformed persons,*
> *Voices of the diseased and despairing, and of thieves and*
> *   dwarfs,*
> *Voices of cycles of preparation and accretion,*
> *And of the threads that connect the stars—and of wombs*
> *   and of the father-stuff,*
> *And of the rights of them the others are down upon,*
> *Of the trivial and flat and foolish and despised,*
> *Of fog in the air and beetles rolling balls of dung.*

This is startlingly bold in its identification with the suffering, with
all those who—in an endearing Yankee-ism—"the others are down
upon." But who could have imagined the end of the list? Whitman
will also vocalize the least likely of actors, the ephemeral fog, the
ignored beetle. These images are figures for the invisibility of the
downtrodden, but they are actual things, too—and what an utter
demonstration of sympathy, how completely unexpected that they
should also be citizens of the world deserving voice and justice.

Later in this same section, the speaker praises his own clean
bowels, the famously "finer than prayer" scent of his armpits, his
genitals— and then, in one of those moves with which Whitman
takes his reader's breath away again, the genitals of the wind, and
even suggests that the daybreak represents a kind of gorgeous
atmospheric come-shot:

Something I cannot see puts upward libidinous prongs,
Seas of bright juice suffuse heaven.

The abiding strangeness! Whence did the nerve to write these poems arise? How did he do it?

One answer to that question has to do with the third form of the unspeakable, that which is wordless, undefined. It is the most difficult form of silence to talk about, since once a word exists for something it does, and the quality of being nameless, outside the realm of speech, becomes irrecoverable.

The polymathic science-fiction writer, memoirist, and cultural critic Samuel Delaney tells an instructive story about this problem in one of his essays. He describes meeting a man in a Times Square porn theater, a shoe fetishist who's passionately turned on, in several wordless encounters, by the writer's sneakers. When Delaney needs to buy a new pair, he figures he might as well make the guy happy, and so he breaks their silence and asks him what *kind* of new sneakers he'd most enjoy. The questioned man is speechless, stricken; he flees; later he returns and manages to choke out only the words "light blue." But though the desired shoes are purchased, the sexual relationship is never the same. Delaney speculates that the man's desire exists in the realm of the unsaid; it has never been brought into the light of articulation, and to do so, in this case, damages or limits, or at least changes, the experience.

That there were words for homosexual behavior in Whitman's day there can be no doubt. Social structures for enabling same-sex congress seem to have been a feature of life in the modern city at least since the later eighteenth century, when the "Molly houses" in London offered a zone of permission for transvestism. Herman Melville, in *Redburn,* carefully evokes the nattily dressed fellows who hang out in front of a downtown restaurant where opera singers perform; he means us to understand what these stylish outfits convey. Historian and theorist Luc Sante describes a nineteenth-century pamphlet that takes as its project the publication of the locations of various quite particular spots of diverse sexual practice in New York City—so that those informed of, say, the address of a bordello featuring willing boys can take special care to avoid this hazard. Trenchant evidence comes from Rufus Griswold's review of the 1855 edition of *Leaves of Grass*:

> *We have found it impossible to convey any, even the most faint idea of style and contents, and of our disgust and detestation of them, without employing language that cannot be pleasing to ears polite; but it does seem that someone should, under circumstances like these, undertake a most disagreeable, yet stern duty. The records of crime show that many monsters have gone on in impunity, because the exposure of their vileness was attended with too great indelicacy.* Peccatum illud horrible, inter Christianos non nominandum.

The Latin, from Blackstone's 1811 *Commentaries on the Laws of England*, indicates the crime of sodomy as that sin which cannot be named among Christians. Surely, placing his specific identification of Whitman's particular form of "vileness" in Latin in a New York newspaper limits the audience for the review severely. What does it mean, to be warned away from what must remain nameless? To be told that one must never commit the sin that is so great it can't be spoken—isn't that necessarily an invitation as well as a warning, an act of pointing to a possibility, just like the self-contradictory guidebook described by Sante? It seems impossible to know, now, if Griswold truly means to condemn the book or to advertise it to a knowing clientele.

None of these examples posits a homosexual identity. Instead, they reveal instances of same-sex behavior. The archives of the nineteenth century are rich with evidence of intense same-sex friendship, passionate attachment. Does sex lie right beneath the surface, like those buds folded beneath speech?

The answer isn't really recoverable, though I can't help but think of a man I met in north-central Vermont, in the 1980s. A native Vermonter from a rural town, he was in his seventies then, and newly and proudly out; gay political associations in Vermont accepted him as a delightful sort of mascot. He told a story that is instructive, placed beside Delaney's anecdote of speechlessness. Near the town of his boyhood was a river that featured one of those delightful Vermont swimming holes, and beyond this inviting spot were wooded islands and farther streams. All summer, the place was the hang-out of adolescent boys, and it was understood among them that they would pair off, wander to some more private spot, and enjoy one another's bodies. This behavior was neither named nor spoken of, and it clearly did not constitute an identity; the teller of the tale did not, in fact, come out for sixty more years! Vermont, in the 1920s, was arguably a nineteenth-century place, and I wonder if this man's experience might not be as close as we could come to a sense of what same-sex practice might have been like before the coining of terms for it, before the imposition of the binary, the rigid enforcing and policing of the newly named heterosexual norm. It is an erotic landscape that appears in the paintings and photographs of Thomas Eakins, and certainly in the poems of Whitman—a free-floating, unfettered homosexual practice that was, to use the terms the poet had gleaned from phrenology, both amative and adhesive at once.

But still not an identity. The boys didn't think they were queers, and presumably most didn't go on having sex with men; that was not an available position for them, just as it wasn't supposed to be such for Whitman. His poems suggest an erotic life that is centered around encounters (often outdoors, but not always) with working-class guys and with younger men. He is at some pains to construct this as an experience of the love of equals, because this notion, a same-sex relation founded on equality (and not the Greek model of transmission of knowledge from older man to younger, or the Renaissance model of boy-loving, or a sort of fin-de-siècle notion of the sensitive esthete enjoying the more animal sexuality of working-class youths, as in Oscar Wilde's "feasting with panthers") is entirely new. Its genesis can be found in the new cities where one can leave the fixed social and familial roles of rural life and decide who one wants to be today. Does this new sense of freedom inform Whitman's slippery use of "you"—and his free-ranging, interpenetrating, omnipresent "I"? The new subject isn't simply a farmer, a son, a father, a teacher, a soldier: the citizen of the new world comes and goes, participates, observes, empathizes, slips into new relations and positions with a freedom the past couldn't have foreseen. How characteristic of its century this new freedom is: like the railroad, it moves you from one place to another swiftly; like the photograph, it allows you to travel in time. One of the more benign projects of industrialism, finally, is the liberation of subjectivity from the bonds of limited roles.

Which is all a way of saying that Whitman inscribes his sexuality on the frontier of modernity; he is writing into being—particularly in the "Calamus" poems of 1860, with their frank male-to-male loving, their assumption of equality on the part of the lovers—a new situation. He does not know how to proceed—he has no path —but he does it anyway. My guess is that he couldn't have written "Calamus," or the boldly homoerotic portions of the 1855 *Leaves*, even ten years later, as the advent of psychology increasingly led to a public perception of the normative, and imagery of the sacred family becomes the object of Victorian romance. As a category of identity—sodomite, invert, debauchee, pervert, Uranian—begins to emerge, so the poems with their claims of a loving, healthy, freely embraced same-sex desire become unwriteable, paradoxically, just as new language of homosexual identity begins to appear. Unwriteable, and, it would seem from Whitman's later remarks, and some of his revisions, barely defensible.

Thus comes about more than a century of remarkably agitated, confused, and fascinating writing about the subject of Whitman and sex, a dialogue (or shouting match) that seems to have begun with Griswold's review, published mere months after the *Leaves'* first edition. A confusion Whitman himself furthered, in his attempt to both say what he felt *and* still reach wide audiences, gaining the love and admiration of his nation. The history of the reading of Whitman's sexuality is a drama in itself, and it shows no real sign of letting up. Depending on your critic, Whitman's an onanist who never touched anybody, or a bisexual fantasist who might have had a *little* queer sex, or a trailblazing sexual pioneer.

What is not at all vague are the needs that Whitman's poems met, the powerful voice they gave or lent to an emergent class of men who had felt themselves isolated and voiceless. The most moving example of this I've seen is Edward Carpenter's book *Days with Walt Whitman, with some Notes on his Life and Work,* published in London in 1906. Carpenter describes his powerful impression of his first encounters with his hero in limpid prose:

> *I was aware of a certain radiant power in him, a large benign effluence and inclusiveness, as of the sun, which filled out the place where he was—yet with something of reserve and sadness in it too, and a sense of remoteness and inaccessibility.*

Carpenter goes on to chronicle a subsequent visit, and then to generalize about Whitman's work, suggesting that the poet extends his affections to women and men alike, circling repeatedly around this theme, then asserting the physicality of these affections, the poet's bodily embrace, and finally coming out with it, late in his text: these affections are expressed sexually as well. It is a thrilling rhetorical performance; Carpenter, clearly, wishes to signal to the flock; he wants the like-minded to find in Whitman their experience reflected, their voices—their soundless voices—carried.

I read the first edition of Carpenter's book, a handsome old green volume, in the library at Rice University. Penciled in the front was an unreadable name in a man's hand; stenciled at the bottom of the page was the name and address of a long-ago bookshop in L.A. What had been this book's odyssey? It had to have been passed hand to hand from one man like me to another, in a more-or-less underground transmission; they had to have known of Carpenter's pioneering work, and perhaps of the courage he took from Whitman. Would any of them have known, later on in the life of this gentle and startling little book, that Carpenter and his partner of forty years, George Merrill, were buried together, in 1929, in Surrey?

I DO NOT WISH TO SUGGEST that the contents of the unspeakable, for Whitman, are entirely sexual, for there is more deep down in his pockets than what obviously resides there. Carpenter and his readers were reaching for signposts of a gay identity when such a thing barely existed, but Whitman is ultimately a queer poet in the deepest sense of the word: he destabilizes, he unsettles, he removes the doors from their jambs. There is an uncanniness in "Song of Myself" and the other great poems of the 1850s that, for all his vaunted certainty, Whitman wishes to underscore. Again and again, he points us toward what, it seems, *must* remain folded in the buds beneath speech, since it cannot be brought to the surface. Here are two instances, the first from Section 50.

> *There is that in me . . . . I do not know what it is . . . . but I know it is in me . . .*

*I do not know it . . . . it is without name . . . . it is a word
   unsaid,
It is not in any dictionary or utterance or symbol.*

The second comes from Section 8 of "Crossing Brooklyn Ferry,"
from 1856:

*We understand then do we not?
What I promised without mentioning it, have you not
   accepted?
What the study could not teach—what the preaching
   could not accomplish is accomplished, is it not?*

In more or less a lifetime of reading these poems, I've never been
able to encounter those last lines without a bit of a shiver. How
does he know this? How does he understand what has happened
to me as I've read his poem—how, just as he predicted, "distance avails not,/ I am with you . . ." He has written his audience into being in this poem, and explained to us something
crucial—something unsayable—about the transmission taking
place. Surely sexuality is part of this transmission—the fact of the
speaker's longing, connected body, its material and sensual presence in the world from which he addresses us—but as sexuality is
inclined to be, it is and is not the entire story. As in Section 29 of
"Song of Myself," the exchange is deeply eroticized, but it points
on past the simple interaction of bodies toward a larger understanding of the structure of the real. Sex colors everything, shapes
every aspect of our perception, and as the erotics of exchange,
of faith, of writing itself, it defines the ethos of participation. Is
desire itself a lust toward the unsayable? Something about Whitman's outsiderness—his participation in what cannot be said, his
huge pressurizing awareness of all that resists language—thrums
in these passages; that presence, felt and almost-named, makes

these poems as alive as the hour they were written. For all their vast claims, there is a silence at their center. He's a genius to use form to point toward this necessary silence, but a further kind of genius—one marked by a nearly unthinkable nerve—is at work in these passages too, where the poem resolutely addresses itself to the underside of speech, our common human possession: untranslatable perception, unvoiced longing, and what glimmers at the edges of knowledge: all we do not know.

NINE

DONE WITH THE COMPASS

In a 1969 issue of *Time,* a magazine my father subscribed to, I found an article describing a new phenomenon: the Gay Liberation Front. The text was accompanied by a photograph of men sitting at a table, organizers giving out information. The one who caught my eye had dark, longish hair under a print bandanna, muttonchop sideburns, soulful eyes. His face hadn't been obscured, he wasn't in the shadows. He wasn't hiding. Handsome as any of the men I admired on the street, in their artfully patched jeans and handmade belts and sandals, he looked like he lived in daylight; he looked like a person who had friends. I couldn't formulate my thoughts about the image. I sat, with the magazine open on my lap, and looked, and hoped that no one would see me looking.

I was sixteen, and not until that moment had I seen an image of an out, confident gay man, one who seemed to live in happy concert with others. It must be difficult to imagine such a blackout of images or information, to conjure such invisibility and silence, if you didn't live through it. If you are a reader too young for this period in American life to seem real to you, I take the fact that it seems unimaginable as a real sign of the progress of freedom in this world.

———•••———

THERE ARE POETS who find their strength in brevity, who use as few words as possible, arranged in the minimum number of lines, to evoke sense perception, emotion, and idea. Whitman, it goes without saying, is not one of those. He is most comfortable on a broader scale. His great poems—"Song of Myself," "The Sleepers," "Crossing Brooklyn Ferry," "Out of the Cradle Endlessly Rocking," and "When Lilacs Last in the Dooryard Bloomed"— each straddle hundreds of lines, providing the poet with room to catalog particulars (*The glories strung like beads on my smallest sights and hearings,* he calls them), to stack up parallel statements, to address his reader, to depart from and return to his argument, and to construct a kind of poetic architecture designed to be mimetic of the process of thinking, and thus draw us more intimately near. This is why his shorter poems often feel like parts of a larger, more encompassing one; even satisfyingly complete shorter pieces such as "To You" and "This Compost" might be seen as outtakes, or gestures in the direction of some overarching intention.

One reason for this is perhaps the speed at which Whitman composed. He said he'd been simmering, before Emerson's New York lecture of 1848, then Emerson's passionate call for a distinctly American poet had set him to boil. Nonetheless, it was seven years before the first edition of *Leaves* appeared, containing twelve poems. Fired by the book's publication, Whitman began to work faster; his second edition, only a year later, contained twenty new poems. One of them, "Sun-Down Poem," later to be retitled "Crossing Brooklyn Ferry," is one of the great poems written in English in its century or any other.

The new look of the second edition is telling. The oversized production of the first, destined for the parlor, its intricately wrought title stamped in gold, gave way to a more streamlined look, perhaps because he was no longer bound to use the large paper his first printer had provided. But I suspect he had recalibrated his sense of audience in a way more suited to his mission; the green book was now sized to fit in a pocket of one of those work jackets Whitman liked to wear, meant to be carried everywhere, and read *in the open air every season of every year of your life*. Hefty, encyclopedic in its proportions, the book came more to resemble the new gospel that Whitman intended, a book that would convince us that *the known universe has one complete lover and that is the greatest poet*.

The third edition of the 1860 edition included 146 new poems—a nearly unbelievable number! Some sixty-eight of these were written between the appearance of the second in 1856 and June of 1857 when the poet was clearly in a kind of creative fever, one that essentially did not subside until the 456-page third collection was headed for the press. This third volume was produced by a commercial publisher, and is indeed more traditional in design. Dropping the models of coffee-table book and portable testament, it looks more like most mid-nineteenth-century books of poems, with small line drawings and ornamental flourishes around the poems' titles. The frontispiece presents the poet in an engraving taken from an oil portrait, Walt Whitman with lush but not yet prophetic locks and a stylish cravat, more Romantic spirit than one of the roughs. Somewhere between two thousand and five thousand copies were printed, and the book was largely well reviewed, and fared better in the marketplace than the earlier editions.

I can't help but wonder what would have happened if Whitman had abandoned his practice of expanding and rearranging his book. Why not write one collection, set it aside, and write another? This is one of the primary ways poets progress; looking at a book you've finished, you don't want to pursue exactly that same path again. A new collection invites us to vary form and tone, try on a new stance, strike out in a new direction and thus view familiar territory from another vantage point. In truth, our obsessions, our ways of making meaning, even our signature vocabulary and syntax often stay remarkably close to where we began; if we're lucky, we just get better at using them. But, as we move from book to book, serious attention to the matters at hand can help to widen the embrace of our work a bit, and just a bit can prove plenty. Suppose Whitman had decided to bring a thread that had been recessive in one book—the abject self-doubt he reveals in the chilling final section of "As I Ebb'd with the Ocean of Life," for instance—and bring it more into the foreground in the next? What unexpected, potentially rich poems we might have had!

Or maybe not. I can see reasons why Whitman would have wanted to go on cultivating the singular field of "leaves" that comprised his book. In a way that is true of no other great poet, his poems were a tool to make something happen; the change he wished to effect, and sometimes believed he could, was more important to him than art. This is why he could later say he wished he'd been an orator instead, when he'd written at least two of the greatest poems in the language. Of course poets themselves don't get to know if they have written anything that will last, but Whitman tells us, in no uncertain terms, that he will be read after his death, by *men and women of a generation, or ever so many generations hence.* I can confidently say that, had I written "Song of Myself" or "Crossing Brooklyn Ferry," I would not be wishing I'd chosen another career.

It's in the 1860 edition that the poet first begins to arrange his poems in clusters, making thematic clumps, breaking one off here and adding another there. He would go on remixing the order for the rest of his life.

This was largely a mistake. It results, at the worst, in sections of poems about the sea, or winter, and this kind of organization inevitably diminishes the work. "Out of the Cradle Endlessly Rocking" takes place on a beach, but it is not "about" the sea, because great poems are not "about" in this way; they are profound reaches into that "furnace of meaning," and they use whatever is at hand—the sea, a ferryboat ride, an unruly field of grass—to get to where they need to go. The "subject" matters until the furnace is lit, and then the poem almost seems to burn its ostensible occasion clean away.

It may be that Whitman arranged and fiddled because he came to understand, over time, that he was losing the capacity to create the magnificent, visionary odes that had launched his career. He would suffer from poverty, and from anxiety over his reception and reputation; as an outsider who both wanted and did not want to be on the inside, he was in a position of near-constant instability. He saw the boys he adored, the ones he hoped might base a newly energized democratic order on their affection for each other, tear one another apart on the battlefield instead, in a war of mind-bending brutality. He wandered from bed to bed for five years in makeshift hospitals, in appalling conditions, offering what comfort and witness he could, and destabilized his own health in the process. He suffered a massive stroke and required help for the rest of his life. How could I expect him to go on writing great poems when he'd already created ones that no one had known how to write in the first place, poems that sail right past what we thought a poem could do?

•••

ONE EXAMPLE OF SUCH A POEM (or poems, depending on how you think of it) is the lyric sequence "Calamus" of 1860—truly a sequence, since the order of the poems and the spaces between them create a larger sense of meaning and presence than any of the individual pieces, strong as they may be, could generate on their own.

The suite's titled "Calamus" after a plant native to Long Island, a wetland dweller the poet described to William Michael Rossetti as *growing about water-ponds in the valley . . . presenting the biggest & hardiest kind of spears of grass—and their fresh, aquatic, pungent bouquet.* Some lines from an early notebook entry probably bring us closer to the plant's charms:

> *Calamus sweet-green bulb and melons with bulbs grateful to the hand*
> *I am a mystic in a trance exhalation*
> *something wild and untamed—half savage*
> *coarse things*
> *Trickling Sap flows from the end of the manly tooth of delight . . .*

We've encountered that boss-tooth before, bringing with it the spilling of liquor, rich recompense and trickling sap.

And indeed, the sequence begins

> *In paths untrodden,*
> *in the growth by margins of pond waters*

evoking some marshy retreat unvisited by casual wanderers, *for in this secluded spot I can respond as I dare not elsewhere.*

There is an old tradition, just how old it's impossible to say, of men seeking sexual congress in the natural world, in settings known to an inner circle but not generally recognized. In the years I lived in Provincetown, on the tip of Cape Cod, and certainly for decades before me and in the decade since I've left, the secluded spot in question was the dunes and salt marsh at Herring Cove, which stretched all the way from the beach by that name around the narrowing spiral of the tip of the Cape, past Wood End Lighthouse and ending at Long Point Light. You never needed to walk that far. On a mild day in winter, men would be wandering in the dunes near the parking lot; in summer, they'd be roaming the edges of the great tidal flat sheltered by the arm of the dunes, in a marvelous shimmer of horizontals, bands of silver water and of beach grass interrupted by the sharp verticals of reeds. You could walk so far into the marsh there was little evidence of a distant road, or a lighthouse, only men naked or nearly so up to their ankles or thighs in warm water, the hunter-gatherers of pleasure. They were the celebrants of what Whitman here calls *manly attachment*, and *athletic love*. He is at pains to name what it is he celebrates, *the secret of my nights and days . . .*

If a poem could have gotten much more forthright in 1860, I don't know how, but no one save men who shared the poet's desires seemed to notice. A wider readership, to the extent Whitman had one, remained blind to the sexual content that seems to us to fairly ooze from the poems. The subject of male same-sex desire remained firmly unseeable.

It may have helped that the "Calamus" section in Whitman's third edition is countered by a mirror double, a group of poems called "Enfans d'Adam." Perhaps even that French title signals us that something is off; why does a poet who vigorously embraced demotic American speech need such window dressing? This sequence is an extended hymn to reproductive sex, and in the second poem of the sequence the speaker announces that he is

> —*singing the phallus,*
> *Singing the song of procreation,*
> *Singing the need of superb children, and therein superb grown people,*
> *Singing the muscular urge . . .*

Some of Whitman's readers, including a surprising number of women, cheered him on, while others shut the book in horror. Was this in fact what made Emily Dickinson give up on *Leaves of Grass*?

Whitman's intent was for these poems to balance the Calamus

poems by embodying the love of women and the joy of heterosexual coupling, but the result is strained. There's even a nasty whiff of selective breeding in it, and ultimately of eugenics. The best of the group is the seventh poem, in which a lover (gender unnamed) addresses another (gender immaterial), in a fierce and uncompromising salutation to what is elemental in us. I don't know that this poem gave rise to Thoreau's comment about the crudity of Whitman's sexuality (*It is as if the beasts spoke*, he sniffed), but I would be delighted if it were in fact a riposte to the uptight Thoreau; it's a deep, full-throated celebration of two people becoming elemental together.

YOU and I—what the earth is, we are,
We two—how long we were fooled!
Now delicious, transmuted, swiftly we escape, as Nature escapes,
We are Nature—long have we been absent, but now we return,
We become plants, leaves, foliage, roots, bark,
We are bedded in the ground—we are rocks,
We are oaks—we grow in the openings side by side,
We browse—we are two among the wild herds, spontaneous as any,
We are two fishes swimming in the sea together,
We are what the locust blossoms are—we drop scent around the lanes,
        mornings and evenings,
We are also the coarse smut of beasts, vegetables, minerals,
We are what the flowing wet of the Tennessee is—we are two peaks
        of the Blue Mountains, rising up in Virginia,
We are two predatory hawks—we soar above and look down,
We are two resplendent suns—we it is who balance ourselves
        orbic and stellar—we are as two comets;
We prowl fanged and four-footed in the woods—we spring on prey;
We are two clouds, forenoons and afternoons, driving overhead,
We are seas mingling—we are two of those cheerful waves,
        rolling over each other, and interwetting each other,

We are what the atmosphere is, transparent, receptive, pervious,
    impervious,
We are snow, rain, cold, darkness—we are each product
    and influence of the globe,
We have circled and circled till we have arrived home again—
    we two have,
We have voided all but freedom, and all but our own joy.

If that is how the beasts sound when they speak, then I am ready to turn and live with them. The poem captures exactly the elemental, descending-to-earth feeling joyful sex can have, an experience that seems to encompass all others, to bring us into contact with many kinds of lives, to awaken us to all we are. My question about Dickinson a few paragraphs ago was a rhetorical one, but I'd like to answer it: Of course not. Enter into evidence this uncharacteristic poem, numbered in the archive of her untitled poems as 249, her own version of *We have circled and circled till we have arrived home again:*

Wild Nights—Wild Nights!
Were I with thee
Wild Nights should be
Our luxury!

Futile – the winds –
To a heart in port –
Done with the compass –
Done with the chart!

Rowing in Eden –
Ah, the sea!
Might I moor – Tonight –
In thee!

The first time I toured Dickinson's house in Amherst, Massachusetts, I was with a small group guided by a docent, and we stopped near the end of our walk through the house (this was before one could enter the Evergreens, the magnificently untouched ghostpalace of Susan and Austin Dickinson next door) before a copy of this poem, printed on a placard on the wall. The docent talked about Dickinson's reputation as the cracked spinster in her white dresses, lowering cookies to neighborhood children in a basket from a second-floor window, a perpetual virgin whispering to visitors from behind a door just a bit ajar, and then she read us this poem. *What do you think?* she asked us. Did Emily Dickinson ever experience sex? And she turned to the poem again, a smile spreading into her eyes.

There is something about *Rowing in Eden —Ah, the sea!* that arrives with the force of utter conviction, which is another form of the voice of experience. The aptness and freshness of the metaphor, the surprise of something it never occurred to me anyone *did* in Eden, and then that breathtaking opening out to the freedom and breadth of the sea—why do these fill me with certainty that Dickinson knows whereof she speaks? It thrills me that I don't know why; the fact that poems do things they should not be able to do, through means not fully apprehensible—well, it makes me treasure them all the harder.

But in truth what I like best here, the lines I might want tattooed on my skin if ever I were to inscribe on myself words rather than the more ambiguous, less nailed-to-meanings image I bear now, are two lines of superb refusal: *Done with the compass —/Done with the chart!* We probably read them first as a sort of reiteration of the fact that the speaker's no longer looking; she doesn't care how the winds blow because she's found her heart's port, and needs no more go a-sailing. But that borders on the sentimental, and so this genius has supplied, inside these lines, a secondary sense. She has entered a zone in which maps no longer apply. Without compass or chart we enter into freedom: nothing but nothing is telling us where to go. The placement of that stressed syllable—*Done*—at the beginning of two lines in a row makes this sound like an outburst, a cry of liberation. She is not afraid of getting lost. With exasperation and joy, she throws away the pointers and directives. *Done with the compass – /Done with the chart:* I say it to myself, sometimes, as a rallying declaration of freedom. The final line of Whitman's ecstatic hymn to lovemaking is entirely in accord here: *We have voided all but freedom, and all but our own joy.*

"Enfans d'Adam" fails to maintain the genuineness of this seventh section, or its sexy appeal. Some of the poems patronize women instead: *To talk to the perfect girl who understands me—the girl of The States.* Others continue to emphasize what Whitman elsewhere called *the procreant urge of the world* over pleasure or intimacy. The speaker sometimes becomes a sexual dynamo of divine proportions:

> *Lusty, phallic, with the potent original loins, perfectly sweet*
> *. . . offering myself,*
> *Bathing myself, bathing my songs in sex,*
> *Offspring of my loins.*

I am no prude, in my reading life or elsewhere, but I find this embarrassing. I understand that it's spoken by an avatar of male fertility, but have those loins really not been praised enough?

——•••——

WHITMAN COULD NOT KEEP his mind on women, even for the duration of a few poems. Here's a sampling of lines from the sequence intended to praise what the phrenologists called *amativeness,* the love between men and women:

> *—the sight of the perfect body,*
> *The swimmer swimming naked in the bath, or motionless on his back*
> *Lying and floating . . .*

And

> *I am for those who believe in loose delights—I share the midnight*
> *orgies of young men . . .*

We know from early drafts of these that he changed some of his pronouns, moving poems from the "Calamus" cluster into this one. It seems surprising that his attempt to balance the homoerotic poems with these was so successful, but the performance was not without consequences: "Enfans d'Adam" was banned in Boston for years, and Whitman would later be fired from his government job because of his frank celebration of heterosexual pleasure.

—••—

"CALAMUS," AN ASSEMBLAGE devoted to the praise of *adhesiveness,* the phrenological term for friendship, what the poet called *athletic love,* moves in mysterious ways. After opening with a sort of invocation, in which the poet resolves *to sing no songs today but those of manly attachment,* and promises *to tell the secret of my nights and days,* the second, mysterious poem turns out to be a hymn to death. It begins with an image of the hair on the speaker's chest, *his scented herbage,* yielding leaves, the pages of his book. This image echoes an equation familiar from "Song of Myself": body equals grass equals text, but now what grows are tomb-leaves. The poet who told us, a few years before, that *there really is no such thing as death* now seems to have moved into another relation to mortality; now he asks *what indeed is beautiful, except Death and Love?* He asserts that love and death are *folded together above all,* and that death may be *the real reality*, which will long outlive life. What are we to make of this somber, rather ceremonial poem, coming from the great celebrant of vitality?

Whitman has made a great movement in the direction of the abject, and I suspect he has placed this poem so early in his sequence of love poems because it is a sort of threshold. The speaker we met in "Song of Myself" cannot, by definition, be lonely, or depressed, because he contains within himself the multitudes, and is a voice speaking for all. From his vantage point no boundary exists between self and other; he shares in all vitality. His life is rooted in the continuously creative forces of being, the pour of something emerging from nothing, the endless recirculation of energy, matter, and language.

That vision has not vanished, exactly, but it has cooled, and the speaker has shrunk to a more recognizable human form; he is part of all the circles of being that surround him and intersect with his individual life, but he is no longer acutely conscious of being unbounded. He is, instead, one who loves, and who is capable of losing the one he loves, and who will himself disappear.

The speaker in "Song of Myself" loves everybody, and needs only comradeship, and in this way floats high above the ordinary human landscape of attachment. But the speaker in "Calamus" wants and needs the specific gravity of an anchoring other. He gives his heart—himself, as it were—to one man, and no such project of finding home in another person's embrace comes without abjection, and terror, struggle, and disappointment. Whitman addresses death directly, at the end of this second section, in one of his wildly bold moves, and says *you will last very long.* Perhaps that's what necessitates placing this section so early in the forty-five-poem sequence: is it the permanence of death that requires us to seek another sort of "death" first, losing and then finding the self again in the embrace of another?

TEN

THE OLD OLD POEM WALT

History and biography have an odd way of singling out detail, some bit of a life that acquires unexpected significance. Here is one tiny element of Walt Whitman's life on Classon Avenue in Brooklyn, in the house where his extended family lived from 1856 until 1859. The New England Transcendentalist and father of the author of *Little Women* Bronson Alcott writes that the poet shared a room with his disabled younger brother Eddie, described variously by biographers as "retarded, probably epileptic," "mentally defective," "helpless and strange in his simplemindedness." It must have been a stormy household. Walter Whitman Sr. had died in 1855; Walt's mother, Louisa, struggled to hold together the household in which six of her eight adult children lived. An older brother, Jesse, possessed a violent temper; his fits of rage would eventually cause him to be committed to the King's County Lunatic Asylum. Walt's sister Hannah married a painter to whom Walt had introduced her, then isolated herself in hypochondria. Whitman, who was devoted to Eddie, would will the younger man most of his possessions, and ensure that, when Eddie died some years after Walt, the brothers would be reunited in the imposing tomb the poet built for himself in Camden.

When Alcott first came to visit in 1856, with Henry David Thoreau and the abolitionist and social Utopianist Sarah Tyndale in tow, Whitman was not at home. But his mother brought the group into the kitchen, where she praised Walt while baking biscuits. Thoreau, apparently, snatched one from the oven without asking her consent. The group returned the next day, and Walt walked them up to the second-floor bedroom. Alcott noted details of the room: the unmade bed, which still bore the impressions of sleepers; the chamber pot visible beneath it.

The detail I keep coming back to is this: there seems to have been no decoration in the room, save that over the mantel were pasted three images representing figures from classical myth: Hercules, Bacchus, and a satyr. Alcott describes them as mounted on the "rude walls" of the room. He asked Whitman which of the images represented the poet, and, depending on the source one consults, either received a shrug for an answer or a was told by Whitman that he was an amalgam of the three. The visitor drew upon these figures in his unforgettable catalog of impressions of Whitman:

> *Broad-shouldered, rouge-fleshed, Bacchus- browed, bearded like a satyr, and rank, he wears his man-Bloomer in defiance of every-body, having these as everything else after his own fashion, and for example to all men hereafter. Red flannel undershirt, open-breasted, exposing his brawny neck; striped calico jacket over this, the collar Byroneal, with coarse cloth overalls buttoned to it; cowhide boots; a heavy roundabout, with huge outside pockets and buttons to match; and a slouch hat, for house and street alike. Eyes gray, unimaginative, cautious yet melting. When talking will recline upon the couch at length, pillowing his head upon his bended arm, and informing you naively how lazy he is, and slow. Listens well; asks you to repeat what he has failed to catch at once, yet hesitates in speaking often,*

or gives over as if fearing to come short of the sharp, full, concrete meaning of his thought. Inquisitive, very; over-curious even; inviting criticism on himself, on his poems—pronouncing it 'pomes'. In fine, an egotist, incapable of omitting, or suffering any one long to omit, noting Walt Whitman in discourse. Swaggy in his walk, burying both his hands in outside pockets. He has never been sick, he says, not taken medicine, nor sinned; and so is quite innocent of repentence and man's fall.

Whitman might have chosen the three images, or perhaps Walt and Eddie did so together, but there's another possibility as well. A young man named Fred Vaughan, who worked on the Fulton Ferry and later on Manhattan coaches, lived with the poet for some time in the Classon Avenue house. Vaughn's letters to the poet, even many years later, make reference to their cohabitation. In 1874 he writes that he'd "been down past our old home several times this summer" and remembers a letter from Emerson Whitman had received "when we were living in Classon Ave." It was common for teenage boys like Vaughn to leave their often crowded homes early and apprentice themselves to an older man, or be taken in as boarders. Vaughan's letters describe his friendship with Whitman's mother; he takes interest in and encourages Whitman's work, and reports, delightfully, on attending a lecture Emerson delivered on friendship. The philosopher said, he writes,

> *that a man whose heart was filled with a warm, ever enduring not to be shaken by anything Friendship was one to be set on one side apart from other men, and almost to be worshipped as a saint.—There, Walt, how do you like that? What do you think of them setting you & myself . . . up in some public place, with an immense placard on our breasts, reading Sincere Freinds!!!*

What charm in those lines! Fred was clearly a smart, affectionate, and witty young man. In the museum of the history of sex the corridors are, inevitably, dimly lit; we can't know exactly what went on, save that the sweet congress of bodies is a perennial shaping force in human lives, a spur and joy, and transformative, for good or ill or some marbled marriage of the two. Is that what took place, under the tutelary spirits of three figures of masculine strength, one a hero, one a god of pleasure, one half-man and half-beast? Walt and Fred enjoyed lots of nude bathing in the East River, on the Williamsburg shore. Fred wrote letters to Whitman all his life. One surviving missive, undated, was enclosed in a separate envelope with another letter in the mid-1870s, after Fred had married and fathered four sons.

> *Walt*
>
> *Driver hour. I loafing in a Lumber Yard at foot of 35th St—Under the shade of a pile of Lumber and sitting on a lower pile.—Opposite and close to me at the pier head a Barque. In the forerigging flapping lazily in the summer breese are a few sailors clothes. From the galley-pipe between the Main and the fore-mast issues a cloud of smoke.—One of the men in blue shirt and bare footed has just come from alooft—where he has been loosening the Mainsail which seems to be wet. He has now gone below I suppose to his dinner.—On the opposite side of the river Wmsbrgh—between the every plying ferryboats, the tugs, the Harlem Boats, and mingled with the splash of the paddle wheels —the murmur of the sailors at dinner.—the lazy flap of the sails. the screech of the steam whistle of the tugs, the laugh and wrangler of the boys in swimming—comes a remembrance of thee dear Walt —*

With Wmsbgh & Brooklyn—with the ferries
and the vessels with the Lumber piles and the docks.
From among all out of all. Connected with all and yet
distinct from all arrises thee Dear Walt. Walt—my
life has turned out a poor miserable failure. I am not
a drunkard nor a teetotaler—I am neither honest
nor dishonest. I have my family in Brooklyn and am
supporting them.—I never stole, robbed, cheate, nor
defrauded any person out of anything, and yet I feels
that I have not been honest to myself—my family nor
my friends

One Oclock, the Barque is laden with coal and
the carts have come. The old old Poem Walt. The
cart backs up, the bucket comes up full and goes down
empty—The men argue and swear. The wind blows the
coal dust over man & beast and now it reaches me –
　　　　　　Fred Vaughan Atlantic Ave 2nd door above
　　　　　　　　　　Classon Ave. Brooklyn

HEARTBREAKING AS VAUGHAN'S RETROSPECTIVE letter may
be, Whitman seemed not so sorry to see him go, although they
did remain friends. Years later, Whitman was troubled by turbu-
lence in his relationship with Peter Doyle, a Washington, DC,
conductor the poet met on his streetcar one wildly stormy night;
Doyle described their first encounter famously: *We were familiar*
at once—I put my hand on his knee—we understood. Disturbed by
conflict between them, Whitman wrote instructions to himself in
a notebook: *Depress the adhesive nature—It is in excess—making life*
a torment . . . Remember Fred Vaughan. But if Vaughan had brought

turmoil to the poet, he may also have been a new sort of muse, occasioning an emotional vulnerability not previously in evidence in Whitman's poems.

—•••—

HAVING LAID THE GROUNDWORK in these its first two poems— one in praise of sexual congress among the reeds, outside any organized framework of social life, the other a hymn to death, praising mortality as the source of these songs—"Calamus" moves into a series of elegantly set pronouncements—public, visionary, indeed Messianic statements predicting the future of *robust love*. They are remarkable for their sweeping, unchecked confidence, their faith in the poet's prophetic position:

> *For I am the new husband, and I am the comrade.*

> *And this, O this shall henceforth be the token of comrades,*
> *this calamus-root shall,*
> *Interchange it youths, with each other!*

> *There shall from me be a new friendship—It shall be called*
> *after my name . . .*

> *Affection shall solve every one of the problems of freedom,*
> *Those who love each other shall be invincible,*
> *They shall finally make America completely victorious, in my name.*

> *I will make inseparable cities, with their arms about each other's*
> *necks.*

These sound like passages from a queer version of the Gospel According to Saint Thomas, a text unknown in Whitman's life-time, and read in almost any light their arrogance is dazzling.

It helps a little to remember that Whitman is, at least some of the time, conflating himself with his book. The speaker in this stanza from "Calamus" 3 is clearly not Walt but *Leaves of Grass* itself:

> *Or, if you will, thrusting me beneath your clothing,*
> *Where I may feel the throbs of your heart, or rest upon your hip,*
> *Carry me when you go forth over land or sea;*
> *For thus, merely touching you, is enough—is best,*
> *And thus, touching you would I silently sleep and be carried*
> *eternally.*

I hesitate at these passages a bit less if I view them as a voice crying out for a group that has none, a group that was newly emergent yet barely even seen to exist when these poems were composed. One can read them as acts of performative speech, as when Allen Ginsberg writes, in "Wichita Vortex Sutra," *I hereby declare the end of the War.* He means Vietnam, and he means his poem to be the chant and spell that begins to end it; in the space in which his poem is heard, in the new space created by the reception of his words, the War is over.

Still, would-be saviors tread dangerous paths, and in fact the wisdom of the seer is called into question; is it possible to be enlightened and so full of yourself at once?

It's a relief when, in "Calamus" 7, Whitman makes room for self-doubt, one of the great correctives. His usual syntax, with its long, confident strides and mastery of asides, suddenly falls to pieces:

> *The skies of day and night—colors, densities, forms*
> *—May-be these are, (as doubtless they are,) only*
> *apparitions, and the real something has yet to be*
> *known,*

(How often they dart out of themselves, as if to con-
    found me and mock me!
How often I think neither I know, nor any man
    knows, aught of them;)
May-be they only seem to me what they are, (as
    doubtless they indeed but seem,) as from my
    present point of view—And might prove, (as of
    course they would,) naught of what they appear,
    or naught any how, from entirely changed points
    of view…

WHILE NO ONE WOULD WANT to read a lot of that, there's something engaging about seeing Whitman tumble over himself, his thinking snarled up in qualifications, in this lurching, going-nowhere tumble. What calms this restless barrage is love; the speaker's anxieties come to rest when *he whom I love travels with me.* Nation-founding ambitions are set aside, the speaker's desires salved:

                    —I am satisfied,
He ahold of my hand has completely satisfied me.

That line, the final one of "Calamus" 7, is a quiet bombshell. It marks the appearance of love for one person in Whitman's work. Read within the chronology of the poet's attachments, *he* who has satisfied the speaker would seem to be Fred Vaughan. I like knowing this because I want to know Whitman more closely, having been so won by the poems, but the identity of the lover doesn't matter really, concerned as "Calamus" is with illuminating singular, archetypal moments in the experience of love, placing them into a chain that acknowledges their radicalism, inscribing a letter sent into the future:

To one a century hence, or any number of centuries hence,
To you, yet unborn, these, seeking you.

These, Whitman has announced, are the songs of adhesiveness, *of manly attachment,* but given his tone and the poems of the opening pages, it's easy to think he means to celebrate affection between men in a general way. Then, at the end of "Calamus" 7, his windy rhetoric and gnarled syntax seem to come crashing down, a hindrance and obstacle now that what he most requires is this, the sheer fact of his lover's hand holding his, and what it brings: an end to anxious questioning, to insistent uncertainty.

. . . I am silent—I require nothing further,
I cannot answer the question of appearances, or that
   of identity beyond the grave,
But I walk or sit indifferent—I am satisfied,
He ahold of my hand has completely satisfied me.

It's no accident that the word *satisfied* appears twice within the span of two lines.

Arriving on the heels of that plain, almost naked moment, "Calamus" 8 marks a crucial point, a pivot, one of those moments in an artistic life when a new path opens and beckons. This twelve-line poem begins with a kind of intellectual and artistic autobiography:

Long I thought that knowledge alone would suffice me –
   O if I could but obtain knowledge!
Then my lands engrossed me—Lands of the prairies, Ohio's land,
   the southern savannas, engrossed me—For them I would live –
   I would be their orator;
Then I met the examples of the old and new heroes—I heard of
   warriors, sailors, and all dauntless persons—And it seemed to

> me that I too had it in me to be as dauntless as any—
>   and would be so;
> And then, to enclose all, it came to me to strike up the songs
>   of the New World—and then I believed my life must be
>   spent in singing;

That's as clear an account of the evolution of a poet's vocation as
we're likely to find anywhere, and for Whitman it is notably economical, its list uncharacteristically compact. The poet wants to
make a single sentence here, albeit a capacious one; he wants us to
keep the logic of the poem's movement in mind, its arc from *Long
I thought* to an account of how he sees things now. Amazingly,
he makes an announcement to the North American landscape,
declaring a change of heart:

> But now take notice, land of the prairies, land of the south savannas,
>   Ohio's land,
> Take notice, you Kanuck woods—and you Lake Huron—and all
>   that with you roll toward Niagara—and you Niagara also,
> And you, Californian mountains—That you each and all
>   find somebody else to be your singer of songs,
> For I can be your singer of songs no longer—One who loves me is jealous
>   of me, and withdraws me from all but love,
> With the rest I dispense—I sever from what I thought would
>   suffice me, for it does not—it is now empty and tasteless
>   to me,
> I heed knowledge, and the grandeur of The States, and the example
>   of heroes, no more,
> I am indifferent to my own songs—I will go with him I love,
> It is enough for us that we are together—We never separate again.

I suppose it is no wonder Whitman suppressed this poem, excising
it from every edition after 1860. He had to, really, since it charted

a direction for future work that he declined to take. Could he, in pursuit of a poetry of intimacy, have abandoned his project as American bard? I wouldn't regret the loss, especially in the poems written after 1860, when an increasingly nationalistic impulse and a sentimental regard for *The States* softens the risky freshness of Whitman's earlier work, compromising the sharpness of his vision.

Had he done so, we'd surely have no Walt Whitman Bridge in Philadelphia, no Walt Whitman Service Area on the New Jersey Turnpike, no Walt Whitman Mall in the town of his birth. High school students would not be reading, as they sometimes still do, "O Captain! My Captain!," a decidedly Victorian performance of grief. His home in Camden would be no museum, and there would have been no money for a tomb. To appropriate a phrase from Elizabeth Bishop, none of these losses would bring disaster. Though his public role as the Good Gray Poet, for well over a century after his death, perhaps even today, has allowed grateful readers to find the bracing openness of a full-bodied freethinker, a man who loved and embraced the body, and honored its joys, if they dug into the thick and cumbersome volume in which he embedded his best work. Had he followed the course he imagines in "Calamus" 8, would we have his poems of intimacy at all?

I love that Whitman imagines—articulately, clearly—the possibility of stepping away from everything he's done, and becoming a poet he'd barely recognize. A poet solely devoted to singing his love for another man, in 1860? Into what silence would he have spoken? One can intuit the answer to that in the fact that Whitman did, after all, publish the most open of texts of same-sex love in his time, and basically no one noticed; no internal apparatus or position from which to read the poems existed. This lends "Calamus" much of its essential strangeness; a poem is being spoken out of a silence so profound that the poet must invent a vocabulary to name his subject, and imagine an audience capable of receiving the poem. An alien speaks to other aliens he cannot yet see, though indeed they will come. Whitman's poem summons Oscar Wilde and Edward Carpenter, Bram Stoker and John Addington Symonds; his poems and his name become a signifier for a category of men emerging toward the century's end, men thrilled beyond measure to find their poet.

But before all that, here, in "Calamus" 11, is one man, speaking to everyone and no one in particular, writing the lyrics he is compelled to write, which have suddenly veered from the oratorical to the evocation of very particular experience, from the big public space of Manhattan streets or the Crystal Palace built for New York's 1853 Exhibition of the Industry of All Nations, to perhaps a tent in the countryside, *in paths untrodden, in the growth by margins of pond waters.* The man who has been universal lover, unbounded, proud of the scale of his lust, emerges on a more human scale, the size of any of us, caught in the thrall of one other.

> *And that night, while all was still, I heard the waters roll slowly*
> *   continually up the shores,*
> *I heard the hissing rustle of the liquid and sands, as directed to me,*
> *   whispering, to congratulate me,*
> *For the one I love most lay sleeping by me under the same cover*
> *   in the cool night,*
> *In the stillness, in the autumn moonbeam, his face was inclined*
> *   toward me,*
> *And his arm lay lightly around my breast—And that night I was*
> *   happy.*

Good-bye, then, to Hercules, Bacchus, and the satyr; hello to merely human love.

AS A BOY—years before that issue of *Time* magazine blew into my hands (on the wind coming from the wings of the angel of history?)—I dwelled under the sign of invisibility. I enjoyed successes in school, and had friends I was forever leaving behind as we moved to a new place, but in my heart I was a member of the one-boy tribe of the Not to Be Named.

Hiding my sexuality meant hiding my body. Even physicality seemed to belong to others; masculinity was a church that was closed to me, and though on some level I longed to join, I didn't have the keys to those locks. I took refuge in being a smart boy, in reading and putting on plays, arenas in which I could excel and thus downplay my failures.

Dramas of inclusion and rejection played out daily at lunchtime and recess. When four smart and interesting fourth-grade girls, skilled jump-ropers who knew many rhymes, would not allow me to be their friend because I was a boy, I didn't know how to say that I was not a boy in the way they thought. My eagerness must have fueled their impulse to send me away. That would have been 1962, on a playground newly scraped from Sonoran desert, and the memory still burns a little; a sense of inarticulate frustration rises in my chest as I think of it. Such stories, many infinitely painful, are legion in the memories of gay men and lesbians of my generation.

We're young enough to have escaped the horrors of aversion therapy, mental institutions, and prison, but old enough to have lived through a weird, nearly total silence, an almost complete invisibility so seamless as to seem unthinkable now, as if an entire culture conspired to say that something evident was simply not there. It makes you crazy, for something you know to be true, know from the very core or root of you, to remain unspeakable.

Enforced invisibility *made* us sick, left us numb or raging, mostly against ourselves, which is why so many took their own lives, and so many others—myself included, at fifteen— tried to.

Children are still bullied for their difference and vulnerability, and not a month goes by but some poor soul who doesn't conform to the codes of how a man or woman is supposed to dress or walk or speak is murdered on the street. But the world has shifted, in my lifetime, with dazzling rapidity. In a city like the one I live in (that city being New York, I have to acknowledge there is no other city *quite* like this one) it's possible to feel that the gender of one's lover is an inconsequential matter, which is where liberation is supposed to lead: to what was once forbidden becoming ordinary.

Gestures of consolation or attempts to instill courage always run the risk of oversimplification. It's too easy to think that once narrow-minded prohibitions are overcome, love and desire are smooth sailing. As if. That's one reason rainbow-decked celebrations of pride, splashy and fun as they are, have a tinge of the naïve about them. Leaving the question of the solidity and nature of the identity we're proud of aside, there remains the fact that freedom to love and have sex with those you choose is in fact freedom to be yourself in notoriously complex realms. From the inside, we know what a confusing, difficult, enthralling terrain utopia can be.

Queer Utopia, the late theorist José Esteban Muñoz said, is always a horizon, configured in our desires, informing our actions and dreams, never exactly reached. True I guess for any utopia, but the ideal has a special poignance for those who have lived far from it; it shimmers up ahead, a kind of aura, the future's shining rim glimpsed above or around our best actions and intentions, our best hopes.

Whitman configures that imagined perfection as a city, a parallel Manhattan, a possibility already latent inside the physical city. Here is the first known version of "Calamus" 24, as found in Whitman's handwriting:

I dreamed in a dream of a city where all men were like brothers,
O I saw them tenderly love each other—I often saw them,
   in numbers, walking hand in hand;

> *I dreamed that was the city of robust friends—Nothing was greater*
> *there than manly love—it led the rest,*
> *It was seen every hour in the actions of men of that city, and in all*
> *their looks and words. —*

And this is the version Whitman published, in 1860, as "Calamus" 34:

> *I dreamed in a dream, I saw a city invincible to the attacks*
> *of the whole of the rest of the earth,*
> *I dreamed that was the new City of Friends,*
> *Nothing was greater there than the quality of robust love—it led*
> *the rest,*
> *It was seen every hour in the actions of the men of that city,*
> *And in all their looks and words.*

The changes are telling. *All men were like brothers, / O I saw them tenderly love each other* has been replaced with an assertion of the city's invincibility, and a suggestion that it will be attacked by *the whole of the earth*—because of that tender love? Is it only in the dreamed city that these lovers are truly safe? The phrase *City of Friends* seems a bit pale to my ear; it might be a motto for a welcoming Midwestern town, or a Quaker summer camp.

The forthright *manly love* is gone, replaced by a less specific *robust love,* and further abstracted by the unnecessary *the quality of.* This isn't a beautiful solution to the problem Whitman faced, which was how to say what he meant in a way that it could be read both by insider and outsider, each finding related but distinct meanings there. But it is a canny one: *robust* suggests health and energy without implying gender. The nearest dictionary yields a remarkably Whitmanian list of synonyms: *strong, vigorous, sturdy, tough, powerful, solid, muscular, sinewy, rugged, hardy, strapping, brawny, burly, husky, heavily built.* The word's Latin root refers to the oak, a

tree evoked elsewhere in "Calamus" as an emblem of a solitary figure of longing, praised by the poet as *rude, unbending, lusty.*

Finally, *robust* needs to be seen in the context of this sequence,
named after a plant that grows in Long Island's marshy ponds
and wetlands, its tall stalk bearing a seedpod like a cattail's but
particularly phallic in appearance. The pond where it grows is
figured as a cruising site on earth and, for Whitman, a location of
erotic connection in the spirit realm as well:

> *. . . a silent troop gathers around me,*
> *some walk by my side, and some behind, and some embrace*
> *my arms or neck,*
> *They, the spirits of friends dead or alive—thicker they come,*
> *A great crowd, and I in the middle . . .*

This is the gathering place of the living and the dead men who
have been members of a secret brotherhood, comrades, *camerados,*
and Whitman anoints himself their singer, their poet, and grants
them the token of their identity:

> *And this, O this shall henceforth be the token of comrades—*
> *this calamus root shall,*
> *Interchange it, youths, with each other!*

I CAN'T READ THIS without thinking of Muñoz's notion of a
Queer Utopia, that edge of promise essential to our lives, a gleam-
ing possibility always up ahead, the glimmer never to be fixed in
place. Never solidified, but not erasable either.

"My America is still all in the making," Whitman once said to
Horace Traubel. "It's a promise, a possible something: it's to come:
it's by no means here. Besides, what do I care about the material
America? America is to me an idea, a forecast, a prophecy."

ELEVEN

BIJOU

*Doubtless I could not have perceived the universe,
or written one of my poems, if I had not freely
given myself to comrades, to love.*

"Calamus" 39

The movie I'm watching—I'm hesitant to call it porn, since its intentions are less obvious than that—was made in 1972, and it couldn't have been produced in any other era. A construction worker is walking home from work in Manhattan when he sees a woman in a short fake-fur coat knocked over by a car as she's crossing an intersection. The driver leaps out to help her up, but the construction worker—played by an actor named Bill—picks up her purse and tucks it in his jacket. He takes the subway to a banged-up-looking block, maybe in Hell's Kitchen, climbs up to his tiny, soiled apartment, nothing on the walls but a few pinups, women torn from magazines. On his bed, he opens the purse, looks at its spare contents, keys and a few dollars. He opens a lipstick and touches it to his tongue, tastes it, does it again, something about his extended tongue touching the extended lipstick . . . Then he's lying back, stroking himself through his jeans, getting out of his clothes; he's an archetypal seventies porn guy, lean, with thick red hair and a thick red mustache, a little trail of hair on his wiry belly. Then he's in the shower, continuing his solo scene, and he begins to flash on images of women, quick jump cuts, but just as he's about to come he sees the woman in fur falling when the bumper of the car strikes her.

That's the end of that; the erotic moment is over, for him and for the viewer, once that image returns.

Chastened, toweling off, he's back in the bedroom, looking again at what spilled from her purse. There's an invitation, something telling her about—a party? an event? someplace called Bijou at seven P.M.

Then he's walking in SoHo—the old SoHo, long before the art glamor and even longer before the Euro-tourist-meets-North-Jersey shopping district: garbage in the streets, cardboard boxes in front of shuttered cast-iron façades. He finds the address, goes in and up, and the movie shifts from the gritty Warholian vocabulary it's trafficked in thus far to another cinematic tongue. An indifferent woman in a lot of eye makeup sits in a glass booth; Bill proffers the invite; she gestures toward a door and utters the movie's only line of dialogue: *Right through there.*

"There" turns out to be a hallucinatory space, its dominant hue a solarized, acidy green. Within that color, Bill moves forward. He confronts the image of his own body in one mirror and then in many, reaches out to touch his own form with pleasure. Time dilates, each gesture extended, no rush to get anywhere, only a little sense of forwardness. In a while there's another body—man or woman?—prone, face-down, and Bill's on top of him or her, they're fucking in a sea of all that green. In a while we can see the person beneath Bill is definitely a man. Then, much later, Bill's alone, lying prone on the floor as if now he's let go, all his boundaries relinquished, and one man comes to him and begins to blow him. Bill lies there and accepts it. In a while another man enters the scene, and begins to touch and cradle Bill's head, and then —no hurry here, no hurry in all the world—there's another. Now the pattern is clear, one man after another enters the liquid field of green that sometimes frames and sometimes obscures—and they are all reverently, calmly touching Bill. They have no end save but to give him pleasure, to make Bill's body entirely, attentively, completely loved.

This is the spiritualized eroticism of 1972 made flesh, more sensuous and diffuse than pointedly hot brotherhood, a Whitman-ian democracy. It makes the viewer feel suspended in a sort of erotic haze, but whatever arousal I feel in imagining Bill's complete submission to pleasure suddenly comes to a halt, as surely as if I'd seen that woman struck down in the crosswalk again, because I realize that all the men in the scene I'm watching are dead. Every one of them, and that the vision they embodied, the idea they incarnated, has gone up in the smoke and ashes of the crematoriums, scattered now in the dunes of Provincetown and Fire Island.

•••

OR THAT'S ONE VERSION of what I felt, watching *Bijou*, Wake-field Poole's weird period piece of art porn. Of course it is not news that the players are all gone now. How beautiful they look, the guys in the movie, or the men in the documentary *Gay Sex in the 70s,* posing on the decks in the Pines or on the porches of houses in San Francisco, eager for comradeship and for knowledge of one another. That is a phrase I would like to revive: to *have knowledge* of someone. It suggests that sex is, or can be, a process of inquiry, an idea that Poole would certainly have embraced.

Watching the movie is just one of countless experiences in which the fact of the AIDS epidemic is accommodated somehow. *Accommodated* doesn't mean understood, assimilated, digested, interpreted, or integrated. Accommodated: we just make room for it because it won't go away.

I don't know what else I expect. What could lend meaning to the AIDS crisis in America? Hundreds of thousands perished because there was no medical model for understanding what was wrong with them, and no money or concerted effort offered soon enough to change the course of things in time to save their lives. They died of a virus, and they died of homophobia. But this understanding is an entirely social one, and it doesn't do much to help the soul make meaning of it all. I have no answer to this problem save to suggest that a kind of doubling of perspective—an embracing of the layered nature of the world— is one thing one could carry, or be forced to carry, from such a shattering encounter. AIDS makes the experience of the body, a locus of pleasure and satisfaction, almost simultaneously the site of destruction and limit. What if, from here on out, for those burned in that fire, the knowledge of another body is always a way of acknowledging mortal beauty, and any moment of mutual vivacity is understood as existing against an absence to come? Presence made more poignant, and more desirable, even sexier by that void, intensified by it.

Maybe the viewer's involuntary gasp, when Bill thinks of the woman hit by the car as he's jerking off, is two-fold—first, the shock of the inappropriateness of it, and then the secondary, deeper shock—that the particular fact of her body is differently understood, differently longed for, when it is seen where it really is, in the world of danger—and that such a perception shakes the desirer out of simple lust and into some larger, more profound realm of eros.

•••

I USED TO LIKE TO GO to a sex club on the Lower East Side, a place now closed through some combination of pressures from the health department, the police, the IRS, and the real estate developers who are remaking Manhattan as a squeaky-clean retail zone. A combination Whole Foods–condo development has opened right down the block.

Beyond a nearly invisible doorway (shades of the one Bill entered in SoHo, long ago), there was a bouncer inside the door, a flirty man who loved jazz music, and then an attendant in the ticket booth ("Right through there . . .") and then a sort of living room where you could check your clothes with the two attendant angels, one black and startlingly shapely, one blond and ethereally thin. They were loving, kind, and funny boys; they looked at the goings-on before them with a sly combination of blessing and good humor, which is just what you'd want in an angel.

Then, beyond a black vinyl curtain shredded so that you could part it dramatically with a swipe of the hand, were two floors, with a stripped industrial look to them—a certain rawness, bare brick and cement, and structures of wood and metal in which to wander or hide, all very plain the first year I went there, and later, redone with branches and dried leaves everywhere, as if an autumn forest had sprouted in the ruins of a factory.

Sometimes it was a palace of pleasure, sometimes a hall of doom. Sometimes when you thought you wanted to be there, you'd discover you just couldn't get into the swing of it. Sometimes you weren't sure you'd wanted to go and it was marvelous. Often it felt as if whatever transpired had little to do with any individual state of mind, but rather with the tone of the collective life, whatever kind of spirit was or wasn't generated by the men in attendance that night, or by the city outside busily thinking through the poem of this particular evening. There were regulars who became acquaintances and comrades. There were visitors who became dear friends. There was a world of people I never saw again, once the doors closed.

Whoever made the decisions about what music to play preferred a kind of sludgy, druggy trance, often with classical or operatic flourishes about it. The tune I'll never forget was a remixed version of Dido's great aria from Purcell's *Dido and Aeneas*. It's the scene where the queen of Carthage, having been abandoned by the man she's allowed to wreck her kingdom, watches his sails disappear out to sea, and resolves to end her life. As she prepares to bury a knife in her breast, she sings, unforgettably: *Remember me, but—ah!—forget my fate.*

It seems, in my memory, that they would play this song every night I attended, always late, as the evening's brighter promises dimmed. There was a bit of a back-beat thrown in that would come and go, in between the soprano's great controlled heaves of farewell and resignation, but the music always had the same effect. I'd take myself off to the sidelines, to one of the benches poised on the edges of the room for this purpose, lean back into the swelling melancholy of the score and watch the men moving to it as though they'd been choreographed, in some dance of longing held up, for a moment, to the light of examination, the perennial hungry quest for whatever deliverance or release it is that sex brings us. It was both sad and astonishingly beautiful and now it seems to me something like the fusing of those layers I mentioned above: the experience of desire and the awareness of death become contiguous— *remember me*—one not-quite-differentiated experience.

MY EX PAUL'S MOTHER has Alzheimer's, or senile dementia. The first sign of it he saw was one morning when, for about a forty-five-minute period, she didn't know who he was. Now she doesn't know who anyone is, or if she does it's for seconds at a time. I was sitting beside the condo pool with her, in Pompano Beach— the Intercoastal Waterway behind us, so that we sat on delicate chairs on a small strand of concrete between two moving bodies of water. *Who are you*, she said to one of her sons. *I'm Michael, your son*, he said. She laughed, the kind of humorless snort that means, *As if . . .* Then he said back to her, *Who are you?* And she answered, *I watch*.

That's what's left for her, the subjectivity that looks out at the world without clear attachments or defined relations. She is obsessed with who everyone is; she is always asking. I wonder if this has to do with her character, or it's simple human need; do we need to know, before we can do or say anything else, who people are to us?

Not in *Bijou*; abstracted subjectivities meet one another in the sheer iridescent green space of sex. They morph together in patterns, they lose boundary; they go at it so long, in such fluid ways, that the viewer does too.

My friend's mother's state is not, plainly, ecstatic; she wants to know where she ends and others begin. The desire to merge is only erotic to the bound.

THE OTHER DAY MY FRIEND Luis asked me if I thought there was anything spiritual about sex. We happened to be walking in SoHo at the time, on our way back from some stores in the Bowery, so we might have passed the very door through which Bill long ago entered into his acidulated paradise. That prompted me to tell my friend about the movie, and my description prompted Luis's question. Luis has a way of asking questions that seems to say, *You really think* that?

I am not ready to give up on Whitman's vision of erotic communion, or its more recent incarnation in Wakefield Poole's pornographic urban utopia. But the oddest thing about Poole's film, finally, is that woman knocked down by the car: why on earth was she necessary to the tale? I suspect it's because even in the imagined paradise of limitless eros, there must be room for death; otherwise the endlessness, the lack of limit or of boundary, finally drains things of their tension, removes all edges. Poole can almost do this—create a floating, diffuse, subject- and object-less field of eros. But not quite; the same body that strains toward freedom and escape also has outer edges, also exists in time, and it's that doubling that makes the body the sexy and troubling thing it is. *O taste and see.* Isn't the flesh a way to drink of the fountain of otherhood, a way to taste the not-I, a way to blur the edges and thus feel the fact of them? Cue the aria here: *Remember me,* sings Dido, *but—ah—forget my fate!* That is, she counsels, you need to both remember where love leads and love anyway; you can both see the end of desire and be consumed by it all at once. The ecstatic body's a place to feel timelessness and to hear, ear held close to the chest of another, the wind that blows in there, hurrying us ahead and away, and to understand that this awareness does not put an end to longing but lends to it a shadow that is, in the late hour, beautiful.

•••

SHADOWS, OF COURSE, lend objects gravity, attaching them to earth.

Luis is right, sex isn't spiritual. The spirit wants to go up and out; it rises above, transcends, flies on dove wings up to the rafters and spies below it the form-bound world. Who was that peculiar French saint who died briefly, returned to life, and then could not bear the smell of human flesh? She used to fly up to the choir loft in church, just to get away from the stench of it. Sex is soulful; sex wants the soul-rich communion of other bodies. The sex of *Bijou* isn't really erotic because what it wants is to slip the body's harness and merge in the lightshow of play, the slippery forms of radiance. That aspect of the film is more dated than its hairstyles, the idea that sex should take us up out of our bodies, rather than farther in. That distance is a removal from knowledge; the guys who are pleasuring Bill aren't anyone in particular, and do not need to be individuated. But that's not soul's interest. Back in the sex club in the East Village, soul wants to know this body and this, to seek the embodied essence of one man after another, to touch and mouth the world's astonishing variety of forms. Spirit says, I watch. Soul says, Time enough to be out of the body later on, the veil of flesh won't be set aside, not tonight; better to feel the heat shining through the veil.

TWELVE

INSATIABLE

I only hope we may sometime meet and I shall be
able perhaps to say what I cannot write.
                              Bram Stoker to Walt Whitman,
                                            February 1876

You did well to write to me so unconventionally,
so fresh, so manly, & so affectionately.
                              Walt Whitman to Bram Stoker,
                                            March 1876

Only a sentence, casually placed as a footnote in the back of
Justin Kaplan's thick 1980 biography of Walt Whitman,
but it goes off like a little explosion: "Bram Stoker based the
character of Dracula on Walt Whitman."

Come again? The quintessential poet of affirmation, celebrant of human vitality—what has he to do with parasitical
phantoms, children of the night? The poet of "Song of Myself"
proclaims his solar confidence; he out-gallops stallions, is *plumb
in the uprights* and *braced in the beams,* and even the smell of his
own sweat delights him with *an aroma finer than prayer.* He
seems himself a kind of sun, radiant and generous, aglow with
an inner heat composed of equal parts lust, good health, and
fellow feeling.

How could the embodiment of lunar pallor emerge from him?

———•••———

WHAT THRILLED WHITMAN was vitality, and Bram Stoker—who'd been championing the older man's poems since his days at Trinity College, Dublin, where he read them in his room "with my door locked late at night"—must have sensed this. He first found the expurgated edition that Rossetti had published in England, then ordered an American edition of *Leaves of Grass,* and proceeded to write Whitman a fan letter—really more of an outcry—about finding in the poems a kindred soul. "I thank you for all the love and sympathy you have given me, in common with my kind," Stoker wrote, and one can't help but read "my kind" in a number of ways, which surely must have been what Stoker intended. The letter—a longish late-adolescent gush, practically falling over itself with hesitation, throat-clearing, and a tumult of feeling—was charged enough for its author that he did not manage to get it into the post for four years, a fact that must place it right up there in the history of delayed correspondence. Once it *was* sent, Whitman wrote an immediate reply; he was charmed by the letter and the note Stoker sent with it. Who wouldn't be, by the description of himself Stoker included, one such a "keen physiognomist" as Whitman might desire?

> *My friends call me Bram. I live at 43 Harcourt St., Dublin. I am a clerk in the service of the Crown on a small salary. I am twenty-four years old. Have been champion at our athletic sports (Trinity College, Dublin) and have won about a dozen cups. I have also been President of the College Philosophical Society and an art and theatrical critic of a daily paper. I am six feet two inches high and twelve stone weight naked and used to be forty-one or forty-two inches round the chest.*

I am ugly but strong and determined and have a large bump over my eyebrows. I have a heavy jaw and a big mouth and thick lips—sensitive nostrils—a snubnose and straight hair. I am equal in temper and cool in disposition and have a large amount of self control and am naturally secretive to the world. I take a delight in letting people I don't like—people of mean or cruel or sneaking or cowardly disposition—see the worst side of me. I have a large number of acquaintances and some five or six friends—all of which latter body care much for me. Now I have told you all I know about myself.

The novelist-to-be visited the poet three times in the 1880s, when the theatrical company Stoker managed toured America. And although their conversations were summarized by Whitman's devoted, note-taking Horace Traubel, who would collect his observations in the nine volumes of his *Walt Whitman in Camden,* I still find myself wondering what they talked about.

———•••———

EVERY ATOM BELONGING TO ME as good belongs to you. I've always read Whitman's startling claim, at the beginning of his great poem, as a generous statement. But if Stoker indeed based his legend of appetite on the poet, then he turns this notion inside out: Every atom belonging to you is mine, your sweat, your tears, your lymphatic fluids, your semen if you're a man, your blood: I own you. That sentence in Kaplan's footnote shocks not because it's a stretch but because—despite the warmth we associate with Whitman and his legacy—it feels right somehow. I recognize him, the craving count, the barely bodied ancient thirst, inside the part of me that shares Whitman's love for the vital ember, the glowing health, the muscle and vigor of men. I wish I didn't.

Every atom belonging to you: your semen, your blood. There he is in the mirror, shadow of the open-collared, slouch-hatted *camerado*.

———•••———

INSATIABLE IS UNSUSTAINABLE. I'm in the parking lot at the natural foods store when the bumper sticker on the Toyota beside me stops me in my tracks. In context it's about consumption and the environment, clearly—we can't go on using more and more resources, producing and shopping and throwing things away, not if there's going to be a lasting human presence on this planet.

I get that, but what shakes me is that I'm reading the slogan in another, not entirely unrelated way. Because I have been insatiable—have forgotten, actually, what it might feel like to be satiated, or perhaps (it hurts to admit this) even to be satisfied. "Satisfaction" is something I stopped seeking in sex, more or less, at least in a physical sense; what I wanted, in my careening tour through the bodies of countless men, through bathhouse and sex club and online hook-ups, was something difficult to grasp. The rhetoric of addiction would describe it as an urge to flee my own sense of lack, seeking and seeking to disguise or ignore or fill an emptiness within—something like the way Carl Jung is supposed to have said to AA's famous cofounder, Bill W., "You were reaching for spirit, you just reached for the wrong kind." And indeed that's one way to view a deep, compelling attraction to bodies, a longing to touch and touch and enter.

I was "partnered"—as postmodern parlance goes, or went, before same-sex marriage began to open different doors—to a man for sixteen years, and there was pleasure and mutuality in our relation. And then there was, more clearly emergent over time, all that was left out, or wouldn't fit. I found this difficult to describe, this sense that not all of me could be expressed within our marriage. I began to use the metaphor of bandwidth, feeling even as I did so that it was partial, barely adequate.

If the self broadcasts on many channels, then he and I could clearly receive one another on, say, three of them, a nice mid-range. Because we were both writers and thus shared a social and professional world of considerable interest, a mandarin realm we could discuss at length with few others, and because we liked domestic tranquility and travel, and shared a deep pleasure in the work of description, trying to articulate what we saw—because of those things, we shared a mutual life. Outside of that: sex, adventure, the night, transgression, surprise, higher and lower pitches of experience. I need to be invited onto the back of a motorcycle and taken somewhere unfamiliar now and then; I welcome a degree of disruption, need a curtain pulled back, a hallway leading into some part of the world I've never seen. He feels that I have undervalued the mid-range, the welcome and comfort of the intimacy that arose from our long association. A friend says that's what marriage is, there's no way around it. Still, I can't help but be hungry for the broader range of experience, the higher frequencies and depths; I need, for whatever reasons, to live on that broader spectrum, or else I wither. I am coming to accept this about myself.

— *The ex-con in construction boots and a towel, smoking a hash pipe, flicking tiny coals and bits of ash from the down of his belly outdoors by the pool, the water-lights rippling over his torso.*
— *The stoned, angelic young man, muscled and pale, opening his body to me and coaxing my fist inside him.*
— *The oil worker who came in from days on the big oil rigs in the Gulf with his ears still ringing and his reddened skin hungry for touch.*
— *The black man from the leather bar in Fresno who stood in front of me and came across my chest, then showed me a photo of his beautiful sixth-grade daughter and wept at how much he loved her.*

— *The beautiful lean-muscled doctor who whispered in my ear for hours about how he wanted me to infect him, covertly, without him knowing it, leaking virus into his bloodstream.*

— *The landscaper who took me to his twenty-third-floor apartment, in a tower overlooking the park, and rested every ounce of his weight on me on his terrace high above the lights of Houston while I lay on the concrete beneath him, entirely happy.*

— *The bare-chested weightlifter in the gym, shorter than I was, thickly built, who stood behind me and guided my arms through a chest exercise as I pulled the cables taut in front of me and squeezed, and then pushed his chest into my back, and held me there, intently, without moving, so that I could feel his sweat and the pulse of his heart.*

Men who wept about their fathers, their brothers, about bullies and gangs, about teachers and counselors and coaches, but fathers most of all, those fountainheads of male woundings, because they sensed I was someone in whose presence they could set down their guard, or just someone willing to listen without judgment. A beautiful, compact hairy young bear from New Jersey—forty-something but nonetheless very young anyway—who shook in my arms, wearing just a clean white jockstrap, because no one had ever genuinely loved him. I didn't judge; it was as if that were part of my purpose: I wanted to know the men who moved through my nights like passing comets, wanted them to feel the pleasure of being known.

———•••———

WHITMAN KEPT LISTS LIKE THAT, in pencil, in his green notebooks, though mine, it perhaps goes without saying, are more graphic. His entries have been the subject of debate; they're just names of men, some with a few descriptive words attached, as if to jog the writer's memory. Not enough to evoke much for a reader. Are they a record of cruising, of men he took to his bed, of men he conversed with and admired, or who he thought might enter in some fashion into his poems? All of the above?

———•••———

A SEX ADDICT? A label like that sits on one like a tight suit, an ill-fitting little cage of identity that must of necessity leave out so many of the regions of the self. That's how I felt, sitting in a twelve-step meeting, talking with groups of fellow users about the drug we had decided not to use. We were collectively defining our identities by what we would not do, and such an act of definition can be a strange, subtle sort of self-murder. I understand that such a radical act might be necessary, in the face of an intractable self-destructiveness, to save one's life. But I can't bring myself to embrace it, because in any such act of self-definition (*I'm Mark and I'm an addict*) the other selves, some of whom are not named because they don't belong in this context, and some of whom aren't named because they cannot be, but remain phantoms, potentialities, shadows, little streams into the larger liquidity— well, all those aspects of oneself are more or less banished from the conversation, and they retreat a little farther away, and then a little farther again.

Addiction is one way to think about it. Jacques Lacan says that all desire is based in a sense of lack. Once we experienced all as a whole, separated neither from the world nor from ourselves, but once a self and other is perceived, then we fall from Eden, and forever after we'll have the sense of something missing, of the irretrievable object—wholeness, oneself, the motherworld that bore us all of a piece. Therefore the veil is the figure of desire. If we tear it away, desire tends to disappear, but as soon as the veil is restored, the well of longing fills again.

Behind every man I want to kiss lies that original desire, which it is my nature and my fate to displace. Though displacement seems hardly the right word, if there is nothing else one can do.

When you have a lot of sex, sex becomes increasingly less narrative. There's less of a story of connection and its development, and more a series of images, like the list I've just written, a photo album of sorts, in which still pictures stand for a succession of bodies in time, in their beautiful or awkward arcs or spasms. Like Cavafy's poems, these remembered snapshots contain rooms of eros: a man who lay back in a sling in his darkened third-floor apartment, his shining red motorcycle spot-lit beside him. Two identical tattooed men, burly rugby players, on all fours, side by side in a bare room in Seattle.

A long green hallway, in an East Village apartment, down which one had to move laterally, since there wasn't room to walk straight ahead, and at the end of it, a room entirely lined with, of all things, mid-century American pottery, arrayed on walls the sun had never touched.

A list, is that what desire makes, finally? As in so many of Whitman's poems, where line after line spins out a careening catalog of what the poet sees, or is, or wishes to be. Ask the collector, the curator, the accumulator of sexual experience, the person who touches and touches what he desires: he is making, on paper or in his head or in his dream-life, a list.

TO AN AMERICAN like Whitman (though there is no American like him, the progenitor of our hopes for ourselves too secret to quite name, the originator of the notion that democracy might be founded in the body, on the affection between bodies), elation in the face of the vital must have seemed an exhilarating rejection of the puritan heritage of division between body and soul. Was anyone ever so sanguine about sex? Blake, maybe, whose work Whitman read, though at what point in his career we don't quite know.

But to a European, perhaps this uprush of energy in the face of the body and its vital fluids had another cast altogether. For Stoker, it may have seemed that what was wan or dead in the self might be refreshed temporarily—and finally, horrifyingly—by the hot juices of those who were more immediately alive. Is vampirism a matter of the overly self-conscious being awakened to life by the vitality of those who are barely self-conscious at all? Is that why Whitman liked stevedores and streetcar conductors and Long Island baymen, the big guys at home in their bodies, who would never think to write a poem?

Or let's say Stoker, who married a woman Oscar Wilde had proposed to before Bram came along, found it necessary to suppress his own desires to the degree that he would project them out onto a sub- or post-human creature, who has no firm foundation in biology, but must feed off the juices of others, without choice or sunlight. And in doing so, perhaps he reversed the gestures of his old idol. Where Whitman had written his beautiful poem of the sexual union between body and soul:

> *I mind how once we lay, such a transparent summer morning,*
> *How you settled your head athwart my hips, and gently turned over*
> *upon me,*
> *And parted the shirt from my bosom-bone, and plunged your tongue*
> *to my bare-stript heart,*
> *And reached till you felt my beard, and reached till you held my feet.*

Stoker offered us a parallel physical situation with an entirely inverted tone:

> *. . . he pulled open his shirt, and with his long*
> *sharp nails opened a vein in his breast. When the blood*

began to spurt out, he took my hands in one of his, hold-ing them tight, and with the other seized my neck and pressed my mouth to the wound, so that I must either suffocate or swallow.

Whitman fuses the erotic and the spiritual, as the kiss to the bare chest begins an epiphanic experience, a moment of peace and of understanding; he's also obscured the gender of the actors here. But in Stoker's novel Dracula brings Jonathan Harker's mouth to his chest in a kind of rape, a horrible force-feeding that can lead only to repulsion and contagion.

And so there it is: the intersection of the chosen and the com-pulsive, of consuming and being consumed, of the celebratory and of erasure.

———◆◆◆———

ADDICTION IS ONE WAY to think about it. But there's also what seems to have been Whitman's view—a mission, if you will, to seek out one's *camerados*, to join in the community of lovers, bound together by desire and affection, to find the common good in our common skin. This vision comes most clear in the "Cala-mus" poems, and in parts of "Song of Myself," and offers primar-ily an imaginative union among men. Whitman's women remain afterthoughts. He grants them freely moving sexual desires, and a position as democratic citizens. He wants them to be participants in the essential, erotic bond that holds his comrades together in the new democratic union, but he can't fully imagine it.

Those lists of men in Whitman's papers— a collector's cata-log, a record of the body's travels? How else will I know the world, if not by touching as much of it as possible, finding in the bodies of my lovers and fellows my coordinates?

———◆◆◆———

OR THERE'S PIERRE TEILHARD DE CHARDIN, brilliant radical Catholic, paleontologist and physicist, who describes our shared atoms this way: "However narrowly the heart of an atom may be circumscribed, its realm is co-extensive, at least potentially, with that of every other atom." We are all co-extensive, and our work is to move toward union; evolution, Teilhard posits, is a collective motion toward greater consciousness. "No evolutionary future," he writes in *The Phenomenon of Man*, "awaits anyone except in association with everyone else." We must know our fellows in order for everything to move forward; it is our spiritual imperative to connect, or else the destiny of the world cannot be completed.

———•••———

A THEORY OF THE POPULARITY of vampire books and movies: we understand that in a consumer culture we are feasting on whatever brings us a feeling of life, that we hunger to be fed in this way, that our freedom to act upon our desires places us in the position of hungry consumers, seeking the next pleasure.

Buy anything and what you've brought into your life has made the world a little less vital someplace else.

And we consume our lovers, of course, as we know the world by mouth.

"By mouth" means to use our lips and tongues to touch, but also to speak, to name. To consume as in tasting. Or as in absorbing, taking on their characteristics or vital energy.

———•••———

GREAT POETS ARE, by definition, undead. The voice is preserved in the warm saline of ink and of memory. It cannot fade; time cannot take away a word of it. The personality, as it breathes through the preserved voice back into the world, is unmistakable: the voice of Walt Whitman is entirely his own. And of all poets, he seems to have understood in the uncanniest of ways that his audience did not yet exist.

He was creating it, summoning readers into being who could receive what he had to say. He speaks to us as if he can push words aside, and make a kind of direct contact with us. He wills himself outside of time—or is it further into it?—approaching his readers in their present moment, as if pushing upward through the skin of the page itself:

> *Closer yet I approach you,*
> *What thought you have of me, I had as much of you—I*
> *   laid in my stores in advance,*
> *I considered long and seriously of you before you were born.*

Who dares to speak this way, to write themselves into the condition of deathlessness?

OF THE MANY POEMS that demonstrate Whitman's daring, "Calamus" 15, later called "Trickle, Drops," is in its way the strangest. He placed it in the yearning, homoerotic "Calamus" sequence for good reason, and I used to think it the creepiest page in *Leaves of Grass*. But in the light of Stoker, I begin to see it differently, though I admit it still makes my skin crawl a little. Who's the vampire here?

> *O drops of me! trickle, slow drops,*
> *Candid, from me falling—drip, bleeding drops,*
> *From wounds made to free you whence you were prisoned,*
> *From my face—from my forehead and lips,*
> *From my breast—from within where I was concealed—Press forth,*
> *   red drops—confession drops,*
> *Stain every page—stain every song I sing, every word I say,*
> *   bloody drops,*

Let them know your scarlet heat—let them glisten,
Saturate them with yourself, all ashamed and wet,
Glow upon all I have written or shall write, bleeding drops,
Let it all be seen in your light, blushing drops.

With his characteristic, canny strangeness, Whitman has done what no one else would have thought to do. He's made the reader the vampire, feasting on the poems, which here expose, in their fierce confessional heat, the poet's naked life. And where "you," Whitman's ubiquitous second person, is nearly everywhere in his work, the reader he wishes to seduce and to claim, here he speaks, for once, to his own blood. He feeds it to us. I feel—as indeed he must have wanted his readers to feel—that he feeds it to me.

How could I refuse him?

THIRTEEN

A LOVING BEDFELLOW

For a long time I lived at least a part of each year in Province-town, at the tip of Cape Cod, one of those places at the end of a road, or the tip of a promontory, that seem not quite attached to the rest of the country. Provincetown's been home or second home to countless gay men and lesbians, to artists, to those in need of a refuge, for more than a century now, and for the time I lived there it served for me as a kind of theater of the imagina-tion. Everything that intrigued me was represented there some-how, on a scale intimate enough to grasp, and the houses and characters, the harbor and its old fishing boats, the salt marshes and crooked steeples became the fixed landscape of my poems, all lit by that distinctive, splendid light.

I met Frank there in 2001; I knew his boyfriend, a year-rounder, and we must have been introduced some afternoon on Commercial Street, where nearly all the social exchange of the village occurs. It was a challenge, sometimes, getting down that street; how many conversations could one have between home and the post office? These constituted an amazing demonstration of the local communications network; once I told someone I had a dentist's appointment on one corner and, a few blocks later, was asked what procedure I was having done; once an acquaintance said, *Oh, I heard you got new glasses,* a statement that indicates just how extensive, and just how desperate for fodder, a gossip network can be.

I found Frank fiercely attractive. I was just shy of fifty then, he closer to sixty, and in terrific shape, with thick-muscled, vascular arms and a strong chest thatched in dense white hair. The perennial allure of the strong daddy, maybe, though it's also true that of gay men of my age and his not so very many survived, so many of us erased in the years of terror between 1980 and 1995. I forget this all the time, and then notice a handsome man my age on the street and feel a little erotic flare shoot up, sometimes burning not so far from incipient tears.

Frank had a boyfriend, and I had a partner, and though no one in this gang of four was entirely monogamous, there was at least decorum to be observed, or consideration. I didn't think about my attraction further until one hot summer afternoon outside Town Hall. The rows of green benches on two sides of the building where people hang out and talk are called the Meat Rack, though anyone sitting there is more likely to be eating an ice cream, waiting for a whale watch, or listening to one of the endearing but less than stellar musicians who play there—each of them, at least in those days, a sweetly cracked combination of damage and a remarkable lack of embarrassment. Whatever I was doing that day, my eye caught Frank standing ten yards away, talking and gesturing in an animated way, his bare chest splashed by sunlight coming through a big maple. What startled me was the way the sunlight reflected from the tops of his nipples; they were thick enough to seem, at this distance, two shafts of light. That was all that was needed to carry a little frisson of erotic memory over the years between that moment and the one in which I write.

All the following year, the shock of September 11 roiled through town; many people there had spent time in the city, or had friends there; one summer resident, a beautiful tattooed Englishman who'd been the boyfriend of someone I knew, was a passenger on the plane that struck the south tower. Grief and confusion, by the following summer, produced an odd, though not inexplicable, symptom.

Every night the open space at the Vault, a small local leather bar, would grow more and more densely populated, as the hour grew later, and when it felt full enough to provide a sense of safety in a crowd, men would begin to touch each other, and, rather unexpectedly, to kiss. They wore leather, or jeans, or shorts; the ones who wore shirts often lost them as the night deepened. And while certainly acts that were undeniably sexual did take place, despite the bar's owner strolling through with a flashlight now and then and growling a little, there seemed a tacit agreement that what we were doing was holding and touching one another in a collective embrace of remarkable intensity, less interested in genital acts than in the creation of a tender, erotic collectivity. Well, genitals were certainly enjoyed, but what stands out for me is the kissing, the eagerness of mouths to find others. I talked to my friend Michael about it one morning, over coffee in the brilliant sunlight in front of his tiny condo over the coffee bar. "All I want to do," he said, "is snog at the Vault." I felt the same way; nothing seemed more interesting.

Frank and I were both in attendance, one of those steamy nights, and the erotic flair that had previously flickered a bit became a full-fledged pyrotechnic event. Eventually we had to escape the suddenly intolerable, airless heat of the bar, but the cool sprinkle of rain on the street was too much. As we sat in the doorway of some closed gift shop, letting the fog-tinged air descend on us and cool the sweat on our chests, he looked at me directly and said, "Do you know Mark Doty? You'd like him."

There are many ways to account for what Frank said: he was a little drunk and perhaps tired; the bar had been dimly lit; he had probably only been able to see parts of me, proceeding more by touch than by visual knowledge; I looked different, with a leather harness over my chest, than I did in the plain daylight of Commercial Street.

I will grant some truth to all of those, but what interests me most is the idea that we were only just returning to ourselves, cooling down in that sheltering doorway. Who or where had we been? Do the trappings or furnishing of identity fall away, leaving us less identifiable, less specifically ourselves? The merge with another, that desire to lose edge or boundary—how does it show in the human face?

THE NEXT FALL, back in New York, I went one afternoon to Frank's apartment. I don't remember if we'd exchanged numbers, or if we saw each other online, on one of the sites that had increasingly become the sexual arena of choice. I hadn't done a lot of online cruising then, and it was exhilarating, going to his place, a high-rise on the Upper West Side, having the doorman contact him to let me in, riding the elevator up, Frank opening the door wearing a pair of gym shorts and a thin gray tank top, and then all that followed.

I don't know how long we'd been "playing" (now nearly a universal euphemism used by the gay men I know, and one that cries out for some examination) when I felt—and could feel that Frank felt—it was time for a pause, a catch-your-breath break. I leaned back, sitting on my heels, toward the foot of the bed, and looked at him, while he sat up against his thick white pillows, leaned his head back, and looked at me, mildly, with a pleasant half-smile.

And then something happened. I would be hard pressed to describe any transition between what I saw first, which was my friend's gray-bearded, strongly sculptured face, and what, after a moment, replaced it. It wasn't Frank who looked at me then, but another man with short gray hair and beard, the same half-smile, but with the visionary dazzle of starlight in his eyes. I was, quite calmly, looking into the face of the Walt Whitman of 1856, the year of the Brooklyn daguerreotype, the picture in which he seems to be slowly and with a great inner radiance returning to earth from wherever it is he's been.

It's pointless, as this juncture, to try to defend or explain myself. For whatever reason, through whatever means, I saw what I saw, and allowed that face to look directly into my own until I couldn't. Then I closed my eyes, and when I opened them he was gone.

I didn't say anything about it to Frank; I can't tell you anything about the rest of our congress that afternoon. I looked out over the Hudson before I left, the reddening sun slanting lower, and went down the elevator and into the street with the knowledge of what I had seen held in privacy. I didn't tell anyone about it for a long time. Later I understood then why I'd gone, that afternoon, to that sleek high-rise apartment, the last place I'd expected, once again, to find myself face to face with a ghost.

—•••—

I'D BEEN READING Whitman a long time before it occurred to me that I might have misunderstood two passages I've talked about earlier here, essential ones. The speaker in "The Sleepers," confused, naked, enters this heavily veiled scene, an encounter beneath a pier at night:

> . . . *and what is this flooding me, childhood or manhood* . . . .
> *and the hunger that crosses the bridge between.*
>
> *The cloth laps a first sweet eating and drinking,*
> *Laps life-swelling yolks* . . . . *laps ear of rose-corn, milky*
> *and just ripened;*
> *The white teeth shining, and the boss-tooth advances in*
> *darkness,*
> *And liquor is spilled on lips and bosoms by touching*
> *glasses, and the best liquor afterward.*

And here a couplet in "Song of Myself," from Section 29, echoes this same sense:

> *Parting tracked by arriving . . . . perpetual payment of the*
> *   perpetual loan,*
> *Rich showering rain, and recompense richer afterward.*

Recompense is not a common word. I took notice, in May 2016, when it appeared in newspapers, after House Republicans gathered at a conference meeting early in the day, preparing for a scheduled vote on an appropriations bill concerned with spending on energy and water. An amendment had been added to the bill that would have prevented discrimination based on sexual orientation or gender identity in the government's hiring of contractors.

The meeting opened with a prayer led by Georgia Representative Rick Allen, who did not mention the bill when he read two passages from the Bible. The "cause" the passage from Romans refers to is the worship of idols, of created things rather than the creator:

26 For this cause God gave them up unto vile affections:
    for even their women did change the natural use into
    that which is against nature:
27 And likewise also the men, leaving the natural use of
    the woman, burned in their lust one toward another;
    men with men working that which is unseemly, and
    receiving in themselves that recompense of their error
    which was meet.

The Revised Standard Version of the Bible, which my grandmother read, substitutes *due penalty* for *recompense,* but the meaning is quite different. There can be little doubt that Saint Paul viewed the payback for same-sex "working" as negative indeed, but *recompense* means simply to pay, perhaps in response to a loss. The King James Bible is likely where Whitman got the word, and if so he must have enjoyed placing it in a new context, in support of other values entirely.

Representative Allen went on read a second text, found in Revelation 22:

18 For I testify unto every man that heareth the words of the prophecy of this book, If any man shall add unto these things, God shall add unto him the plagues that are written in this book:

19 And if any man shall take away from the words of the book of this prophecy, God shall take away his part out of the book of life, and out of the holy city, and from the things which are written in this book.

If indeed the congressman from Georgia means what I think he does, invoking a plague as the consequence of failure to follow Paul's prohibitions, I want to tell him that I have known many men and women who every day inscribe the book of life, in our holy and ruined cities, in places I am certain he has never been. He and his fellows went back into that chamber, four days after one of the largest mass shootings in American history, in a gay nightclub in Florida, and voted again to kill that same amendment. Could the message be any plainer? He believes we deserve to die.

———•••———

WHAT I ACTUALLY WANTED to say about *recompense,* and about *the best liquor is spilled afterward,* is that perhaps those images aren't necessarily solely orgasmic, as purely sexual as I'd thought. After the recompense, yes, *sprouts take and accumulate,* suggesting that what Whitman elsewhere calls *the fatherstuff* has fertilized the earth. Whitman was terrifically interested in body fluids, especially semen, blood, and tears; these appear in the poems with considerable frequency, called by various names.

But both of Whitman's delirious passages about orgasm end in *afterward*.

Is *afterward* the glow of satisfaction or calm rest, the pleasure of being held, or being adjacent to a body at rest—what William Blake, the other great long-lined poetic visionary of Whitman's century, called *the lineaments of gratified desire*? After my own long and restless pursuit of what sexual congress might deliver, I find that what I like best and value most are these moments of physical intimacy, of warm ease with the man I love. To hold and be held, to be almost still together, to occupy the space we have created, where, for a little while, there's just this.

"QUEERNESS," José Esteban Muñoz wrote, "has an especially vexed relationship to evidence." Where does one go, for proof of anyone's sexual experience? Or proof of apparitions? Despite the advent of queer theory and a flowering of progressive literary study, there are a troop of Whitman biographers and scholars— as well as Whitman himself!—who will tell you Whitman was not queer. They are wrong, and he was lying. How can I claim this so firmly? As I have just told you, I have been to bed with the man, something you are unlikely to hear another living speaker say.

I offer this half in jest, but my insistence on the felt understanding of Whitman's gay readers is no joke. He infuses his descriptions of men's bodies with such palpable longing that anyone sympathetic to such desires cannot miss his intent. Gay men mostly grow up in hiding even to this day. In hiding they learn to listen attentively, to read the signals around them, to know who and what is safe, where lies judgment and where the solace and good company of their own kind. If you characterize such perceptions as projection or wishful thinking, you simply erase the character and capacity of a great many of Whitman's readers.

Case in point: a single passage, two lines from early on in the 1855 edition of "Song of Myself."

> *As God comes a loving bedfellow and sleeps at my side*
> *all night and close on the peep of the day,*
> *And leaves for me baskets covered with white towels*
> *bulging the house with their plenty . . .*

This invites us to read in two ways: that God Himself arrives in the form of a loving bedfellow, or that a bedfellow arrives in the way that God would. Perhaps for Whitman there isn't really so much difference. And of all the things a visitor divine or otherwise might leave behind, baskets covered with white towels? Not just swelling, like rising dough, but actually *bulging* the house? What makes these lines feel so ferociously sexy? Is it because of those *buds folded beneath speech?*

Muñoz again:

> *Historically, evidence of queerness has been used to penalize and discipline queer desires, connections and acts. When the historian . . . attempts to document a queer past, there is often a gatekeeper, representing a straight present, who will labor to invalidate the historical fact of queer lives . . . The key to queering evidence, and by that I mean the ways in which we prove queerness and read queerness, is by suturing it to the concept*

of ephemera. Think of ephemera as trace, the remains,
the things that are left, hanging in the air like a rumor.

And there indeed is Walt Whitman's mild, beneficent face, calm, curious, open, still lit from within by some trace or remainder of starlight.

THE
THIRD
SOURCE

—•••—

FOURTEEN

I LOVED WELL
THOSE CITIES

Years back, on a steamy evening in early June only a year or so before her death, the fiction writer and activist Grace Paley and I walked across the Brooklyn Bridge. By twilight the city had already built up that store of heat that sends everyone who can hurrying out of town in July and August, but we faithful gathered at the foot of the bridge on the Manhattan side. We were there for the Bridgewalk, an annual event organized by Poets House, a library and literary center that's a mainstay of the life of poetry in New York. We heard a poem or two, and then perhaps three hundred lovers of our private-yet-open art began the walk up the arc of what Hart Crane called "the most beautiful bridge in the world." The traffic was loud, making the cables hum, but there was a breeze blowing from the south, cool air scuttling across the impossibly wide expanse of water, lifting the white gulls. I couldn't look without Crane's lines echoing and singing in my head, the first lines of his hymn to the modern, made thing that might lift us up:

How many dawns chill from his rippling rest,
The seagull's wings shall dip and pivot him
Shedding white rings of tumult, building high
Over the chained bay waters Liberty—

What a vision of dazzled light that is, the dipping and pivoting bird leaving in air the white rings of his passage, the stirring tumult of motion that washes around our local goddess, our city's dream of who we might be.

Grace was herself an avatar of Liberty, a lifelong advocate for the poor and the denied, and the sort of born New Yorker who was comfortably herself wherever she traveled, at least one woven bag over her shoulder full of leaflets, chewing gum, and the loose pages of her short stories and poems. She moved seamlessly between art and activism and holding her handsome dark-skinned grandson on her lap:

> Here I am in the garden laughing
> an old woman with heavy breasts
> and a nicely mapped face
>
> how did this happen
> well that's who I wanted to be
>
> at last a woman
> in the old style sitting
> stout thighs apart under
> a big skirt grandchild sliding
> on off my lap

That early evening she stood with her legs spread wide, as if she herself (maybe all of five feet five inches?) were a sort of colossus, her white cotton blouse flapping in the wind, and read Marianne Moore's "Granite and Steel." When she came to the poem's exclamatory line *O steel! O stone!* she read it in her finest New York accent, and shouted it out over the vibration of traffic thrumming the bridge cables with her fist in the air.

•••

THE FIRST WELLSPRING of Walt Whitman's greatest work was a radical experience of reality, magnificent and disruptive; and the second the transformative power of a life of uncharted desire. The third is perhaps a gift of circumstance. He was a citizen of a newly great city, one that had just awoken to its own modernity and vigor, a potential without precedent. When the poet was born in 1819, somewhere around 120,000 people lived there; by the time he was at work on *Leaves of Grass* in 1850 the city had grown to over half a million, becoming by far the nation's largest.

Great cities require their poets, and New York seemed to summon Whitman into being, charging his voice with its own brash, self-inventing confidence: *City whom that I have lived and sung in your midst,* he wrote, *will one day make you illustrious.* He's as sure of himself as the city that spawned him, full of swagger and bluster, as if he had a direct channel to the genius of the place.

Over the nearly thirty years that Whitman reworked his book, adding new poems, shifting and combining, sometimes deleting others, he revised many individual lines. Here, in chronological order, are all the versions of line 497 of "Song of Myself"—the first time a puzzled reader of the 1855 edition would have encountered the author's name:

> *Walt Whitman, an American, one of the roughs, a kosmos*
> *Walt Whitman am I, of mighty Manhattan the son*
> *Walt Whitman am I, a Kosmos, of mighty Manhattan the son*
> *Walt Whitman, a kosmos, of Manhattan the son,*

The big voice of "Song of Myself" stands back from exhortations and praise to introduce itself, announcing that Walt Whitman is a universe. And what has given rise to the awareness of that vastness? A city. His spiraling, hectoring, crowded poem, with its universe of observed details melded to metaphysical rhetoric, seemed to Emerson "a remarkable mixture of the Bhagavad Gita and the New York Herald." He'd already experienced some glorious dissolution of the ordinary limits of selfhood, but it's New York City that makes the poem's sense of scale possible, and supplies much of the characters who people its intricate, quickly yet sharply sketched landscape.

It's safe to say that more people appear in "Song of Myself" alone than in the entire body of work of other nineteenth-century American poets. Whitman seems eager to see that Americans of every sort walk onto the grand stage of his poem: working men and women, slaves, artists, farmers, soldiers, African Americans, Native Americans, trappers, the disabled, the mentally ill, prostitutes, *venerealees*. All are given attention. After a passage in which the poet admires a *negro* who *holds firmly the reins of his four horses,* Whitman continues:

> *I behold the picturesque giant and love him, and I do not stop there,*
> *I go with the team also.*

> *In me the caresser of life wherever moving, backward as well as*
>   *forward sluing,*
> *To niches aside and junior bending, not a person or object missing,*
> *Absorbing all to myself and for this song.*

The caress of Whitman's gaze travels *wherever,* and he employs a nautical term, *sluing,* meaning to turn or twist a mast or boom around on its axis, which has the interesting effect of making his attention seem both fluid and entirely in his control. These remarkably economical lines suggest that the poet's gaze equals touch, and that his perception absorbs the world's body, democratically, into the body of his song.

—••—

MAYBE IT ISN'T SO GREAT, the distance from claiming oneself a citizen of the *kosmos*, inseparable from the great stream and pulse of life, to being a resident of Manhattan. Since I live there myself, I'm aware that some readers will see my conflation of New York and the cosmos as a symptom of a certain narrowness of vision. Maybe so, but New York is, after all, the very image of the fullness of being, a capital of the human. What is unavoidable here is the grand range of human feeling, every aspect of who we are more or less on continuous display. Ambition and aspiration, triumph, pettiness, despair and hunger, vanity, rage, sorrow and delight: everything about us *shows* here, and cannot quite be tucked away, which is why most Republicans and all those who'd like to control the lives of others tend to despise it. New York City insists, as it pretty much seems to have always done, on including everything.

Every great city participates in this sense of dimensionality, but there's just one New York, and this city's been celebrating and selling its beautiful self for two hundred years now; its myth is visible and shared. We're the Emerald City, Metropolis, Gotham, and Tomorrowland. What is the city you see in ruins, in cinematic visions of the future? Liberty's crown spikes above the deserted shore of *Planet of the Apes,* and our half-ruined towers rise out of the water in Spielberg's *A.I.* New York is for us, as it was for Walt Whitman, and then for Hart Crane and Frank O'Hara after him, modernity itself.

That great chain of poets—to which I'd add Langston Hughes, Muriel Rukeyser, James Schuyler, and Adrienne Rich, and make room for Tim Dlugos and Eileen Myles as well—has come to embody this city's collective life; civic scribes, note-keepers of the urban soul. It's no mere accident, nor bias in my list-making, that every one of them is queer; San Francisco may be our zone of permission but New York, in an unexpectedly sublime way, is our zone of indifference, so big and ambitious and forward-looking that it simply doesn't *care* who you happen to be, as long as you consent to be a part of its huge, flashing, various life.

Or don't consent, and see if the city gives a damn.

Cities, Lawrence Durrell suggests, have more will than people do; we express *their* characters, embodying their obsessions and particular stances toward the world. If nineteenth-century New York invented Walt Whitman, he returned the favor. His voice seems to emerge from immensity, from this confluence of waters, the Harbor, the East River, and what he called "the lordly masculine Hudson." It is spacious, even sprawling, and shaped by winds blown in from who knows where. Like his city in the era in which he published the best three editions of his mighty book, he is a speechmaker, a huckster, a salesman, a retailer of gorgeous possibilities, a fan of the future, a democrat, a mixer of races and creeds and languages, a collector, a list-maker, an optimist, a realist, a visionary, possessed of almost boundless ambition, and lacking a shy bone in his body.

These are not necessarily the characteristics of Walter Whitman Jr., born in Huntington, Long Island and raised in Brooklyn, but they are certainly the traits of his creation Walt, *of Manhattan the son,* who came to wear that city as confidently as he does the slouch hat in his book's frontispiece.

Thoroughly conscious of his image, Whitman liked to be photographed, and went to some lengths to pose, and to shape the way he was represented to his audience. In the Walt Whitman Archive, an online trove maintained by the University of Iowa and a model of the way a digital archive can make vast amounts of material readily available, there are 128 photographs of the poet, a very large number for a man of his times. The pictures range from a rather oily-looking dandy in 1840s New Orleans to the scruffy exemplar of cosmic consciousness caught in the Brooklyn daguerreotype of 1856, and even to an appalling bit of later promotional flak in which the poet, in a rustic pose, placidly studies a butterfly perched on a finger he holds up in the air. Whitman claimed, to Horace Traubel, "we were good friends: I had quite the in-and-out of taming, or fraternizing with, some of the insects, animals . . ."

The butterfly, now in the Library of Congress, was a cardboard prop. This must be one of the earlier examples of an artist manipulating his image for public consumption, offering readers a view of the person who writes the poems, a glimpse of his character and attitudes. Is a pasteboard butterfly a violation of the reader's trust? Do such acts of advertisement necessarily violate or contradict a promise of authenticity, that feeling of the genuine that seems near the core of Whitman's work?

The question points to one of the ways in which Whitman embodied modernity, and was perhaps one of its first true celebrants. To make sense of him, we have to move past a binary opposition, since in that light he must be either sincere or false. The fact that he performs sincerity, with his paper prop wired to his index finger, does not mean that his tenderness toward the world, or his stance toward his readers, is insincere. This performance is a display designed to project the poet's persona to a future audience, and thus "sell" the reader his book by selling an image of its author. (Lying to Horace is perhaps another matter . . .)

This same dynamic is at work when Whitman, certainly one of the most intimate of poets, stages his intimacy with his readers. His great poems proceed from a kind of contract with the audience, a promise that we are being taken into confidence by one committed to us, although he does not yet know us, one who wishes he could push away the cold type and ink and paper between us, and speak to us individually, directly, with the intimacy and conviction of a lover:

> *This hour I tell things in confidence.*
> *I might not tell everybody, but I will tell you.*

To publish these lines is, of course, to *tell everybody*. Much as he wants to take us into his confidence, seduce with the warmth and directness of his voice, he's also making one of his sly jokes: he's created an intimacy with all the doors and windows open, in which *you* could be anyone at all. Even as I laugh at the line, I feel the gesture of his arm around my shoulder, drawing my ear nearer his mouth. What is the difference, in a poem, between performed intimacy and the real thing? What, in a work of art, is not performed? Whitman, perhaps more than any poet before him, explored and exploited poetry's strange duality. In the best poems, we feel the poet's breath, the almost-physical presence of the speaker created by all the tools at the writer's disposal. I sometimes feel that Walt has just walked into the room, as present now as he ever was, a sensual, breathing body that he somehow seems to have constructed of nothing but words.

Can a poet be blamed for trying on the spirit of the times, for making use of the enticing illusions photography and the new visibility of advertisement offered? This was a man who, after all, wrote and published how many reviews of his own book, and splashed a private letter from Emerson, the most respected American literary intellectual of the day, on the back cover of the second edition of *Leaves of Grass* without so much as asking for permission. Whitman viewed neither self-publishing nor self-advertisement as a problem; they were part and parcel of the gallopingly expansive capitalist spirit of the day. New York, where marketing was, in essence, invented, remains a world capital of self-promotion to this day.

———•••———

TWO DECADES BEFORE the sham butterfly, when Whitman was writing his best poems, he was already positioning himself for his public, shaping the way he'd be viewed, a process for which it would not be inappropriate to use the current, unpleasant word *branding.* Ted Genoways, an observant scholar, realized a few years ago there were at least two versions of the introductory engraving printed in the first edition of *Leaves of Grass*—one version showing considerably more of a bulge in the poet's trousers than the other. Dissatisfied with the initial version, Whitman seems to have ordered up a revision. Copies of the first edition were bound as needed, and he made sure to replace the older engraving in newer copies en route to the bindery.

Another Whitman scholar, Ed Folsom, suggests that Whitman actually chose to replace the bolder image with the more modest one. My own sense of the Walt Whitman of 1855 suggests that he'd have chosen to reveal more rather than less, an idea perhaps supported by an 1856 review of the book by Sara Willis.

Writing as Fanny Fern in a May 1856 review of the book, Willis seems to nod—hilariously—to the image. After remarking with approval that the poems were "not submitted by the self-reliant author to the fingering of any publisher's critic . . . till they hung limp, tame, spiritless . . . ," she acknowledges that some have charged the poems with "coarseness and sensuality." She does not agree, and responds boldly:

> *Sensual? The artist who would inflame, paints you not nude Nature, but stealing Virtue's veil, with artful artlessness now conceals, now exposes, the ripe and swelling proportions.*

Where Whitman's poems could have "hung limp," they instead display "ripe and swelling proportions." I like to think of the poet and the reviewer having a good laugh over what had to be a bawdy inside joke.

———•••———

THE WALTER WHO CROSSED Brooklyn Ferry to enter into Manhattan's teeming life found there, as did countless young men of his time, a freedom and mobility they had never known. They came from farming towns, as jobs were shifting to the cities; American urban centers of the 1830s and '40s suddenly required vast amounts of new housing, spawning crowded rooming houses and teeming flats. Thus unleashed, the men required entertainment, fellowship, and company; it's no accident that this is the moment when the first push for temperance laws appears, and new attempts to legislate demeanor. Back in Huntington, there was no escaping the fact that you were Walter Whitman Sr.'s son, Jesse Whitman's younger brother; in the city, as much of a generation discovered, you were who you seemed to be, that moment, that day, in the brisk and delicious air of possibility.

This was exactly the sort of prospect that confronted the young Hart Crane, stepping off the train from Cleveland around 1917, and later the young Frank O'Hara, arriving in Manhattan near the end of the 1940s. From what I see among young gay male poets I know the city still offers them that high-octane mix of exhilaration, community, anonymity, adventure, and joy. If there's a bite in the mix, a flash of something bracingly bitter in the cocktail, so much the better. It is an entirely modern response to the city. Every face William Blake confronted in his walks near the Thames betrayed to the Romantic poet "marks of weakness, marks of woe," and William Wordsworth, looking out at the same city from London Bridge, found he liked London best when everyone was asleep. But for young American poets, especially the gay ones like Elizabeth Bishop and May Swenson, the city was one teeming, living catalog of possible futures, a great stage, and each newcomer was welcome to join the perpetual performances, in all their rich variety. What Cleveland or Worcester, Massachusetts, or Logan, Utah, could barely imagine on the menu is daily fare here: taste what you will.

Thus it seems entirely right that Whitman's words from "Crossing Brooklyn Ferry" are cut into the railing on the East River at Fulton's Landing in Brooklyn, where the ferry used to land and depart:

> *Flow on, river! Flow with the flood-tide, and ebb with the ebb-tide!*
> *Frolic on, crested and scallop-edged waves!*
> *Gorgeous clouds of the sun-set! drench with your splendor me,*
> > *Or the men and women generations after me . . .*
> *Stand up, tall masts of Manahatta! Stand up, beautiful hills of*
> > *Brooklyn!*

And on the other side of Manhattan, chiseled into a similar rail on the Hudson, is a line from Frank O'Hara: *I can never relax if I am more than a mile from a record store or some other sign that people do not totally regret life . . .* And between them? Brooklyn Bridge, which needs no inscription to belong to Hart Crane, who studied that *frozen trackless smile* day and night from the apartment in Brooklyn Heights where its chief engineer, Washington Roebling, had once lived, supervising the completion of that magnificent arc of stone and steel from his wheelchair after he'd lost the use of his legs, coming up too swiftly from a submerged diving bell deep beneath the river. Crane saw in the Brooklyn Bridge not only the myth of American possibility but an emblem of the spirit's arc flung between islands, a cable-strung curve he saw as the *harp and altar of the fury fused.*

WHITMAN PUBLISHED A POEM in 1860 he called "City of My Walks and Joys." When he republished it, he changed the title, raising the stakes considerably.

CITY OF ORGIES

City of orgies, walks and joys,
City whom that I have lived and sung in your midst
    will one day make you illustrious,
Not the pageants of you, not your shifting tableaus, your
    spectacles repay me,
Not the interminable rows of your houses, nor the ships
    at the wharves,
Nor the processions in the streets, nor the bright
    windows with goods in them,
Nor to converse with learned persons, or bear my share
    in the soiree or feast;
Not those, but as I pass O Manhattan, your frequent
    and swift flash of eyes offering me love,
Offering response to my own—these repay me,
Lovers, continual lovers, only repay me.

The poem celebrates much of what Whitman loved about the booming, hustling New York of those years, even if it concludes by saying that none of its marvelous attributes reward him save the continual current of desire, the flashing currency of looking and offering. (That sex is so often spoken of in economic terms in these poems—*repayment, perpetual loan, recompense*—reflects the expansive capitalist ethos of the day.) The poem corrals all its urban pleasures into a single sentence, so the sexual charge seems to spill into all its elements; even the construction of the sentence, with its cascade of negations, is a buildup to the delayed gratification at the end.

The speaker likes to boast, as New Yorkers do till this day.

That second line's wild claim seems charming when you imagine reading the poem when it was new, a declaration of a young poet's bravado. His faith in his own poems is of a piece with his sexual self-confidence; he knows the *frequent and swift flash* of his own eye will be met with the same. It makes me think of those hip-hop lyrics wherein the speaker swaggers his way through town, talking up his own allure.

Subtle and overt gazes ricocheting among strangers, the spark of connection threading the streets: this is one of New York's perpetual parades. For the most part these perhaps-encounters are imagined for seconds only; a few go a bit further, and a very few are realized. The luster of street cruising dimmed, during the AIDS epidemic, and never really returned to the full-fledged theater of sexual possibility it used to be, at least for gay men. The culture that came after values above all else ambition, and the money and recognition that flow from it, and tends to focus the gaze of those on the street not on one another but onto little handheld screens. Nonetheless, we present ourselves, we take notice, and not all that happens on those tiny screens concerns wealth, or the corporate world; which of their portfolios are the gazers checking? What sort of investment do they seek? Is it *recompense richer* they have in mind?

—•••—

THE PAGEANTS AND TABLEAUX of Broadway thrilled Whitman, and the panorama and processions of the city served as a template for the grand catalogs of his poems, in which the world parades by in all its engaging variety. Posters, newspapers, and photographic records of the times brim with spectacle: florid displays of the world's marvels, of scientific achievements and industrial products, of wealth and athletic achievement. Horse-drawn carriages racing up what had once been a deer path running along the spine of the island, the pomp of inaugurations, rowdy firemen whose muscles rippled beneath their clothes, even the officious civic spectacle of his own funeral: Whitman loved a parade. New York was on the march all the time. It's a challenge to imagine the radical novelty of it. America had seen itself as provincial, but suddenly wealth, appetite, and pride made our city near the pulsing heart of things, all abuzz and alight: the steam-whistles of departing ferries, the bristle of masts in the harbor, the steepled skyline, rows of houses, the gas-lit allure of music halls, theater, opera, places to dance or attend lectures, *men and women crowding the streets,* shop windows stocked with things to want. An invention new to America, plate glass, made these last come into their own; here was a world of things to be desired, elements of possibility, new ways to look and to be seen.

The new technologies of glassmaking also gave New Yorkers a marvel: the Crystal Palace rose at Forty-Second and Fifth Avenue in 1853, in what's now Bryant Park. Built for the Exhibition of the Industry of All Nations, it was constructed in the shape of a great cross, like a cathedral, its iron structure supporting a skin of glass, with a central dome a hundred feet wide. Solid and transparent at once, it was like nothing New York had ever seen.

The inaugural show, which everyone called the Crystal Palace Exhibition, boasted four thousand exhibitors. Its loose rubric was capable of admitting practically anything: industrial products, consumer goods, steam engines, the largest crocodile ever captured. Here's a sampling of the exhibition catalog's long list:

- *Minerals, Mining and Metallurgy, and Geological Mining Plans and Sections.*
- *Substances used as Food.*
- *Machines for direct use, including Steam, Hydraulic and Pneumatic Engines, and Railway and other Carriages.*
- *Naval Architecture, Military Engineering, Ordnance, Armor and Accoutrements.*

- *Philosophical Instruments, and Products resulting from their use (e. Daguerreotypes), Maps and Charts, Horology, Surgical Instruments and Appliances.*
- *Manufactures of Cotton.*
- *" of Silk.*
- *Paper and Stationery, Types, Printing and Bookbinding.*
- *Wearing Apparel.*
- *Iron, Brass, Pewter, and General Hardware, including Lamps, Chandeliers, Kitchen Furniture.*
- *Perfumery, Confectionery, Toys, Taxidermy.*
- *Musical Instruments.*
- *Fine Arts, & Sculpture, Paintings, Engravings. etc.*

Whitman, rapt, must have moved from aisle to aisle, again and again taking out the little green notebook he carried to scribble a phrase or the name of something that interested him: some quick descriptions of the newly discovered fossils on display, for instance—the saurian who'd figure in a late section of "Song of Myself"? He might as well be walking through one of the vast catalogs he hadn't written yet, like the list of persons in action that comprises Section 15 of the poem:

> *The pure contralto sings in the organloft,*
> *The carpenter dresses his plank . . . . the tongue of his foreplane whistles*
> *   its wild ascending lisp,*
> *The married and unmarried children ride home to their thanksgiving*
> *   dinner,*
> *The pilot seizes the king-pin, he heaves down with a strong arm . . .*

And so on, for sixty-six lines, in which I count seventy-four characters or groups of characters, something like a human version of the exhibition: here we are, on display in our labor and activities, in our disparate natures, working or idling, victorious or suffering, desperate or at ease. The poet's eye takes us in swiftly, as though he were a spirit flying just above the rooftops, able to see into lives below. Or as if, walking the streets of New York, he saw into lit windows and down dim hallways, into the rooms of surgeons and of prostitutes, into the galleries and ballrooms, onto the wharves. Strangely, his visions do not feel like a progression; he does not move through or above space in a sequential way. A line about old black men hoeing in a field is followed by one set in a ballroom, then followed by a young man awake in a garret bedroom listening to the rain. Whitman's perception of these human scenes is simultaneous; he observes them from a position outside of space, as it were, traveling anywhere, the motion of consciousness all that's needed to propel him. His carefully curated list of human actions comes to us in the present tense; it's all happening now, all seen at once.

Some readers find Whitman's catalogs tiresome; for me they are almost endlessly exhilarating. His quick gestures of description sharply evoke what he wants us to see and hear. Take that carpenter, for instance, how *the tongue of his foreplane whistles its wild ascending lisp*: say that line aloud a few times and you can't help but hear and feel the up-shifting pitch of the plane-stroke, as the resistance felt in the consonants of *the tongue of the foreplane* gives way to the windy glide of *whistles its wild ascending lisp*. I admit I do not know what a foreplane is, but Whitman certainly did, and this draws my attention to the word *king-pin,* too, in the four lines I've quoted above. The language of trades is a lexicon we have largely lost, as manufacturing and craft are a diminished part of everyday American life; the things we use are made elsewhere. These are words Whitman might have learned from spending time with the capable workingmen he admired, or from his own work as a carpenter, housebuilder, and printer, or he might have written them down in his notebook, as he strolled the Crystal Palace, studying the enormous array.

Whitman also knew to vary his lists, a subtle but effective means of sustaining interest. Sometimes a parenthetical comment offers a careful bit of observation that makes the line before it more arresting, and far more sad:

> *The lunatic is carried at last to the asylum a confirmed case,*
> *(He will never sleep anymore as he did in the cot in his mother's*
> *bed-room;)*

You don't need to know about Whitman's developmentally disabled younger brother Eddie, or his irrationally angry older brother Jesse, both committed to institutions, to feel the pathos in this line, though surely his own experience lies behind it.

A few lines later, Whitman's gaze stops on not a person but a part of a body:

> *The malform'd limbs are tied to the surgeon's table,*
> *What is removed drops horribly in a pail;*

Poets are often advised to go in fear of adverbs, avoiding them as much as possible. But try removing *horribly* from the line above and you'll see what a brilliant usage this is; it emphasizes the detached quality of the limb, how truly dreadful and alien parts of our own bodies can be when they are no longer joined to the whole. It's no longer even a specific thing, this limb, simply *what is removed,* which makes the line convulse, as it were; the horror of it creates a departure in tone from the sorrow of the lunatic a few lines above. Whitman knows that keeping the tone at play, in motion, is crucial here, as are the intrusions of subjectivity (which *horribly* surely is) that keep his list from turning dry or impersonal. Here is a marvelous example of that sort of intrusion, just a few lines later:

*The young fellow drives the express-wagon, (I love him, though I
    do not know him;)*

The bracing directness of the parenthetical statement breaks
through what actors call the fourth wall, as if the poet stepped
out from behind his catalog to address his readers directly. *I love
him*— how plainspoken can you get? What energy this avowal
gives the poem, adding an affectionate, lusty disclosure to the
mix. Now it seems the poem can go anywhere; what might this
voice *not* reveal, what all might it sweep up in its energetic path?

Energy is the key notion; the sections of Whitman's poem
generate movement as they create pattern and artful variation.
Their patterns seem either to resemble the incoming rush of a
tidal river, a mounting current carrying everything along, or—
as in the case of Section 15, this beautiful exhibition of human
types—they feel cyclonic, as if the poem establishes a spinning
motion, the speaker turning or whirling in a kind of rising prayer,
one offered not to a god above but to the vast possibility of awareness we are.

NEW YORK PULLS ME UP out of myself, just as it must have done
for Whitman. The singularity of the self is constantly called into
question. This can seem a diminishment or an enlarging, a source
of despair or of elation: how welcome it is sometimes to be just
one of an innumerable tribe, not the center but a flashing leaf in a
grove of leaves both similar and endlessly varied. One of the mul-
titude walking this moment on Broadway toward endless possible
destinations.

The first time I taught a graduate poetry workshop at Colum-
bia University, I was struck by the way we'd talk for three hours
each week over every aspect of my students' poems, from a semi-
colon in line 3 to a poem's attempt to inhabit some profound

human conundrum, and how the micro- and macro- levels of the poem might speak to one another to create a form for feeling and thought. It was a joy to build this exhilarating, exacting kind of focus together. But the moment we walked down the steps of Dodge Hall and turned the corner toward Broadway, a magnificent randomness took charge, and the poem that had loomed so large as we gathered around it at the table was dwarfed, put into perspective, as it should be. I imagine many urban dwellers love this feeling, that moment when you step out of your building and whatever has preoccupied you goes flapping away like a burst of pigeons rising all at once, wing and wind carrying them out into this pulsing, indifferent life.

Of course you also have to get out of New York, else you can feel depleted, drawn, your life parceled out into a movement between many small chambers, room to room, from a dark apartment bedroom to a brighter tiny kitchen, to the pet food store where they're open even though the power isn't back on yet and you shop the aisles with a flashlight, and stumble on the teenage Arab boy who works there taking a nap in a dark spot at the end of a row of shelves. You need to be somewhere where you hear less of other people, are not caught up in the endless waves of their conversations, where there is more space between—well, everything.

Everythingness—by which I mean a great, symphonic fullness, where the streets seem to swell with the rising pressure of all that might occur, where every note on the scale will be struck, then struck again in combinations that no one could have expected or foreseen—is one of Manhattan's signature characteristics. That's what it was like the night we drove in from the east end of Long Island after Hurricane Sandy in October 2012. A black, ominous lake had appeared where the entrance to the Midtown Tunnel into Manhattan should have been; the many lanes of the Long Island Expressway merged down to three and then simply plummeted into the waters of . . . Averno? But the Brooklyn Bridge was open, and we drove across that still-lit span down into a city so dark as to seem bewitched, punished by some sorcerer for what transgression? The streetlamps of the south end of the island were out, as were the stoplights; the headlights of very slowly moving cars, and not many of them at that, provided the only illumination save for candles in apartment windows and the occasional flashlight in a passerby's hand. People walked more tentatively; I had the thought that these weren't people, but ghosts, and that it must have been this dark in some parts of the city in Whitman's day, the years of the seamy, sometimes wildly dangerous downtown Luc Sante chronicles in his book *Low Life*. Suddenly it seemed possible to understand that crazed, tumultuous passage Whitman later excised from his poem "The Sleepers," when the speaker joins a fractious, bacchic parade and winds up naked under a pier someplace—doing what exactly? What all might the citizens of this city get up to, in such a permissive and unmapped darkness?

Just as you were one of a crowd, I was one of a crowd . . . Daily, as a citizen of Manhattan, I am part of living throngs—on the sidewalk, underneath the intersection of Fourteenth Street and Seventh Avenue while we wait to catch an uptown train, most pressingly at Penn Station, when at busy morning or late afternoon hours we pour through the corridors away from and toward our trains. We are great streams released, pouring around the pretzel vendors and bagel stands, the drugstores and ATMs and soldiers in desert camouflage carrying before them huge weapons to save us from phantom dread. IF YOU SEE SOMETHING, SAY SOMETHING the signs proclaim, but something is seen every second, in the world of strangers like ourselves so vast it threatens to drown us, though in some miraculous way the clashing millions stride in disparate directions and we mostly do not collide, are rarely knocked down, and most of us do not recede to the sides of the huge rooms or narrow halls in terror, most of us keep moving. When I come back late at night from anywhere the station is a temple of fluorescent sorrow, a few people striding forward but many who are still or nearly so, ruined or broken, like ancient statues set at random on a plain of stone. I move among them on my way to the A or C or E train; they move very little, though some begin to turn to me a pleading look, or begin to mutter pleas they have down by heart: *help me get something to eat, I'm cold, I can't, I have children, I have nowhere, will you* . . . If you stop you may begin to enter into a contract with damage, moving into a relation whose end will be the limit of what you can do growing louder and more terrible. To move through without looking, to withhold your eyes from theirs, makes you complicitous, erases you as much as it does this city's cracked-out and crumpled. *Stand up*, Whitman enjoined, *for the stupid and crazy*. What would he have done, midnight in Penn Station, hurrying home from a late night at his teaching job, an official custodian of the language passing through a dim place where speech is reduced to please and moan, and declarations of the ways the broken have been made more so by what tunnels inside them, the radio waves, the Lord's secret transmissions, the voice of night itself?

Even in that crowd, there is another voice, another witness, the poet who walks with us and stands at the edge of every living American crowd now. One thing Walt Whitman has become is an attitude toward the fact of being numerous. Sometimes his gaze informs the throng crowded into the subway, many of us stealing glances at the little boy sprawled wide, asleep and happy on his seven-foot-tall black father's wide lap, or at the mariachi band that out of nowhere strikes up a warbling ode to the joy of merely circulating. Or the prophet seated beside me who speaks to me, after I give a dollar to some self-proclaimed homeless woman who holds a stunned-eyed child by the hand and recites the story of her eviction in a toneless monologue. *You don't know,* he says, I believe speaking of alms given to one who might or might not be telling the truth, *He comes like a thief in the night.*

———•••———

ONE MORNING I WAS STARTLED by a sudden movement in my third-floor window, which turned out to be the waving of the not-too-full but still reasonably brushy tail of a gray squirrel, who was burying an acorn in a terra-cotta window box. How long did that creature have to look to find a bit of earth accommodating enough to dig? In our stretch of Chelsea it's many a block to a park, and the plane trees and gingkos grow out of squares cut into the sidewalk, fenced with metal railings, or in big Parisian-style planters in front of buildings with money and a sense of style. That day it was those ten tiny talons versus Manhattan, and though the fellow seemed a cheerful soldier of tenacity, I wished I could give him a break.

———•••———

THE NEW YORK OF 1853, like the Crystal Palace, offered viewers the known world on display. How much Whitman wanted to include in the exhibition hall of his poem! The Egyptian Gallery on Broadway in SoHo, whence came his notion of grass as *a uniform hieroglyphic;* the thrilling vocal performances of the Italian opera singers he'd review for the *Brooklyn Eagle,* which give us his *orbic tenor.*

Most potent perhaps were the ideas crowding into his awareness from the flourishing decade before the prospect of war began to loom over the hopes of those years. Whitman drank in Emerson's lectures, with their insistence that the natural world and our own native inclinations could educate the soul, and he encountered, through him and other Transcendentalists, the first translations of sacred texts from Asia breaking upon these shores. New currents of feminism spoke to freedom beyond traditional constraints, posited the equality of the sexes, and dared to propose the reality of women's sexual desire; such thinking inevitably questions the nature of masculinity, interrogating what we claim as "natural." Dr. Sylvester Graham, whose surname lingers still on boxes of crackers served in every preschool in the nation, preached that a high-fiber diet could cleanse the blood, and the spirit along with it. Phrenology provided a map to the self, through the study of the shape of the head, where specific areas of the skull revealed strengths or deficits of character. Nude sunbathing could restore our native energies, and sexual freedom might keep them flowing; communal living might reform the social order, address inequity, and forge new social contracts founded on respect and affection. It was not an uncommon thing, to propose a new gospel.

A maximalist, a fan of multiplicity, Walt Whitman loved the climate in which he found himself. Was there ever a poet less likely to sign on to the maxim that less is more?

The challenge that abundance presented to him was that of synthesis and structure: how to make something of a burgeoning whole that is both coherent and various? Too much coherence and the poem excludes the exuberant chaos of the world; too much disorder and the thing falls apart. A poem needs to be orderly enough to hold our attention, to make us feel that we are being guided through the exhibition, and needs to leave room for slippage and surprise, for those productive disruptions that characterize the real.

It's probably indicative of Whitman's struggle to shape the poem that he had a hard time titling it. What we know as "Song of Myself" was first printed, confusingly, beneath the words *Leaves of Grass,* which may refer to this poem or may mean the whole book. In his 1856 edition, he calls it "Poem of Walt Whitman, an American," a blandly descriptive label. In 1860, he simply calls it

"Walt Whitman" and so the title remains until 1871, when the poem received the title we know, the far better one.

I understand why he thought to call the poem "Walt Whitman." The poem is a great spiraling tour of a personality, flush with its obsessions and desires, both overt and repressed, a catalog of the information and evidence the world brings to the speaker's body, a guide to what he loves, a consideration and recasting of the idea of selfhood, and a meditation on what can be said and what cannot. What holds this vast interior road trip together is an unmistakable voice, a creation of remarkable durability and range: garrulous, intimate, haughty, ironic, sly, confiding, dismissive, grand, teasing, wise, sometimes obtuse or mysterious, and decidedly American, surging with the vital energies of New York City in its brash hour of new strength. With this extraordinary instrument, at full strength at the very beginning of his career, he strides onto the stage of American poetry and simply takes possession of it, even though hardly anyone knew he had done so.

THE
FOURTH
SOURCE

FIFTEEN

STUCCO'D
WITH QUADRUPEDS AND
BIRDS ALL OVER

Whitman's first edition came gushing into sight, borne high on the energy of a new vocabulary: a supple, colloquial, as-yet-unwritten speech, rich as the lexicon of Chaucer or Shakespeare—poets who also heard, in their times, their language renewed. This splendid flood is the fourth source of Whitman's greatest work, and helps to account for his poems' radical new-ness, since spoken American English is more than a lexicon: it brings with it a tone, a stance toward experience and the world.

Plants and animals that inhabit islands are one of the richest areas of inquiry for evolutionary biologists; what happens to a species separated from its origins and changing under the conditions of new demands? American English, in Whitman's time, had for two hundred years lived at an increasing distance from its sources on the other side of the Atlantic, long enough to acquire a distinctive character.

What went into it? The camp-talk of hunters, trappers, woodsmen, miners around small fires in a large continent. Native American place-names, their melodious euphonics wildly foreign to white people's ears: Nantucket, Mattapoisett, Montauk. And names for rivers: Susquehanna, Lackawanna, Mississippi. Rhythms of scripture and hymnals, immigrants and pioneers, echoing in the voice of the angel who translated the tablets of

New World scriptures unearthed in upstate New York by Joseph Smith as he plowed his fields. More place names: Canaan, Mt. Pisgah. The sung and spoken words of slaves, bringing, through no choice of their own, new words, new inflections, and music. The patois created by white writers and performers attempting to represent (and thus to market) African American speech. Words and phrases from the far West, reflecting new geographies and geology, mountains and deserts presented in engraved images for those who'd never see the untamed territories, terms brought back by explorers, soldiers, miners, and failed settlers. The languages of trades, industry, and commerce, their lexicons multiplying radically at mid-century, with the mounting successes of new industrial and manufacturing processes. The talk of carpenters, stage coach drivers, and dock workers, city slang, speech of the up-to-the-minute, or the underclass, or the temporary worker, speech of the displaced, the incarcerated, of thieves. Of sailors, fishermen, and baymen. The demotic, as distinct from the talk of the salon and library. Part of Whitman's project was the importation of a great deal of speech previously considered unpoetic, either because it was too colloquial, too American, too arcane, or too technical, or because it just hadn't occurred to anyone to put a word like *foofoo* (a slang term for a fussy, fancy man or dandy) or *yawp* (an outcry) in a poem yet. American poets before Whitman wanted to prove themselves worthy of the name, and a conservative, traditional diction might be one demonstration of their mettle.

Whitman's influence in this area is so profound that it seems difficult to imagine, now, a contemporary American poet *not* writing in some version of spoken American English.

Literary language is not alien to Whitman either; the cadences and anaphoric patterns of the Bible ring through *Leaves of Grass*. This passage from Matthew 6, in the King James Version of the Bible, exemplifies the way the gospel authors (or Jesus himself?) interpreted the "book of nature":

28 And why take ye thought for raiment? Consider the
lilies of the field, how they grow; they toil not, neither
do they spin:

29 And yet I say unto you, That even Solomon in all his
glory was not arrayed like one of these.

Updated just a bit in diction and syntax (*why should you think,* for
instance, instead of *why take ye thought*), those lines strike me as
a likely bit of some lost section of "Song of Myself." Might even
Whitman's title be a revision of the Song of Solomon, another
great love letter to the divine?

The 1850s saw the publication of another New Yorker's under-
praised masterwork. Likewise intoxicated by the unruly beauty
and freshness of American speech, Herman Melville published a
sui generis hybrid of a novel melding sailor slang with Elizabe-
than drama, Emersonian essay, and, of course, those precise and
technical descriptions of whaling that have driven many a reader
to distraction. The great American books of the 1850s—*The Scarlet Letter, The House of the Seven Gables, Moby-Dick, Walden, Leaves
of Grass*—and the dazzling, private poetic career of Emily Dickinson represent an awakening, a willingness to go out into the new
world and *look,* and to be, as Emerson promised, instructed. In
this spiritually rich, investigative literature, a new country finds
its *gravitas,* and a position from which to speak. But for all their
American-ness, their lives out of doors, their directness and courage, their struggles with guilt, or the solitude of a vast continent
or an equally vast interiority, or with a white whale—these writers nonetheless seem isolated characters who've been up all night
reading, as it were, trying to reconcile the landscape and towns
around them with Isaiah and Matthew, Shakespeare, Marlowe
and Milton. They dwell out on an edge, one that allows them to
see their own time and place, its sources, its crises and its pros-
pects, and that never allows them to feel quite at home in the

world. Of the lot, Whitman seems the most at ease, the most pleased to be in human company. Though even his essential loneliness still shows through—a sense that there is a "Me myself" apart from the camaraderie, one who watches. One of the Transcendentalist visitors from New England who'd traveled out to Brooklyn to meet him in the house on Classon Avenue objected, later, to the hearty way Whitman greeted, and was greeted by, practically everyone passing by. Should a poet be this sociable? Was Whitman acting a part; did he stand, lonely observer, somewhere behind his warm performance of belonging to the social world? It's worth noting that, though Thoreau and Alcott may have distrusted Walt's friendly exchanges, the activist Sarah Tyndale stayed after the two men had departed, and her long conversation with the poet became the basis of an enduring friendship.

THE FRESHNESS OF WHITMAN'S LEXICON comes from an interest in and affection for language itself, its unexpected connections, surprises, and sensuous delight, the way some words seem to move tongue, lips, and teeth in unexpected combinations. The way some words—*wallow, guzzle, tumble, souse,* and *spray*—spoken with attention to the physical experience of voicing them are simple sources of delight.

But the affection and interest shown to passersby on the Brooklyn sidewalks that rankled Whitman's visitors was the mark of an energetic, inclusive curiosity about others. An eagerness to encounter, without regard to status, class, or education, must also be a source of Whitman's wide-ranging vocabulary. How did they speak, the Long Island baymen who made their living from the salt marshes and coves along the sound? The stage coach drivers who urged their horse teams to rattle at bracing speeds going up and down Broadway, their pace sometimes approaching the death-defying?

Through me, the poet writes, *many long-dumb voices.* But we don't really hear, in Whitman, the speech of others. Is there a line of dialogue in all his poetry? He renders perception and experience in a voice unmistakably his. But he subsumes other presences, human and animal, absorbs them as it were, and wants to serve as witness and advocate. The pages of *Leaves of Grass,* especially the three early editions, present us with a diverse cast of characters, most of them scarce indeed in the work of the poet's contemporaries. These are the texts of the witness who wanders the world, day and night, city and fields, and is not blind or deaf to the suicide *on the bloody floor of the bedroom,* the lunatic who *will never sleep anymore as he did in a cot in his mother's bedroom,* or the prostitute who *draggles her shawl* as *her bonnet bobs on her tipsy and pimpled neck.*

What the poet has to give—the nourishment of his verse, the bracing and salutary news his poem brings—

> . . . *is the meal pleasantly set . . . . this is the meat and drink*
>   *for natural hunger,*
> *It is for the wicked just the same as the righteous . . . . I make*
>   *appointments with all,*
> *I will not have a single person slighted or left away,*
> *The keptwoman and sponger and thief are hereby*
>   *invited . . . . the heavy-lipped slave is invited . . . . the*
>   *venerealee is invited,*
> *There shall be no difference between them and the rest.*

It seems odd, for modern readers, to find the slave included in this list of those who are morally compromised or ill, but it is primarily an accounting of those who have not been able or allowed to speak. Whitman wants to listen to them, and he seeks to make of his art a banquet that feeds the despised and outcast as well as the privileged. His inclusive impulse extends toward people of color again and again, especially in his relished accountings of reality in Section 13 of "Song of Myself:"

> *The negro that drives the huge dray of the stoneyard . . . .*
> > *steady and tall he stands poised on one leg on the string-piece,*
> *His blue shirt exposes his ample neck and breast and loosens over his*
> > *hipband,*
> *His glance is calm and commanding . . . . he tosses the*
> > *slouch of his hat away from his forehead,*
> *The sun falls on his crispy hair and moustache . . . . falls on*
> > *the black of his polished and perfect limbs.*

That, by the way, is a fine example of the energy Whitman gains through dilating his sentences. Conventional punctuation would make at least five sentences out of this passage, and if you try reading it that way it marches prosaically along. But if we read it as written, allowing the poet the brief pause of the ellipsis or comma instead of the full stop of the period, then the sensory information here seems to arrive in a single moment of perception, and the breathless speed it gathers underscores the speaker's admiration for this *commanding* figure with his *polished and perfect limbs.*

Many a writer of color in the first half of the twentieth century found in Whitman a model of a white writer who embraced a wide range of humanity in his work without apparent prejudice. "Song of Myself" alone offers repeated instance in which slaves are presented empathically: the runaway slave *limpsey and weak,* or *the quadroon girl sold at the stand,* or the older black men—*woollypates*—who *hoe in the sugarfield* while *the overseer views them from his saddle.* Fewer of them, it's safe to say, had read Whitman's journalism (some of which was not reprinted until relatively recently) or perused accounts of some of his later remarks. It is expecting the miraculous, I guess, to expect that any person completely escapes the racial attitude of his or her times, but nonetheless it is strange to see the poet who presents the human presences in his poems with such egalitarian warmth slipping into confused and sometimes reprehensible positions. There's one particularly depressing example, in a passage the poet later deleted from his prose text *Democratic Vistas*. Concerned with the difficulty of integrating new groups into a democracy, he notes that it will be *much harder* to integrate blacks than it was to bring into American society *the millions of ignorant foreigners* who had arrived during the previous fifty years. How then will we be able to assimilate, when slavery ends, *a powerful percentage of blacks, with about as much intellect and calibre (in the mass) as so many baboons.* He does not, as some have complained, call citizens of African descent "baboons," but by using that particular simile, he may as well have; the damage is done. And what could be more of a textbook example of racist speech than that parenthetical assertion? How can he claim to know the intellect and worth of the whole of any group?

This passage from "I Sing the Body Electric" says, to my mind, what's most crucial when it comes to Whitman and questions of race. Here the speaker observes a man, a slave up for auction, and slips into the role of an auctioneer who says to his audience of potential buyers the things they'd never want to hear. I've said that Whitman is not an ironic poet, but this passage is a splendid, cutting exception, spoken from behind the thinnest of masks, and you can't miss the poet's rancor, and his rage at those who think themselves so above another human being that they actually think they can *buy* him.

> *A slave at auction!*
> *I help the auctioneer . . . . the sloven does not half*
>   *know his business.*
>
> *Gentlemen look on this curious creature!*
> *Whatever the bids of the bidders, they cannot be*
>   *high enough for him,*

For him the globe lay preparing quintillions of years,
      without one animal or plant,
For him the revolving cycles truly and steadily
      rolled.

In that head the all-baffling brain,
In it and below it the making of the attributes of
      heroes.

Examine these limbs, red black or white . . . . they
      are very cunning in tendon and nerve;
They shall be stript that you may see them.

Exquisite senses, lifelit eyes, pluck, volition,
Flakes of breastmuscle, pliant backbone and
      neck, flesh not flabby, goodsized arms and
      legs,
And wonders within there yet.

Within there runs his blood . . . . the same old blood . . . .
      the same red-running blood;
There swells and jets his heart . . . . There all passions
      and desires . . . . all reachings and aspirations:
Do you think they are not there because they are
      not expressed in parlors and lecture-rooms?

This is not only one man . . . . this is the father of
      those who shall be fathers in their turns,
In him the start of populous states and rich re-
      publics,
Of him countless immortal lives, with countless
      embodiments and enjoyments.

How do you know who shall come from the off-
spring of his offspring through the centuries?
Who might you find you have come from yourself,
if you could trace back through the centuries?

What is required to confront history, I think, is an allegiance to complexity, a refusal to oversimplify. The truth here is that Whitman managed, in poems like the one above, to see right through the racist conventions of his day, and to understand that human beings shared *the same red-running blood.* And he made some appallingly racist comments, in conversation and in editorials, which are indefensible.

———•••———

MELVILLE PACKED THE PAGES of his visionary novel *Moby-Dick*—a book of startling existential bleakness, but so energetic that it is somehow hopeful nonetheless—with nautical terms, and with the names of tools and of atmospheric conditions, providing a lexicon for American writers ever after. Hart Crane's work alone borrows beautifully from Melville both individual words (*leewardings*) and whole phrases (Melville's waves roll by *like scrolls of silver;* Crane describes them as *scrolls of silver snowy sentences*). A great book is a kind of raft of language, carrying words into the future. Whitman's a word collector, filling his green pocket notebooks with terms he might later use, for their heft and color, their character and tone, as well as for the way they might open doors to new perspectives. He's engaged by the language of the sciences, for example, as evidenced by his borrowings from the lexicon of New York's Crystal Palace exhibition, at which examples of practically everything human endeavor had created up to 1853 were on display. All the latest findings of the sciences were there too—crystals and fossils and botanical specimens—as well as splendid examples of various arts. The exhibition filled one of those fashionable structures, a sort of huge conservatory of iron and glass made possible by new technologies, and to Whitman it must have seemed like a model of his own brain, or of the repository and index of all of life he wanted the self to be. He roamed the aisles, penciling words and notes in one of the small green notebooks he favored. Thus in "Song of Myself" appear lines like these:

> *I find I incorporate gneiss, coal, long-threaded moss, fruits, grains,*
>   *esculent roots,*
> *And am stucco'd with quadrupeds and birds all over . . .*

Gneiss is a "high-grade metamorphic rock," subjected to high temperatures and levels of pressure, and it's characterized, like the poem's vocabulary, by layers of different materials. *Esculent* is an adjective meaning "suitable to eat," something of an improvement over the merely edible. *Stucco'd* is the completely unexpected term here; who but Whitman can we imagine thus plastered in animals and birds, a marvelous, comic image for the inclusive self? In this half-sentence are to be found words from geology, botany, construction, and zoology. Whitman was a magpie of a collector, one who could seamlessly conjoin discourses, and make from multiple lexicons a hybrid speech. Or, perhaps, what one might think of as a dwelling place.

LOAFE, WORMFENCE, I GUESS, hankering, the sniff of green leaves, pokeweed, Kanuck, Tuckahoe, Congressman, Cuff, have you reckoned, limpsey, gamut, silliness, woolypates, squaw, all out, tipsy, luckier, Chattahoochee, Altamahaw, Buckeye, stuck up, fancy-man, rowdyish, the fish-smack pack, carlacue, foofoos, a suck and a sell.

These are words and phrases that simply would not have appeared in poetry written in the English language before 1855.

Many more could be added. It's hard now to imagine the sense of the new they must have carried, to try to summon how startling it must have been to find them on the page. The word *gulch*, for instance, made its first appearance in print in 1850, but five years later Whitman is *afoot with his vision* and his spirit *wanders along the ruts of the turnpike along the dry gulch and rivulet bed.* The word has a strongly physical quality; the hard *g,* the low-pitched vowel sound *uh,* the way the throat is required to make a sort of swallowing motion to produce the sound *ulch.* No surprise then to find the Oxford English Dictionary suggesting the noun may come from an onomatopoeic North American dialect verb meaning *to swallow.* Many of the words in my quick list have this kind of thick, impasto texture of consonants; they wake us up to the sheer sound of words, their richness and variety; there's a level of pleasure in just saying *fish-smack pack* or *foofoos* aloud. These words splash onto the page in Whitman's first edition, as if a dam holding back a flood of new speech had been dynamited, all at once, by the force of a single poem.

—•••—

DELVING INTO ETYMOLOGIES, I'm surprised to find that many of the words or phrases I hear as American aren't necessarily native in their origin. In this signature line, *I sound my barbaric yawp over the rooftops of the world,* that thoroughly Yankee-sounding *yawp* turns out to originate, at least as a verb, in Middle English. It must be the poet's tone, his ability to subsume words into the most decidedly American-sounding of voices.

In a few years' time, Whitman would begin to put what he'd previously have considered affected speech and poeticisms back into place—attempting to lively up what I imagine he knew were rather flat later poems with bits of French, tired apostrophizing, and other unconvincing gestures. Who, I ask you, is likely to be won over by a phrase like *Democracy, ma femme!*?

When an artist works alone, without the company of the like-minded, in a climate not especially supportive of the project, it's difficult to sustain the courage required for the new. Or when vision is cooling, and the artist can't find a way back to the sources of her vitality, then gestures trying to be artful might begin to substitute for the real thing.

Or, when an artist hungry for validation finally receives some, there's a temptation to play to those who offered it, and with that comes the risk of imitating oneself, producing paler, anemic versions of the vital art that you made with no notion of where it was headed, before you'd made anything to imitate.

THE IDEA OF MODERNIZATION, the adaptation of poetic speech and forms to American voices, doesn't seem to have concerned Whitman's contemporaries much; it wouldn't be until a decade after Whitman's death that free verse began to mount any serious challenge to the formal tradition. Early reviewers noted the barbarism of his utterance, as if this were not a carefully crafted literary production but something out of the poet's control, the work of an unschooled or outsider artist.

Here, for instance, is the reptilian Rufus Griswold, writing in the *Criterion* in 1855:

> *It is impossible to imagine how any man's fancy could have conceived such a mass of stupid filth, unless he were possessed of the soul of a sentimental donkey that had died of disappointed love. This poet (?) without wit, but with a certain vagrant wildness, just serves to show the energy which natural imbecility is occasionally capable of under strong excitement.*

Whitman actually chose to reprint this review, along with others, in the back of the 1856 edition. Did he think that a bit of controversy might help attract an audience? Did he think it was funny? I can't help but feel, reading *stupid filth* and *without wit*, a pang of sympathy. More or less the same has been said of me, though not quite so directly, and there is no consolation for it, save perhaps to note that one would be hard-pressed to locate a copy of the collected works of Rufus Griswold, canon-maker though he was in his day.

An unsigned review of one of Griswold's anthologies, published in 1843 and quite possibly written by Edgar Allan Poe, deftly makes the point:

> *What will be {Griswold's} fate? Forgotten, save only by those whom he has injured and insulted, he will sink into oblivion, without leaving a landmark to tell that he once existed; or if he is spoken of hereafter, he will be quoted as the unfaithful servant who abused his trust.*

Griswold had some strong words for Whitman's content, but much of his objection seems formal and class-based, as if the poet had made an intolerable breach of etiquette. *Stupid, donkey, without wit, vagrant wildness,* and *natural imbecility* are here to remove the poet from the category to which poets *should* belong, the highly literate, whose cultivated work wears its formality for all to see, as opposed to the "natural imbecility" of *Leaves of Grass. Natural* here means artless, which is surely how Griswold thought of Whitman's choice of poetic forms. The free verse Whitman invented, with its rangy lines of varying length, its relaxed, speech-based rhythms, and its use of the stanza as a unit of thought, with the white space between stanzas intended as a space of reflection— well, that form became, because Whitman made it work so elegantly and "naturally" to advance his poems, the template for most American poetry after early-twentieth-century Imagism.

Whitman demonstrates that neither rhyme, regular meter, nor regular stanza patterns are needed for a poem to be a song. And that, in fact, new and complex sorts of meaning and singing can emerge when the poem is not confined by a predetermined form. Unbound, the free-verse poem finds a new template: the act of inquiry.

I want to return to the electrifying lectures of 1843 delivered by Ralph Waldo Emerson at the Boston Athenaeum and at the New York Society Library in Manhattan, one of which was titled "The Poetry of the Times"— an early version of an essay that would later be called "The Poet." Whitman was in the New York audience, and would have heard these words, or a draft of them:

> *For it is not metres, but a metre-making argument, that makes a poem,—a thought so passionate and alive, that, like the spirit of a plant or an animal, it has an architecture of its own, and adorns nature with a new thing. The thought and the form are equal in the order of time, but in the order of genesis the thought is prior to the form. The poet has a new thought: he has a whole new experience to unfold; he will tell us how it was with him, and all men will be the richer in his fortune.*

If you think of the freely shifting rhythms of Whitman's lines as a sort of meter, then Emerson's words become an apt description of the kind of free verse Whitman would teach himself to write, in which content generates form, the poem an embodiment of the motion of thought.

Whitman heard Emerson's words—*we have yet had no genius in America*—as challenge and clarion call. So, I imagine, did Henry David Thoreau. Fueled by that same heat, his own questions and sense of the nature of things affirmed, Thoreau penned some of the most muscular and engaging of American prose, and launched a tradition of autobiographical writing, chronicling encounters with the natural world, that continues to thrive a century and a half since the publication of *Walden*.

But the poems of the prophet of civil disobedience are another matter. Here is "The Thaw."

> *I saw the civil sun drying earth's tears —*
> *Her tears of joy that only faster flowed,*
>
> *Fain would I stretch me by the highway side,*
> *To thaw and trickle with the melting snow,*
> *That mingled soul and body with the tide,*
> *I too may through the pores of nature flow.*
>
> *But I alas nor tinkle can nor fume,*
> *One jot to forward the great work of Time,*
> *'Tis mine to hearken while these ply the loom,*
> *So shall my silence with their music chime.*

Fain and *hearken* distinctly belong to Poetic speech; the other words here are ones we might use every day, but there are no distinctly American words, in part because the speaker seems to be holding himself above common speech. The inversion of syntax reinforces this elevation: *I too may through the pores of nature flow*, as opposed to *I may flow through the pores of nature, too*—or, more painfully, *But I alas nor tinkle can nor fume*, which defies rephrasing. Readers of poetry in the nineteenth century were used to such posturings, and perhaps it's not even fair to call them that; they were part of the poetic rhetoric of the day, just as aspects of the poetry of our moment will doubtless seem like mere conventions to readers of the future. But the result feels so stiff and arch!

If I play with the second stanza, freeing it from its corset of form in order to make the sense more clear, the impulse behind the poem starts to come to life. Something like

I would like to lie down by the side of the highway,
and thaw and trickle with the melting snow,
then my body and soul would be mingled with that water,
and I too would flow through the pores of nature.

That's not great, but it removes a certain degree of distance between us and the poem's central, Whitmanic impulse: to fuse, to melt away.

Thoreau wrote prose of undeniable vigor and richness, with the aura of the genuine to it. No reader of *Walden* could forget that sleeping insect caught in the wood of the tabletop who whirrs urgently, disruptively into life when the wood's warmed by the heat of an iron. The image of a thaw seems central to him; he wants the ice-locked soul to awake.

Why then is "A Thaw" so awful? It isn't Thoreau's fault that *tinkle* has taken on a secondary meaning now, as countless mothers have found it a useful onomatopoeic euphemism, thus rendering *But I alas nor tinkle can nor fume* even more ridiculous. The problem goes deeper than that; there's a fatal mismatch here between form and content. By *form* I mean the poem's regular iambic pentameter and regular rhyme scheme, which lead the poet to traffic in inversions, twisting syntax till it's actually a good deal of work just to make grammatical sense out of stanzas two and three. By *content* I mean not just the poet's idea—that he'd like to lie down and melt, but can't—but something like his speaking character, the cadences of his voice and thought, the way he moves his body, breathes, his stance toward experience. Compare Thoreau's lines to Whitman's:

I depart as air, I shake my white locks at the runaway sun,
I effuse my flesh in eddies and drift it in lacy jags.

These feel far more adventurous, in part because Whitman's lines are much richer in verbs, and he chooses more active ones: *depart, shake, effuse,* and *drift* come to us in just two lines. *Runaway* is a completely unexpected adjective here; the passage comes only eight lines from the end of "Song of Myself" when Whitman says that *the past and present wilt* because he has filled and emptied them. He speaks, here, from another position in time than that which his readers occupy; he is preparing to bequeath himself to the dirt *to grow from the grass I love* but he also waits for us, we who will find our way to his voice in the future. He doesn't doubt for a moment that he can *effuse* his flesh and *drift* it, which is pretty much what Thoreau seems to have in mind with wishing his body to *tinkle* and *fume,* those things he cannot do.

Obviously, I prefer Whitman's bolder stance, though in fact a perfectly good poem could be written about the inability to join in with the flow of the world. The reason Thoreau hasn't written it is that his formal bindings provide him with too tight an enclosure; he can't explore the idea, ask questions, investigate the problem his poem wants to consider because he is committed to this antique packaging whose only sign of modernity is the odd little unrhymed couplet at the beginning, though that too is delivered in perfectly regular meter.

A great part of Whitman's accomplishment was to simply sidestep the matter of rhyme and meter, and thus free himself to compose poems that constructed a different kind of music, out of repetition, marvelous sonic effects and forward-moving cadences. Since these often took as their formal structure the shape of argument, it's no surprise that he wanted to be an orator, since he would have had a wider influence that way. He couldn't have known what his innovations—the ways he opened both formal possibilities and new territories for content—would mean to poets to come, both in his home country and around the world. He'd hoped to change his country, to provide the founding text of a new order. What he changed was poetry, which indeed does change the world, but quietly, a reader at a time.

THE
FIFTH
SOURCE

SIXTEEN

DEMON OR BIRD

"Out of the Cradle Endlessly Rocking"—published first in a journal in 1859, and then in the 1860 edition of *Leaves of Grass* as "A Word Out of the Sea"—is one of the strangest and most haunting of American poems, and a startling inquiry into why we make art. The poem begins with an evocation of a remembered night's walk through fields and woods near the center of Long Island, down to the shore: a landscape of Whitman's childhood, more than a century before that land became the deracinated expanse of suburb and strip mall it is today. This nocturnal excursion is narrated in one gloriously extended sentence, layered and crystalline, and occupies a stanza unto itself.

Whitman's opening lines are usually lucid, encapsulating what's to come the way an orator might begin by sketching an argument. But this walk to the shore, the boundary between the solid and the unstable, between what we know and what we don't, begins in a luminous swirl and scramble. The poem starts by placing and disorienting us at once, setting us unmoored in a wild night of instruction. Birdsong and the ceaseless sound of the September sea called the boy to the beach at night, and call down the years to the adult poet's memory, bringing him to a place of origin, the desolate ground where, he will learn, all songs begin.

Out of the cradle endlessly rocking,
Out of the mocking-bird's throat, the musical shuttle,
Out of the Ninth-month midnight,
Over the sterile sands and the fields beyond, where the child
    leaving his bed wandered alone, bareheaded, barefoot,
Down from the showered halo,
Up from the mystic play of shadows twining and twisting as
    if they were alive,
Out from the patches of briers and blackberries,
From the memories of the bird that chanted to me,
From your memories sad brother, from the fitful risings and
    fallings I heard,
From under that yellow half-moon late-risen and swollen as
    if with tears,
From those beginning notes of yearning and love there in
    the mist,
From the thousand responses of my heart never to cease,
From the myriad thence-aroused words,
From the word stronger and more delicious than any,
From such as now they start the scene revisiting,
As a flock, twittering, rising, or overhead passing,
Borne hither, ere all eludes me, hurriedly,
A man, yet by these tears a little boy again,
Throwing myself on the sand, confronting the waves,
I, chanter of pains and joys, uniter of here and hereafter,
Taking all hints to use them, but swiftly leaping beyond them,
A reminiscence sing.

Whitman's syntax creates a driving but fractured motion, as if we're viewing this scene through a prism of memory that breaks time into planes of light and action. Three lines begin with *out*, telling us this meditation comes from the sound of waves, from the music of a mockingbird, and from a September midnight.

But then the pattern shifts, and the next four lines commence with *over, down, up*—and *out* again; this scramble of prepositions mimic the boy's path to the shore, but more than that they blur action and agency; this is a physical world inextricable from one lit up by the movements of the spirit. *Down from the showered halo/ Up from the mystic play of shadows twining and twisting as if they were alive* suggests a mist-ringed moon and a walk through a fantastic leaf-shadow realm, but it also evokes a soul coming into being, that which has descended from above and rises into new life out of the womb, *the Ninth-month midnight.*

Eight lines begin with *from,* a list of origins of this reminiscence that swiftly turns into an exploration of the sources of this poem, and of poetry, which is made of *the thousand responses of my heart never to cease.* Whitman makes a startlingly modern gesture, overtly including in this poem the moment of its composition, when *from the myriad thence-aroused words . . . from such as now they start the scene revisiting . . .* That *now* is the moment when he first inscribes the words that come

> *As a flock, twittering, rising, or overhead passing,*
> *Borne hither, ere all eludes me, hurriedly . . .*

What an alive, anxious description of how it must have felt to write *this* poem, the possible words hurrying, calling out, streaming as if through the air, carried by some wind that will, if he's not quick enough, sweep them away! But it's equally possible to read that the speaker's the one who is "borne hither," drawn to the birdsong, to the rush of language and the shoreline of vision not by volition but by some signature inscribed within him, an undeniable imperative.

The game this sentence plays with time is dazzling. It remembers a moment in the past while making elements of that moment—a walk to the beach—feel timeless, figures for a soul's coming into being. It gradually reveals itself as a chronicle not of one walk to the shore but of many and ongoing ones, and then it establishes a present, the moment of its composition and the moment in which we are reading it. These two *now*s unfold side by side, parallel lines separated by an elastic amount of time between them. For the writer, the moment is receding before the ink of the words that inscribe it has dried. That distance increases as the poem travels further from the writer's hand into print, into the attention of readers, into the silence of libraries. If you could hear this distance in time as it lengthens I think it would have a deepening sonority, a piece for solo cello growing more gravid and resonant.

Whenever a reader picks up the poem and lends it voice, silently or aloud, the moment of composition is, as it were, restored, lit up before a background of elapsed time. For the poet, the poem fuses *here and hereafter*; for readers the "present" of the text is our past, and its "future" our present. Whitman understood this paradox, and put it to remarkable use, addressing an audience he rightly anticipated would appear, and establishing his own voice in a position of startling atemporality. For the reader, the sound the poem makes is that of a door gliding open. As in Dickinson: *You there —I here—with just the Door ajar.*

•••

IN ITS CONTINUOUS CHARACTER, its unbroken, repetitive movements, this sentence evokes the shoreline itself, in the forward rushes of sound, the feeling of small retreats, a line of water breaking into foam, a line of thinking revising and regrouping, now qualified, now urgent . . . But enough.

•••

"OUT OF THE CRADLE Endlessly Rocking" is a libretto for a two-character opera, a feverishly theatrical one. The boy who'll grow up to speak the human part of the poem comes to the beach, each day, to hear the song of a pair of nesting birds, studying them intently, *peering, absorbing, translating*. The last verb in the list is key; even before he understands the nature of his calling, the young man is already acting as a poet, turning experience into language, importing the unreadable into the realm of words.

Translating is also a crucial verb here because, in the very next line, the birds begin to speak. We're offered an italicized translation of their tune, whose spirit and intent the listener understands. The birds sing of their union, undaunted by winds and weather or where in the world they are, *minding no time/ While we two keep together*.

Love makes them unmindful of time, but of course time is likewise unmindful of them. The she-bird disappears. *Thenceforward*, the poet tells us

> *. . . all summer in the sound of the sea,*
> *And at night under the full of the moon in calmer weather,*
> *Over the hoarse surging of the sea,*
> *Or flitting from brier to brier by day,*
> *I saw, I heard at intervals the remaining one, the he-bird . . .*

The young poet hears an elegy, a lamentation of extraordinary beauty. The Orphic bird *pour'd forth the meanings which I of all men know*, he tells us, in a phrase that collapses any separation between the listening boy and the remembering man. Enraptured by such grave beauty, the boy returns repeatedly, careful to make no disturbance, so as not to interrupt the song.

> *I have treasured every note,*
> *For more than once dimly down to the beach gliding,*
> *Silent, avoiding the moonbeams, blending myself with the*
> *shadows,*

Recalling now the obscure shapes, the echoes, the sounds
    and sights after their sorts,
The white arms out in the breakers tirelessly tossing,
I, with bare feet, a child, the wind wafting my hair,
    Listened long and long.

What a gloriously gothic passage! Moonbeams, the breakers tossing their foam like the white waving arms of the drowned, obscure shadows hiding a sleepless, barefoot boy enchanted by a gorgeous outpouring of grief. Entirely rapt, the boy is *listening to keep*—a deft description of the poet's attention to the world. If "hearing" is essentially a passive experience in which we receive whatever sounds are audible, then "listening" implies a spectrum of action: concentrating, submitting, discerning, identifying, categorizing, noticing nuance, "translating" the emotive and intellectual meanings of music into language—meanings we both apprehend and create.

    The boy Whitman must indeed have listened long, as the bird launches into a bravura set-piece: a sixty-two-line lament, punctuated by forty-one exclamation points. The bird's stacked apostrophes (*O night! . . . O rising stars! . . . throat! O trembling throat!*) become increasingly fevered:

Shake out carols!
Solitary here, the night's carols!
Carols of lonesome love! death's carols!
Carols under that lagging, yellow, waning moon!
O under that moon where she drops almost down into the sea!
O reckless despairing carols.

In notebook entries sketching out the poetic principles of his first edition, Whitman enjoined himself to employ *a perfectly transparent, plate-glassy style, artless*; he favored *clearness, simplicity, no twist-*

ified or foggy sentences. "Out of the Cradle" is twistified and fogged right and left, its sentences bending time and doubling back upon themselves. Surely one of its sources is Poe, with his creaking spirit-bird whose single word seals a loss inside the unyielding passage of time. The other is grand opera, those sumptuous pageants in which neither feeling nor vocal ornament is restrained. Whitman resisted European opera at first, preferring an American music more direct and, he thought, readily accessible. But the influx of thrilling Italian opera singers who began to appear in New York in 1847 won him over entirely. The many greats included Alesssandro Bettini, thought to be the tenor characterized in these lines from "Song of Myself:"

> *A tenor large and fresh as the creation fills me,*
> *The orbic flex of his mouth is pouring and filling me full.*

Whitman's feel for the physicality of music, the bodily transformations involved for both performer and listener, is on superb display here. No singer compelled him more than Marietta Alboni, a contralto who also sang soprano roles, and who "used to sweep me away as with whirlwinds," he said. For Whitman, opera is rapture, a mode of lifting the self up and out. *I hear the trained soprano,* he writes, again in "Song of Myself,"

> *The orchestra whirls me wider than Uranus flies,*
> *It wrenches such ardors from me I did not know I possessed them.*

RAINER MARIA RILKE, the great German poet who bridges Symbolism and the modern era, was sixteen years old when Walt Whitman died. In the ninth of his *Duino Elegies,* he speaks of the importance of our relationship to the objects of this world and our responsibility to "translate" them into ourselves, through seeing and naming them so completely that some essence of them dwells within us. Toward the end of the elegy, he addresses the earth, here in Stephen Mitchell's translation:

> *Earth, isn't this what you want: to arise within us,*
> *Invisible? Isn't it your dream*
> *To be wholly invisible someday?—O Earth: invisible!*
> *What, if not transformation, is your urgent command?*

What does being on earth ask of us? The world wants to be rescued from evanescence, to be translated into an immaterial realm that does not perish because it was never exactly alive. To become, in other words, poetry—either in the poem the poet writes out of engagement with things, or in the interior "poem" of anyone who loves the world, the never-said words we come, over time, to carry within us. Rilke's reply to the earth's command is one of the loveliest sentences I know, in the original German, and in English: *Erde, du liebe, ich will.* Earth, my love, I will.

Whitman is thought of as a poet of exuberance, and rightly so. He pledges affection without reserve, and makes bold claims (*I am the poet of the body, and I am the poet of the soul*) without qualification. But his account of the experience of hearing the world's call, the moment of receiving his *calling,* is far more ambiguous than Rilke's affirmation. Whitman's conflicted myth of origin may well be the most emotionally ambiguous moment in all his work. The song that makes the boy want and need to sing begins and ends in pain; its singer cannot be consoled. But the certain knowledge it imparts to the poet is thrilling. Who among us is ever able to say, as the poet does, *now in a moment I know what I am for?*

But this knowledge is childhood's end. The work of the adult artist rises within him. *Never more shall I escape,* he tells us, launching a cascade of *never more*'s that echo the single, awful word of the raven that forecast, fifteen years earlier, another American poet's fate.

Never more shall the reverberations,
Never more the cries of unsatisfied love be absent from me,
Never again leave me to be the peaceful child I was . . .

Now he knows what he is for: to be a solitary singer charged with naming all that's passing, raising a song commensurate with the love of what vanishes. This means to be forever unsatisfied, since no song can be entirely adequate, and no accounting of loss restore what's gone.

. . . before what there in the night
Under the yellow and sagging moon,
The dusky demon aroused—the fire, the sweet hell within,
The unknown want, the destiny of me.

The bird—demonic now in its power to compel, to bring the boy's true nature to the fore and charge him with purpose he is not free to refuse—presents an understanding of the poet's work more troubled than any Whitman would have articulated before. The poet can neither turn away from death nor complete the endless work of elegy. And therefore come *a thousand songs, clearer, louder and more sorrowful than yours.* No one song will do, no word hold what it is to love what disappears, which is to say what it is to be human, and therefore the only choice (since silence is unbearable, to one who whose purpose is to sing) is more songs, more words, more attempts to this time get it right.

What persists, no matter what is said or sung or written, is the gap between the words and the world, and it is *the destiny of me* to address it, *the unknown want*: the need, desire, compulsion, privilege, or joy to sing into that space, the unsayable. Under the spell of *my dusky demon and brother,* the poet makes his book.

•••

IN THE VERY FIRST SENTENCE of the poem, Whitman hinted at *the word stronger and more delicious than any,* and he returns to that word after the boy has been confirmed in his vocation. Then the word rises, whispering over and over: *death*, spoken with a kind of longing, as the speaker is laved in the word by the sea.

> *My own songs, awaked from that hour,*
> *And with them the key, the word up from the waves,*
> *The word of the sweetest song, and all songs . . .*

This awareness of death, a profound fascination with it, is the fifth of Whitman's sources. It seems paradoxical, for death to be generative; but for him this darkness, fountaining and still at once, is the necessary presence that mothers all songs.

SEVENTEEN

THE STRONG AND DELICIOUS WORD

You wouldn't know, until you drive in a ways, that the gates of Harleigh Cemetery open onto rolling, hilly land, where many graveled roads curve off from the main stem, inviting confusion. If you want to find the tomb of Walt Whitman, you're on your own; there's no sign to mark the way. Perhaps Camden, New Jersey, fears the poet's grave might be a hangout for bohemians and the unruly, though more likely this battered community just has other priorities.

Down a hill to the left, there's a small valley, a dip obscured by trees and the bulks of old tombs. Whitman's monument is there, in a buggy, moody place, and behind it, on a ridge thick with scrappy trees, rise the terraced levels of an art deco hospital built some forty years later. The tomb stands by itself; the only adjacent headstone appears to have toppled years ago. The monument was scooped into the side of the slope, and constructed of just a few very large pieces of brooding, bluish granite. The open door feels like the entrance to a cave.

Door isn't quite the right word: the unimaginably heavy plinth of stone is set so that it seems ajar. (*You there—I here...*) A padlocked iron gate blocks the way in, grillwork decorated by a scrap of faded plastic flowers, but through the opening you can see a wall of granite, and six flat marble rectangles marking where at least some of the Whitmans lie, in this order:

LOUISA	GEORGE	EDWARD
LOUISA SR.	WALT	WALTER

Thus Walt himself lies beneath his sister-in-law Louisa, his war-hero brother, and his mentally disabled brother Eddie, to whom he left a good deal of the proceeds of his estate, though Eddie died later the same year Walt did. He is between his parents, Louisa and Walter, whose bodies he had moved here from their original resting places on Long Island.

Whitman was offered a plot in the cemetery the year it opened, 1889, in exchange for a poem about the place. He picked out the spot himself, and set to fund-raising for the tomb, but never delivered the poem. The structure he designed cost four thousand dollars in 1891, nearly double—as biographer Jerome Loving points out—what he had paid for his house. Stand back to take in the monumental granite top-piece and you can easily see why: that huge triangular stone must have cost the earth to transport. It makes the whole structure vaguely Greek, vaguely gothic, and distinctly pressed down toward the earth. At its center, chiseled in blunt lettering, WALT WHITMAN. The poet has subsumed the other Whitmans buried here, or perhaps it's more fair to say that he has surrounded himself for the voyage with chosen company.

What did he think of the tomb? When he visited the site to view the work in progress, his housekeeper Mary Davis wrote, "Mr. Whitman won't be paler when he is dead than he was when he had alighted from the carriage and down into the tomb. He leaned up against the wall . . ." Whatever the case, the funeral itself, in March 1892, was a ceremonious affair. Spectators lined Haddonfield Road; a big tent was erected near the grave (where would they have put it? perhaps the ornamental pond with its somewhat casino-ish jet of water is a later addition to the scene). There were speeches. It was an event of a piece with the expansive civic mood of the day. A strand of boosterism, with its optimistic fellowship of developers, entrepreneurs, and opportunists, is the external side of Whitman's fervent embrace of American energies. Perhaps the love of comrades, the affectionate company of fellow spirits making home and love in the wilderness, is, in its basest form, the Camden Rotary.

Peter Doyle, the DC streetcar conductor Whitman called his "tenderest Lover," stood at a distance during it all, up on the slope away from everyone. Doyle said he never really liked Whitman's literary friends. His presence haunts descriptions of the event, and perhaps shades the tomb itself. John Burroughs, a naturalist who was a friend and admirer of Whitman, described Doyle "up the hill, twirling a switch in his hand, his tall figure and big soft hat impressively set against the white-blue sky." What to do, if you were nervous, and felt unwelcome, or wanted to look on and yet set yourself apart from the hoopla and speeches? Twirl a stick.

A modern stone installed a few feet in front of the tomb seems a similar gesture. The slick black granite's inscribed with a passage from the end of "Song of Myself":

> *I bequeath myself to the dirt to grow from the grass I love,*
> *If you want me again look for me under your bootsoles.*

Whoever ordered those lines etched in stone, their text now partly worn away after only thirty or forty years, must have been aware that Whitman's flesh has been bequeathed to nothing; it is crypted where no grass takes root. Of his bodily organs, only the brain isn't interred here; being "abnormally large," it was removed for study at the American Anthropometric Society. The organ is said to have been dropped there by a clumsy lab assistant, and destroyed.

If you want me again look under your bootsoles. Does whoever selected the text for this monument mean to tell us not to bother to seek here? Should I abandon this pilgrimage? Many others, of course, have made it too. Some evidence of their passing is the only cheering thing in sight: bits of graffiti knifed onto the bark of birches: MAE + LOUISE and I LOVE YOU WALT.

•••

AM I ANNOYED with Walt Whitman for having a tomb? It seems an emblem of the public self, that side of Whitman's character that sought attention and approbation, and led him to do harm to his own work through too eager an embrace of externals. Because he—along with Emily Dickinson—wrote the most courageous American poems of their century, I rail against his attempts to turn outward and write crowd-pleasing poetry.

But we tend to be hard on heroes. I might think instead of the hard truth of being close to penniless, and how welcome the income brought through the occasional honorarium, or a newspaper's fee for a bit of timely verse. Or of the Civil War, and the years of attending to ruined bodies, an endeavor as physically challenging as it was utterly heartbreaking—particularly for one who'd once hoped that the love of comrades might be the foundation of our social order. Or think of the physical robustness of Whitman in his thirties, and the increasingly debilitating illnesses that darkened his later years, the stroke that left him unable to walk, entirely dependent on a chain of attendants.

The Whitman who dismisses mortality is the famous one; *The smallest sprout shows there really is no death*, he announced as he walked onto the stage of American poetry. If the self is porous and multiple, and "I" *am not contained between my hat and my bootsoles* but range freely across space and time, if bodies become grass, and grass becomes text, and the world's one vast recirculating stream, what difference could individual death make?

This great gust of fresh air is countered by a certain gothic strain in Whitman, as American as those sad urns carved in shallow bas relief on early headstones, the weeping willows and winged death's-heads of old burial grounds. For a spirit that roamed restlessly, entering into every jot of the teeming life around him, stillness must have held a deep allure. If you are everything and everywhere, how restful it must seem to be no one and nowhere.

In the nine lines of the penultimate stanza of "Out of the Cradle Endlessly Rocking," the word *death* actually appears ten times, enough to make one consider that the poet may be rather more than half "in love with easeful death" like Keats, and enough to demonstrate that he is more a brother to the grave-besotted Poe than at first appears to be the case.

> *My own songs awaked from that hour,*

the poem's final stanza begins,

> *And with them the key, the word up from the waves,*
> *The word of the sweetest song and all songs,*
> *That strong and delicious word which, creeping to my feet,*
> *(Or like some old crone rocking the cradle, swathed in sweet*
>   *garments, bending aside,)*
> *The sea whispered me.*

Delicious? I don't know that I can go that far, but indeed there's something here beyond or behind this relishing of mortality. The poet becomes himself, his songs awakened, when he understands that the world around him is saturated with death, that every single thing exists next to its disappearance. The great overarching self of Whitman's early vision is deathless, yes, but to be everyone is to be no one in particular, and in an odd way to be everyone is to be alone, since there can be no other. When the Self dissolves into a world of separate selves and death becomes real, love becomes a pact with grief; what is gained then is the inescapably poignant fact of individuality. There will never be another you, and I love the stubborn particularity of you because you will disappear.

The elision of a preposition in that final line is a poeticism, of course; we understand that Whitman means that the sea whispered its single word, repeated incessantly here, *to me*. But because he does not inscribe the word *to*, he places a parallel meaning beside the first. *The sea whispered me* can be read to mean *I am that word the water repeats.*

•••

WHEN I PICK UP the phone there's that outer-space sound of static, and Alex says, *I'm all right*. We have been together for five years. We struggle, but I don't doubt that we love each other, in our unstable, volatile bond.

All conversations that begin with *I'm all right* are terrible. It means, *It's not as bad as the worst thing you're thinking*, offered as a preemptive gesture of reassurance or consolation—but how can the listener help but feel paralyzed with fear as to what's about to be said? Even though the inner mechanisms are hurrying to construct a narrative (*he's able to call, his voice sounds more-or-less all right*) to forestall terror.

He says he's had an accident, on his motorcycle. There was a deer, another car, a man stopped, the police are there now, he's all right, can I come, can I bring a broom? His voice, threading through all that galactic static (the sound of the police radio behind him, added to the random noise of cell phone transmission?) sounds so far away I don't want to hang up, but he says *Come, I'll tell you later, I'm all right*, so I do. I am all but immobilized, though I know I have to find my shoes, a jacket, my keys, a dustpan and broom—*to clean up the glass,* he'd said, which made me shiver.

Then I'm driving on a road I usually love for how unlit it is, how you can take the measure of the night there, and be startled by the wide-awake presence of the stars, either as crystalline singularities or as washes of light like the place I imagine that static on the phone line came from. I remembered the dustpan but not the broom. I briefly consider going back for it and think better of it. I'm focused on trying to keep my speed down, studying every grove and cluster of trunks in my headlights for flashes thrown back from the retinae of deer; they're restless with desire, this time of the year, on the move.

It's never seemed farther to Town Lane Road, the slow curves through the woods that end at Deep Lane as the road straightens then crosses a big field, past the horse barn and farm stand and a still-standing skeletal row of sunflower stalks, if there were light enough to see them. Then, looping through woods, past the mailboxes of darkened houses, up ahead a way, pulsing red light, two police cars, one on either side of the road. And near one of them, looking down into the lank grass beside the asphalt for some lost thing, Alexander.

I remember the way I held my shoulders and back, as if I were creating a kind of armor in myself not unlike the rigid plastic in Alex's jacket, which certainly saved him from much greater injury. The dense, plastic- and metal-infused cloth was torn at the elbow, the blue and silver helmet's sparkle marred by scratches and a gouge on one side where he'd struck and slid.

He'd been riding at a blessed thirty miles per hour; a truck came toward him, headlights filling his gaze so he couldn't see the deer just behind it, poised to spring. As the truck passed him his field of vision filled with an amber field; there was nothing in front of him but deer, featureless, a carpet of fur. And then he was separated from the bike, in the air, and here the story breaks.

His first—and characteristic—words, spoken while still prone, on the pavement, were "I'm all right," a hypothesis tested by speaking it aloud to the air and the late crickets. It seemed to be true, primarily. He could, with effort, stand up, begin to straighten up.

The Hispanic woman driving the truck stopped, and emerged just as he was beginning to stand, to demonstrate he had come near one of the gates of this life and wound up again on this side, more or less intact. She let loose an excited cascade, in Spanish, of which Alexander caught a bit, his attention fixed mostly on the continuing project of attempting to stand upright. Even in the first of the sensation that was condensing into pain the way a film of moisture will precipitate from a cloud of mist, he had the presence of mind to be annoyed that she was talking about herself. He was aware that he was surrounded by the small pieces of shattered windshield—and what had become of the hapless deer? Knowing him as I do, I imagine this may well have been the moment when he thought to ask me to bring a broom, so that he could clean up the road.

When he asked the driver to call the police, she tucked herself swiftly back into the truck and fled. Who knows what the consequences might have been for her, if she had no Green Card, or if the responding officer might be without sympathy for her kids at home? How would you make that decision, between offering assistance to one who could at least stand and speak and the loyalties that might send you driving away? I don't know whether or not she waited to see him stretch and move before she got out of her truck, but I am grateful to her, that she did get out, did come to his side before she sped into the night.

A few minutes later another driver called the cops, and then stayed till they arrived. By the time I got there the evidence had been examined: the nose of the bike had cut a long, deep groove into the pavement; there was a puddle of oil into which I promptly stepped, even after I'd been warned not to; the policemen helped to push the bits of glass out of the road. They looked for any sign of the deer—nothing. Had a flank or hind leg glanced off the nose of the bike? We hoped for that. We looked—nothing. The awful flashing of the red lights formed an angry cloud in my head that prohibited clear thinking. Alex seemed stunned, able to walk, slowly, bent forward, looking for something. The police wanted to go home, and in few minutes we understood that they were waiting for us to call a tow truck.

On the drive home the strength that had animated Alex to stand up, look after himself and the wreckage, look for the deer, to talk to the police and call me, ebbed away almost visibly, as in that mythological image of the great statue animated by the molten metal within until the valve at its ankle is opened, and out pours the life-force of it, as its color drains and its motion slowly comes to a halt. He didn't want to go to the hospital. He wanted to rest. I got him up from the passenger seat, his arm over my shoulder, and he very slowly leaned and hopped his way up the driveway, up the low front steps into the cottage door, onto the edge of a chair, where he perched a few moments before he sank onto the floor, where he'd remain for hours.

It's hard to say how much of what kept him there was physical pain. He'd been holding the body of the motorcycle between his thighs as he was torn up from it, and he'd hit the pavement at thirty miles an hour, helmet and shoulder and elbow sliding along it. But there was some other gravity as well, a sort of bruise left by the experience of nearly leaving physicality, or of knowing that he could have. He tells me the story of the accident, in detail, the story that is not a story at its center, where it becomes unstable, shot through with uncertainty, the night of Town Lane Road blowing through it.

Then his talking slows, longer pauses between phrases, and then no more phrases, though his eyes are open. Both the dogs have come to lie beside him, and curl quietly there. Ned is stretched out fully, his back fit to Alex's belly and chest, and George has laid his smaller body beside Alex's face. Both dogs are holding still, not asking for attention or for stroking; they seem to be playing some other part, as witness and companion. They're doing their work. My phone's at hand, and I use it to take some pictures of the three, the still, conjoined company. A kind of bulwark the living make.

—•••—

MY OWN SONGS AWAKED *from that hour,* Whitman writes of the moment when the demon-bird's lyric of grief fueled in him a poet's vocation,

> *And with them the key, the word up from the waves,*
> *The word of the sweetest song and all songs,*
> *That strong and delicious word which, creeping to my feet,*
> *(Or like some old crone rocking the cradle, swathed in sweet*
>   *garments, bending aside,)*
> *The sea whispered me.*

In what way is death the key? Is our mortality so much the chief feature of us that who we are cannot be known without it? A gate swings partway open, now and then; we can't really see inside it, but things as they are seem changed by the way the air around us begins to pour ahead through the door. One of us could have gone through, but here we are, warm together, quiet: Alex, Ned, even little George, lying together in the soft lamplight, on the living room floor. They seem to be floating there, above their own shadows, and at the same time the bodies seem to have taken on weight, solidified with the fact of limit. I know, the dogs want to comfort him, something they seem to take as part of their jobs in this life. But I seem to catch, in their faces as well as his, something else, as if what they were doing just now was giving active attention to being present together, in the fact of their common lot.

And my work in this life?

None of this will go unrecorded. I will see and say all of it, as clearly and deeply as I can, re-entering, lifting experience in the direction of another dimension of time, where everything I have loved can be known again, more fully, that my joy in it might increase as I take the measure of what I have lost. And my grief may increase as well; Alex and I loved each other, and held together through a troubled and volatile relation as best we could, and in a while we ended it. I truly wish him every good in this life. *Sweet hell?* Maybe, but so be it.

EIGHTEEN

WHAT IS IT THEN
BETWEEN US?

Whitman's signature gesture, and his great accomplishment—setting aside, for the moment, the invention of American free verse, the elevation of colloquial speech into an astonishingly flexible, workable mode of poetic discourse, and the first open inscriptions of same-sex love since the Renaissance—lies in the way he reaches through the curtain formed by words, paper, and ink, stepping into the readerly present with a directness and immediacy that have never lost their power to startle. These lines from "To You," a meditation on what the essence of a self might be, are a prime example:

> Whoever you are, I fear you are walking the walks of dreams,
> I fear these supposed realities are to melt from under your feet and
> hands,
> Even now your features, joys, speech, house, trade, manners,
> troubles, follies, costume, crimes, dissipate away from you,
> Your true soul and body appear before me,
> They stand forth out of affairs, out of commerce, shops, work, farms,
> clothes, the house, buying, selling, eating, drinking, suffering,
> dying.

Whoever you are, now I place my hand upon you, that you be my poem,
  I whisper with my lips close to your ear,
I have loved many women and men, but I love none better than you.

I read this passage to Alex, who first admired it, then laughed at what he saw as a manipulative gesture, a means of seduction. Hucksterism, self-promotion, putting one's product out there for all to see—these essential American activities came booming into their own in Whitman's day, as the latter half of the nineteenth century invented marketing and publicity. How could a newspaperman fail to understand the power of an artfully shaded turn of phrase, how a memorable or rhythmic slogan made an object desirable, an idea attractive, a political position agreeable? Only recently a graduate student at the University of Houston turned up a forgotten Whitman text, a grooming and exercise manual intended to be serialized in a number of papers—a guide for men to self-presentation, advice for men who wanted to shape how they were seen. Such endeavors might have seemed vain, after the war, when Whitman had spent his days walking from bed to bed in makeshift hospitals, bringing oranges, candy, and postage stamps to mutilated young men. He listened to their stories, read letters from home aloud to those who, blinded or illiterate, could not read them themselves, took dictation for their letters home, and sat by them when they died. But even then the poet was sending press releases to the *Boston Globe,* noting the charitable work "the poet Walt Whitman" had undertaken. Self-promotion? Of course. Had he not had a knack for it, we would have no first two editions of his book, perhaps no book at all. He wanted to stand in the light of visibility and admiration, as the reviews of his own work he published anonymously demonstrate.

But to my mind there is such profound conviction in the second stanza of "To You" that the moment in which those lines were written and the moment in which they are read collapse, as Whitman must have intended them to do. Reading is a privacy occupying singular moments in time, but the reader who made pencil notes in my facsimile of the first edition fifty years ago and I seem to have had the same experience at particular passages. When readers share this sense of contact with *the poet himself,* his warping of time is further compounded. The poem bends the time-space in which it resides; it goes on gathering together instants of fusion between then and now, between *then* and the way we experience the then *now,* and between him and me, him and you, you and me, a whole company of us who cannot see one another now, though I am tempted to say, as the Christian pastors I grew up hearing might have said, we will sometime.

———•••———

WHITMAN WANTED—with a passion seemingly as strong as any in his life—to be read, in his time and ours. In all his huge body of work I can find mention of only two things he wishes to possess: the love of a comrade and the attention of the reader. This latter desire is not bound in time; *I considered long and seriously of you,* he writes in "Crossing Brooklyn Ferry," *before you were ever born.* What good is the song of myself without you to hear it, or to join in?

The love of a comrade and the attention of the reader: these desires (which have no clear boundary between them) reach effortlessly across years and cities, then centuries and continents. No poet has spoken to the audiences of the future with such certainty that they are *there,* listening. Nowhere does this address ring as clearly and hauntingly as it does in "Crossing Brooklyn Ferry," a poem that wins hands-down any competition for the most uncanny of American poems. In 1856, when the poem was written, Whitman had the barest handful of readers; what poet—even one with a large audience in his or her own time—has the nerve to summon to attention those not yet born? Shakespeare, in the sonnets, and probably no one else.

I want to say that Whitman has succeeded in this project more than he might have dreamed, but the poem provides every evidence of a writer who, as Edward Carpenter said of him, "knows exactly what he is doing." For us, the poet's attention seems to beam from a point in the past *and* to shine from a continuous present that exists in our immersion in the poem. The poem makes a *now,* as the speaker addresses us directly, as he has been speaking to readers, in increasing numbers, for 160 years. He becomes, as he said of himself, a *uniter of here and hereafter.* Is that a way of saying that he makes himself a ghost, no longer human exactly, but a presence who dwells in time in a way we don't know how to chart?

———•••———

THE LOVE OF A COMRADE. The time when the greatest erotic charge lay, for me, in the slipstream of men of New York or Houston or Los Angeles, whatever large city I found myself in, the flashing masculine currents and shoals Walt Whitman also enjoyed (*firm masculine colter it shall be you*) seems to have passed, for me. Not that my head can't be turned, or that a random flirtation doesn't arouse interest or even action on my part, but I recognize now where a sense of satisfaction lies for me, a feeling of coming to rest. Though that arriving at anchor, against the beautiful long form of my lover's body, is no passive harboring, but something more like Dickinson's "rowing in Eden."

We met online. I enjoyed the lightness and freshness of Ethan's company, and his dedication to giving pleasure. He'd appear from time to time, and we'd take mutual delight in an evening. We had knowledge of one another in the present tense, which turns out to be a lovely way to get to know someone. Over the course of ten years—during which I was first newly divorcing myself from Paul, and much later leaving Alex—we underwent together a kind of alchemical process I can't claim to explain. In a while we acknowledged that having sex became making love. The difference in our ages—he is twenty-three years younger than I am, and achingly beautiful—and circumstances, our domestic situations, all that seemed to burn away, till we were left with two naked bodies and two equally unclothed subjectivities, rapt with each other all the time we were together. Of course one of us would be preoccupied now and then, less than fully present, but the extraordinary thing is that for those years our congress became both warmer and hotter, increasingly an occasion that seem lifted up above all the rest, a time out of time.

SOME THINGS ARE SO INHERENTLY METAPHORIC that a poet need only point to their existence in order for the meanings they embody to emerge; surely Brooklyn Ferry and the bridge that would take its place late in Whitman's life belong to that category of being. The ferry between islands (running more or less from near the old Fulton Street Fish Market, near South Street Seaport, to Fulton's Landing in Brooklyn, just south of the bridge) linked two boroughs, making a unity of disparate parts. Such boats had, in the underworld, ferried the Egyptians, Greeks, and Romans into the land of the dead, linking the lit and shadow realms, though the journey was generally offered in only one direction. Brooklyn Ferry shuttled citizens back and forth on a regular schedule; its constant motion seemed an inevitable emblem of ongoingness, as riders poured on and off, or stood their moment by the railing as pennants flapped and the masts of a hundred ships gleamed along the docks. The casts changed, but the scene remained essentially the same, and thus every passenger stood in relation to every other, all of us connected by our voyaging.

The bridge that John Augustus Roebling and his son Washington Augustus Roebling would build, allowing walkers and vehicles to arc in the air above nearly the same course, was likewise emblematic. The gothic arches of its two great pylons, as well as its cables strung like harp strings, inevitably suggested religious associations. Its skyward curve seemed a physical embodiment of our aspirations. As Whitman took possession of Brooklyn Ferry as an emblem of human continuity in time, so sixty years later Hart Crane crowned "the most beautiful bridge in the world" with a superb crown of appositives, a litany of poetic names:

> *O harp and altar, of the fury fused . . .*

> *. . . thy swift*
> *unfractioned idiom, immaculate sigh of stars . . .*

> *O Thou steeled Cognizance whose leap commits*
> *The agile precincts of the lark's return . . .*

Crane's rhetorical heights work to lift our vision, intent on illuminating the spiritual dimensions of the bridge. If that splendid final example above strains against sense, it does so to show us Brooklyn Bridge as itself a great metaphysical poem. How to read *commits?* Does the poet mean that the leap *commits* in the way one commits a crime, or that the leap commits in the way one pledges loyalty to something? Or should we turn to the Latin *committere*: to connect? Can one do any of those things to *the agile precincts of the lark's return?* The phrase is so gorgeous that I don't care about the answer to my question.

Crane works near the limits of language, while his predecessor employs plainer speech to evoke his vision, rendering both the sensory experience of the ferry (*the glories strung like beads on my smallest sights and hearings*) and the spiritual dimension the poet apprehends through that experience. Whitman's poem introduces the idea of historical continuity gradually, persuading or seducing us through an attentive naming of things interspersed with rhetorical passages that make the spiritual and temporal realms they propose seem as real as *the heights of Brooklyn to the south and east.*

"Crossing Brooklyn Ferry" was first called "Sundown Poem," proof positive that the slogan promulgated by Beat poets, "First thought, best thought," is not reliably the case. The poem's elegant sections advance its argument while simultaneously building a superbly realized model of the physical experience of riding a ferryboat across one of the world's busiest rivers, navigating a crowded and richly drawn universe of things on, above, and around New York Harbor.

As with a number of Whitman's poems, this one was published first without any division into sections. The sections were an excellent choice; they allow the intensity of the poem's argument to build, and they lend resonance to those lines that end sections as well as to those that begin them. The first of the poem's sections begins:

> *Flood-tide below me! I watch you face to face;*
> *Clouds of the west! sun there half an hour high! I see you*
>   *also face to face.*

Much is established here: a pattern of direct address to various elements of the scene (*Clouds of the west!*), as though it were important simply to call the parts of the world by their names. To be *face to face* with flood-tide, cloud, and sun suggests that those aspects of the world *have* faces; they are our fellow travelers, accompanying us on our journey in time, our movement across the waters; the poet acknowledges their presence as players on the great stage of the day.

The speaker turns then to his fellow passengers, who are, he

says, *more curious to me than you suppose*. This is a rather mild assertion. The poet doesn't say in what way he might be curious; the
wording suggests an interest less than passionate. Whitman's
understatement allows him to go a little farther, asserting an
interest in those who'll ride the ferry far in the future.

> *And you that shall cross from shore to shore years hence, are*
> *more to me, and more in my meditations, than you might suppose.*

There are many reasons one might be curious about the citizens
of the future. The poet isn't ready to disclose his; he knows he
must begin quietly, building a context in order for his argument
to strike us as plausible. As a true free-verse poet startlingly ahead
of his moment, he uses the act of composition as a way to discover what he thinks, to develop his own understanding of what
may be, at this point in the composing of the poem, only dimly
apprehended. The question he proposes—*what are you to me, passengers of the future?*—reverberates in the silence between sections.
I like knowing that Brooklyn Ferry runs again now, on a slightly
changed route, so that Whitman's question may indeed travel
directly toward those he intended to hear it.

Though whether or not we ride that ferryboat across the East
River, we are *passengers of the future,* are we not?

——•••——

EACH OF THE TWO STANZAS in the second section of "Crossing
Brooklyn Ferry" is a single sentence, and each has its own focus.
The first sketches out a position concerning the self—understood
not as an isolate entity but something more like a dialogue
between awareness and world. It's a list of phrases, but it manages
to form a remarkably clear and compact exposition of Whitman's
radical understanding of subjectivity: "I" is an ongoing, dynamic
relation, a subjectivity joined to and sustained by everything "out-

side" it. The speaker is dazzled and nourished by the physical world as it appears in this moment: *The glories strung like beads on my smallest sights and hearings.*

But his experience is not bound solely in space; the stanza mentions *all hours of the day; the similitudes of the past, and those of the future; the others that are to follow me.* The self is extended in time as well as in space, a confluence of what's been and what's to come; we are shifting, unbounded, admitting and responding to everything "outside" us.

> *The impalpable sustenance of me from all things, at all hours*
> *of the day;*
> *The simple, compact, well-join'd scheme—myself disintegrated,*
> *every one disintegrated, yet part of the scheme:*
> *The similitudes of the past, and those of the future;*
> *The glories strung like beads on my smallest sights and hearings—*
> *on the walk in the street, and the passage over the river,*
> *The current rushing so swiftly, and swimming with me far away,*
> *The others that are to follow me, the ties between me and them.*
> *The certainty of others—the life, love, sight, hearing of others.*

How elegant the compact line, *The current rushing so swiftly, and swimming with me far away*; the poet effortlessly places us *here* and far away at once, a bit of evidence for a claim he's soon make, that *distance avails not.* The *certainty* of others in all this fluidity is perhaps the only firm anchor here; we can be sure of being bound to a chain of human others unfolding ahead of us. That thought becomes the driving principle of the second stanza.

> *Others will enter the gates of the ferry, and cross from shore to shore,*
> *Others will watch the run of the flood-tide,*
> *Others will see the shipping of Manhattan north and west, and*
> *the heights of Brooklyn to the south and east,*

Others will see the islands large and small,
Fifty years hence, others will see them as they cross, the sun
    half an hour high,
A hundred years hence, or ever so many hundred years hence,
    others will see them,
Will enjoy the sunset, the pouring in of the flood-tide,
    the falling back to the sea of the ebb-tide.

There is no mention here of the past; the poet's concern is for the contact he can make with the future, how he might extend himself *ever so many hundred years hence*. No end-times thinking here, no looming apocalypse. There's something deeply comforting in Whitman's confidence in the presence of those who will come after him; he's heartened by the fact of their persistence, just as he takes comfort in the pouring in and falling back of the tides that end this stanza.

MAYBE THERE IS A MOMENTUM generated in the making of great poems that propels them beyond the reach of ordinary time; perhaps some have the power to step out of the flowing-forward. This would explain how the poems of Emily Dickinson, carefully copied into the forty handstitched booklets she kept inside her desk, called out to be found, to begin their long blossoming into the world, and how you might, in the still hours of the night, from a fussy Victorian guesthouse in Amherst, sense still from across the street the roiling activity of a restless presence, a relentless intellect dwelling in the ceaselessly self-consuming energy of its omnidirectional doubt. Or feel the distilled sorrow of John Keats pour into you in half a house near Hampstead Heath. Or see the face of Walt Whitman appear above the shoulders of a bedmate on a winter afternoon early in the twenty-first century, in an apartment tower in Hell's Kitchen. These presences are not

Dickinson, Keats, or Whitman themselves, but something more miraculous than any ghost: an intervention in reality committed by the power of art.

Have their poems fixed something of the soul in time, as William Everson said the book could? Their lights, broken through the prismatic gaze of readers, come beaming into the present. I understand that this is a wildly romantic notion to set on the table at this point in history, I make no claim to understand how such a thing is possible, I am certain only that the power released in those acts of making, in which the poet brought an unrelenting concentration to the embodiment of presence, a gift to the future—that heat seems to remain in the world for a very long time.

———•••———

SECTION 3 OF "CROSSING BROOKLYN FERRY" begins with a deep, headlong dive into the heart of the poem, perhaps precipitated by the tides that poured in and ebbed at the end of the previous lines. The poet is ready to state his case directly:

> *It avails not, time nor place—distance avails not,*
> *I am with you, you men and women of a generation,*
>   *or ever so many generations hence,*
> *I project myself—also I return—I am with you, and know how it is.*
>
> *Just as you feel when you look on the river and sky,*
>   *so I felt,*
> *Just as any of you is one of a living crowd, I was one*
>   *of a crowd . . .*

Avail means to have value, worth, or efficacy; the inverted syntax here suggests that Whitman drew the word from the Bible. Space and time do not have the power to separate us, or at least to separate the poet who speaks to us from the *living crowd* we are. I don't know why that last line above feels so achingly poignant. Perhaps the answer lies in the strange and subtle thing the poet's just done, a shift in tense one barely notices. *I am with you,* he writes, but by the end of the following line, and still within that single sentence, his presence is located in the past: *Just as you feel when you look on the river and sky, so I felt.* Whitman was thirty-seven when he wrote that line, but he speaks to us as one already dead, and thus the line that follows, *Just as any of you is one of a living crowd, I was one of a crowd,* comes with a particular emotional tone, a melancholy relish. For the first time the poet positions himself as a citizen of the past, one who speaks to us from the dead, recalling the physical proximity he loved, the jostle and thronging life around him. In the space of a line he has joined the great company of the dead, taken up residence outside of time—although he hasn't left us, not by a long shot.

As if to demonstrate that he is fully there, present on that now-vanished ferry, just as he might be fully "here" in any moment in an ongoing present, Whitman fills the rest of Section 3 with a splendidly alert catalog of what the crossing offers the senses, observed so exactly we feel as he intended:

> *I watched the December sea-gulls, I saw them high in the air*
> *   floating with motionless wings oscillating their bodies,*
> *I saw how the glistening yellow lit up parts of their*
> *   bodies and left the rest in strong shadow . . .*

The precision of observation, the detail of those shadows, seems to inscribe this section with a signature: *I, Walt Whitman, saw this.* The man loved these crossings, as he wrote in his compilation of prose notes, sketches, and meditations, *Specimen Days: I have always had a passion for ferries; to me they afford inimitable, streaming, never-failing, living poems.*

His cascade of physical detail does not shy away from the spiritual. It portrays a material world not transcended by spirit, but imbued by it:

> Had my eyes dazzled by the shimmering track of beams,
> Looked at the fine centrifugal spokes of light round the shape of
> my head in the sunlit water . . .

That halo is not of another world but of this one. It's echoed in a poem I've mentioned earlier, "To You":

> Painters have painted their swarming groups and the
> centre-figure of all,
> From the head of the centre-figure spreading a nimbus of
> gold-colored light,
> But I paint myriads of heads, but paint no head without its
> nimbus of gold-colored light . . .

The poet-muralist here sees on every head a golden aura of divinity; Whitman here seems to echo the English poet perhaps most akin to him, the visionary William Blake: *Everything that lives is holy*. We know that Whitman read him, at some point in his life, but not when. A Mrs. Gilchrist, an English champion of Blake's poems, took a great shine to Whitman's work. A widow, she voyaged to America with the intention of marrying him, a project she abandoned, settling for friendship and eventually heading home.

THE TWO SECTIONS that follow are stately, superbly written pieces of oratory, reiterating the poem's assertion of the connection between the speaker and *men and women to come*. Each time it recurs, this claim seems to gain in import and implication, and to swell toward greater confidence. The Whitman who does not believe that time or space can limit the reach of his voice gains his stride now, and sounds his boldest notes:

> *These and all else were to me the same as they are to you,*
> *I project myself a moment to tell you—also I return.*
>
> *I loved well these cities,*
> *I loved well the stately and rapid river,*
> *The men and women I saw were all near to me,*
> *Others the same—others who look back on me, because*
>   *I looked forward to them,*
> *(The time will come, though I stop here today and tonight.)*

This is the first time that the speaker looks into the future and discovers there a reciprocity. Who are those who look back *because I looked forward to them*? Citizens of the city of robust friends? Poets who bend back their gaze to meet the extraordinary presence who has established a new relation to time in these pages? Have I looked back to Whitman because he has all my life, though I did not know it, looked forward to me?

Those lines are the entirety of the poem's shortest section, and I imagine it's the most concise in order to let its final line ring into the silence that follows. The statement is parenthetical, an aside, almost a whisper. It reframes the ending of "Song of Myself" (*I stop somewhere waiting for you*) by simply stating that the meeting between Whitman and his reader *will* happen; he doesn't just wait for us but knows we are coming. He may have stopped just for a day or night's rest; he may have "stopped" because, on the day of composing this poem, he has become part of the past—has, in essence, died, though he will live for another thirty-six years, and though his voice, speaking now from the past he transforms into a continuous present, remains audible, available, proof of his presence.

THE POEM'S NEXT SECTION begins with a question: how many years have elapsed between the writing of his poem and your reading of it—scores, hundreds? *Whatever it is,* he reiterates, slightly varying his statement from Section 2, *distance avails not, and place avails not.* The repeated phrase is a sort of spell, intended to intervene in the movement and character of time by establishing a new position from which to speak.

The bonds—affections, cities, questions—the poet knows he shares with his readers, though they may be hundreds of years apart, overrule any sense of separation. Two remarkable statements complete this argument, two radical propositions placed just at the section's close.

The first is a claim as mysterious as anything in Whitman's poetry: *I too,* he writes, *had been struck from the float forever held in solution.* What can he mean? It sounds like a sort of manufacturing method, some industrial vocabulary he might have gleaned from the Crystal Palace exhibition—but I can find no evidence to support this idea. *Struck* as sparks might be struck? Each more or less identical, as the poet suggests in another poem:

> *Men and women passing in the streets,*
> *If they are not flashes and specks, what are they?*

Or *struck* as we say coins or medals are struck from a mold? Is the *float* something solid, like a bar of silver used in an electroplating process, from which molecules of silver might be transferred to another, waiting surface? Or should we think of the float as something liquid or in suspension, in the sense that Whitman uses the word in "Song of the Open Road":

> *Something there is in the float of the sight of things that*
> *provokes it out of the soul.*

It in this line is wisdom, and the float in question is the procession of objects before our eyes. Is *the float forever held in solution* then a perpetual flux, an endless source from which we are each, in some way, catalyzed—so that, whatever our differences shaped by history and culture, language and social position, we are, at the flashpoint of our beginning, joined?

If we are all *struck from the float forever held in solution,* whatever it may be, sparked or minted or catalyzed from that same source, then how to account for individuality? The lines that follow answer, forming a second proposition:

> *I too had received identity by my body,*
> *That I was, I knew was of my body, and what I should be,*
> *I knew I should be of my body.*

Out of the range of categories a person might occupy, how many are determined by the flesh itself? Male or female, trans or intersex, gay or straight, and what of the range of human skin tones, or the other characteristics we consider aspects of "race" with all the social, culturally determined consequences they bring with them? Tall or short, ecto- or endomorph, hairy, smooth, symmetrical or misaligned: they seem nearly endless, the myriad ways the self is shaped by the particular givens of the body, though we aren't always certain what's a given and what is not. It's only through the body, Whitman asserts, through sense perception, that we know we exist.

To what degree did the scale of Whitman's own body shape his sense of the primacy of the physical? A tall man for his time, he stood over six feet in his thirties, large-framed, barrel-chested, an imposing presence. I imagine him reclining, leaning back, filling that small bedroom in Brooklyn his visitors recorded, almost too much for the room that contained him. Did Bronson Alcott note the presence of the chamber pot under the bed because he felt, in that little space, that Whitman's body was too much with him? His boys must have loved being held by him, pressed against the wide shore of that broad chest! If "Walt Whitman" was a construct, a self created by Walter Jr. who could move in the world with a new social ease, greeting other citizens as equal, seeing himself reflected in the energies of all around him, was that creation an extension of the body he was given?

All this puts me in mind of the Tibetan Buddhists' idea that what continues in us—the bit that endures, going forward from life to life—is simply awareness; that's our core, the wide-awake part of us that registers where we are, taking in the world. The rest—biography, character shaped by family, circumstance, culture? Perhaps that's just identity received by the body, and when the body's gone all that is, too—leaving you simply a sentience, a gaze looking out at the world.

———•••———

THREE YEARS AGO NOW, I went to Paris for two weeks, to teach and to breathe in the beautiful winter of that city, all lustrous grays and smoky charcoal. In the summer it can be hard to see Paris behind the throngs in the avenues, the tour buses, the restless crowds in the big square in front of Nôtre-Dame. I loved the astonishing fireworks in July on Bastille Day, seemingly shooting from every crevice of the Eiffel Tower, filling the sky with glowing smokes and streaking trails, but in winter Paris is intimate, the great mask the city lifts to protect itself from the tourist hordes set down. The warm light of shop windows and café doors draws the traveler in, and Paris can be understood in an entirely different fashion.

I was there with Alex, for part of the stay, but I was lonely, too. He stayed on in Europe, to visit family in Germany, while I returned, happy to do so, to fetch our two dogs from the perfect-but-pricey sitter they both adored. Almost as soon as Ethan and I saw each other, at my apartment in the city and then heading out to my little house almost at the very tip of Long Island, we understood that what was between us had changed. How had it happened? We were so deeply, entirely happy to see each other; we seemed bathed in a common light, of which we were the source, a glow that warmed us both. There was no line between this intimacy and desire; I've seen in the past how coming closer to a man can make lust begin to fade, as though it were otherness that had fueled it all along. Nothing like that happened; our lovemaking became deeper, more immersive. I had forgotten, or come to doubt, that sex with someone you love is an entirely different thing from the other sort—which is not undesirable in itself, certainly not without pleasure. It's a matter of magnitude, of what leads one to step into one's largest self, and to enter into experiences that inscribe themselves so deeply into us as to become benchmarks in a life, unforgettable.

There isn't a single thing, I believe, that is meant by "being in love." That phrase is poor shorthand for a range of feelings and relations that are crucial to us, and that I've only begun to differentiate in retrospect. I wouldn't deny or demean any of my adult loves, though I understand that I haven't always made wise choices in relation to them. What I would say is that I have never loved anyone in quite the way I do Ethan. We spent a long time coming to know one another physically, in the present tense, and from our bodies all else has proceeded.

When I say I have never loved anyone in the way I love him, is that a tautology? Since only he could produce the particular set of responses in me that he does? What is more subterranean, less available for examination than the way we love? What I know for certain is that this complex of feelings, this knowledge gained through the body, through experience and trust, is woven together in me, around me, into something that feels like a dwelling place.

⁘

THE NEXT SECTION of Whitman's poem goes farther in claiming the poet's connection to us, his likeness to anyone who reads him. *It is not upon you alone the dark patches fell,* he writes, in a slyly constructed phrase, since it's nearly inevitable that the sort of weaknesses of character or psychological failings to which Whitman admits in this section are the sort none of us wants to own, and because we're loathe to air them we're far more likely to think them either ours alone or far less widely shared than they are. *The dark threw patches down upon me also,* he continues, and speaks openly of his uncertain relation to his claims to knowledge:

> *The best I had done seemed to me blank and suspicious;*
> *My great thoughts, as I supposed them, were they not in reality*
>   *meagre? would not people laugh at me?*

This sort of doubt, if expressed a year earlier in "Song of Myself," would have deflated that symphonic poem like a balloon slipping out of one's fingers before the opening's been tied. These lines demonstrate how profoundly Whitman's speaker has changed. He burned with certainty, in the radiant vision of "Song of Myself," flush with the apprehension that there is no separation between self and other. This was no mere idea, but an experienced insight that must have shaken Whitman to the root, and thrown all of life open to reconsideration. One does not, in the grip of such ravishment, doubt.

But no one, save perhaps those who become divinities, can live there. The enlightened soul, come down from the mountaintop or out from the cave, still has to move through the streets where so much depends on you and me, yours and mine, bought and sold, held and desired. All the failings in the energetic, animal catalog of sins the poet claims as his own are only possible when one believes one *is* an individual, that there is actually such a thing as an *other,* who may have what you do not, and thus inspire your envy, your calumny, your rage, resentment or lies, guile or lust. The list tumbles out of the poet's mouth and pen with the ferocity of something held back, offered to us here not just to put us on equal footing but because it has been impelled by necessity. I hear this most clearly in the magnificent line of mostly monosyllabic words, jabbing like repeated thrusts: *Blabb'd, blush'd, resented, lied, stole, grudg'd* . . . And then, a line later:

> *Was wayward, vain, greedy, shallow, sly, cowardly, malignant;*
> *The wolf, the snake, the hog, not wanting in me . . .*

These are extraordinary things to say about oneself, as the poet descends from his sunlit position of knowledge to the realm of the *dark patches,* the wallow and struggle of those creatures who stand, here, for unbridled and self-serving appetite.

With this section—one that goes to such lengths to show us the speaker's humanity and cravings, what he has in common with us—comes a startling recognition: the Walt Whitman who speak to us in this poem is, in many ways, a better one. There is something untouchable in the freely circulating, splendidly free speaker we know from "Song of Myself": he's gone beyond attachment and craving, since everything around him *is* his, or him. He desires nothing, really, except to be heard.

But in "Crossing Brooklyn Ferry" a speaker who is surely brother to that one lives in a paradoxical position. He is no longer dissolved in unity, no longer entirely boundless, though he can see beyond the ordinary limitation of space and time. He knows that his listeners await him, centuries in the future, and that he will not cease speaking as long as there are readers, as long as words inked on a page are understood to represent a heightened version of human speech, and someone believes that insight might be held in suspension in the music of finely tuned language, and that such a suspension might form a stay against time.

Or not a stay: not just a means of fixing a voice, as a recording does, but a means of preserving something of the presence from which that voice speaks, a presence that was human and has now gone on beyond that (though affable, confiding, hopeful), continuously available to us through the agency of a mere poem, holding out—apparently without end—a now and a now and a now—for those readers who will come, and stand in our places in the future.

IT NEVER OCCURRED TO ME to question, exactly, the circumstances William Blake had in mind when he wrote his famous visionary lines

> To see a World in a Grain of Sand
> And a Heaven in a Wild Flower
> Hold Infinity in the palm of your hand
> And Eternity in an hour.

I first read them in the 1960s, as a very young man, and I'm sure I saw them cited in texts concerned with the expansion of consciousness, a description or distillation of the sort of thing that might happen when a psychedelic substance opened the doors of perception. Blake, as far I know, had no need of chemical assistance; his dead brother's ghost and his own propensity to vision brought him to extraordinary vantages. He loved and honored sex. Who could forget the wonderful story of a neighbor coming to call and finding Mr. and Mrs. Blake, nude but for helmets, reading Milton aloud in the back garden?

Thus it seems not illegitimate to read these four lines as a description of heightened sexual congress, when perceptions of space and time seem to dilate, and it becomes difficult to tell earth from heaven.

I want to place one moment here, *one of the glories strung like beads,* a moment above the city, in suspension, one that might stand for Ethan and me, for what we made together, how we continue, and how we might be seen, by readers *of a generation,* or if I am lucky *of ever so many generations hence.* An hour, or hours, outside of time, and therefore contiguous with the past, the present, and the future, not because of what I write here but because that night was, always, unbounded.

We often met, because of our complex domestic arrangements, in hotels. On the night I'm thinking of it was an inexpensive, serviceable hotel just south of Midtown. Because the city had been swept, early that evening, by a blizzard, there were few other guests, and the clerk at the desk gave us a room on a high floor, twenty stories up, looking south. I was there first, getting things ready, and when Ethan arrived—that cold fresh aura of new snow all around his hair and collar—I had turned out the lamp, so that the only light in the room came from the generous snowfall that had silenced our city, downtown laid out before us in fine detail, though everywhere softened and rounded by mounds and drifts. We embraced, we looked out into the night with our arms around each other, and it was hours before either of our hands left the skin of the other. We were alone up there, entirely with one another, and our city, both intimate and immense, cold and breathtakingly lovely, lay at our feet, and the snow ensured that for all that night and well into the morning, neither of us would leave the room.

Blake says that God "does a Human Form Display/to those who Dwell in Realms of Day." I am grateful that Ethan is a fallible, thoroughly human, irreplaceable man, but I do believe that something of what is most true and most radiantly alive in the world is made visible to me through him, in his beauty and kindness, and in the ferocious sexual heat of him. And not just in "Realms of Day," but also in the chartless, snowy precincts of night.

---•••---

WHITMAN BUILT HIS POEM so that each section makes possible the one that follows it. The *hot wishes* of the "dark patches" section give way to a riff on the pleasures of proximity:

> *I was called by my nighest name by clear loud voices of young*
> *   men as they saw me approaching or passing,*
> *Felt their arms around my neck as I stood, or the negligent*
> *   leaning of their flesh against me as I sat,*
> *Saw many I loved in the street or ferry-boat, or public assembly,*
> *   yet never told them a word,*
> *Lived the same life with the rest . . .*

The speaker was a body among bodies, and loved the touch of them, and though he dwells in intimate relation, called by his *nighest name,* he never speaks his deepest feeling. Because his desire would not fit with their unself-conscious physicality? Because he is both one of them and apart, conscious that he plays a part in a pageant, that he is both participant in this moment in time and at once looking back on it from the vantage point of the future?

From that viewpoint the next section begins with a startlingly direct address to the reader, one that feels increasingly uncanny as it proceeds:

> *Closer yet I approach you;*
> *What thought you have of me, I had as much of you—I laid in*
> *   my stores in advance,*
> *I considered long and seriously of you before you were born.*

It's strange to think the poet draws nearer to us, through the agency of his poem, and stranger still to think that our relation is reciprocal, that our awareness of him exists in proportion to the concern he has previously extended to us—a proposition that seems a conundrum until one thinks that for Whitman the moments of the poem's generation and of its reception have fused. Now—as signaled by Whitman's shift to the present tense here—there is one continuous moment in which he reaches toward us as we turn to him. This fusion has made possible the wildly disruptive sentence the poet places next:

> *Who was to know what should come home to me?*
> *Who knows but I am enjoying this?*

It's the last thing I'd have imagined. The poem has worked to establish for its speaker a position in time unlike any we've known—or, if the greatest poems speak to us both from the hour of their composition and from an ongoing relationship with the reader, no one has ever quite articulated this. The poet has struggled here to name our commonalities, to position all of us along a grand historical line of those who cross and will cross the river, and out of his triumphant merger with the future, he—well, he enjoys himself. He delights in his position, loves finding us and being found by us. It is a pleasure, he discovers, to be some version of immortal, and this leads him to praise the world that is his, *my river and sun-set, and my scallop-edged waves of flood-tide.* He praises those who clasp him by the hand, and call him by his *nighest name,* in happy intimacy, and wonders at that *which fuses me into you now, and pours my meaning into you.*

At this moment, which to my knowledge has no equivalent in any other poem, save perhaps for the Bhagavad Gita, or the speech of the voice from the whirlwind in Job, the poet has created a vision of the world for us, a richly detailed painted scene, ferryboat, masts, clouds and passengers and haloed reflections in the current—and then simply pushed all that aside, seeming to step out from behind the curtain. He began with the plainest of statements asserting his presence, here and now: *Who knows but I am enjoying this?* And then:

> *What is more subtle than this . . .*
> *Which fuses me into you now, and pours my meaning into you?*

That is, something has been transmitted outside of, or beneath, or above, language. Poems are composed of nothing but language, so this isn't possible. But *We understand then do we not?* I believe him wholeheartedly when he writes, *What the study could not teach—what the preaching could not accomplish is accomplished, is it not?*

THE REST OF THE POEM is a glorious shout of encouragement to every element of the scene Whitman has drawn; the poet energetically participates in each bit of the action of his poem, praising the things of the world as "beautiful dumb ministers" who bring to us elements of our own souls, or *the* soul. The *you* and *I* that have dominated the stage resolve into a *we* fully enamored of earth, and the poem ends with a hymn to appearances, a cascade of praise for the world apprehended by the senses:

> *Appearances, now or henceforth, indicate what you are,*
> *You necessary film, continue to envelop the soul,*
> *About my body for me, and your body for you, be hung our divinest*
> *   aromas,*
> *Thrive, cities—bring your freight, bring your shows, ample and*
> *   sufficient rivers,*
> *Expand, being than which none else is perhaps more spiritual,*
> *Keep your places, objects than which none else is more lasting.*

You have waited, you always wait, you dumb, beautiful ministers,
We receive you with free sense at last, and are insatiate henceforward,
Not you any more shall be able to foil us, or withhold yourselves from
    us,
We use you, and do not cast you aside—we plant you permanently
    within us,
We fathom you not—we love you—there is perfection in you also,
You furnish your parts toward eternity,
Great or small, you furnish your parts toward the soul.

But in fact, no matter how apt this ending is in its enthusiasm, even its joyous humility (*we love you*), it is, in an odd way, after the fact. It's a beautiful, necessary downshift, a closure that eases us out of the poem, many lines after "Crossing Brooklyn Ferry" has performed its central work: a genuine, barely imaginable intervention in the nature of the real.

The great drama of the poem, by the time we come to those final passages, is over. It ended with the triumph of the questions that conclude the penultimate section, questions that assume their own answers:

We understand then do we not?
What I promis'd without mentioning it, have you not
    accepted?
What the study could not teach—what the preaching
    could not accomplish is accomplished, is it not?

These are paradoxical, impossible assertions: the *buds folded beneath speech* have flowered, and borne fruit: that which cannot be said has been not only said, but understood.

I knew, somewhere behind every word I have written about Walt Whitman, that I would arrive at this moment, which is the poet's greatest glory, and the exegete's inescapable defeat. The poem sails on into heaven, where no gloss or paraphrase or explanation can go.

The reader in me believes in words, the poet in what lies beyond them. I wrote every page of this book, in a sense, to lead to this one, where Whitman steps forward from the scene he has built onto the barest stage, and looks at us face to face, and where I step back from the stage I have built, and cease my fountain of appreciation and interpretation, and allow him to still my hand and my lips, and mark here my silence as his words accomplish what words cannot.

ACKNOWLEDGMENTS

———•••———

Portions of the text appeared, often in different versions, in *Conjunctions, Granta, The Sienese Shredder, Story Quarterly, The Virginia Quarterly Review,* and *Tiferet,* and in the anthologies *The Best American Essays 2012, The Pushcart Prize XXXIV: Best of the Small Presses, Who's Your Daddy: Gay Writers Celebrate Their Mentors and Forerunners,* and *The Inevitable: Contemporary Writers Confront Death.*

———•••———

THIS BOOK WOULD NOT have been possible without the work of many a scholar and biographer. I want in particular to acknowledge my debt to Paul Zweig's superb *Walt Whitman: The Making of the Poet,* published in 1984 and still the biography of choice. I'm also indebted to Charly Shively's *Calamus Lovers,* to Gary Schmidgall's edition of Whitman's selected poems, to conversations with Robert Hass and his excellent annotated edition of "Song of Myself," and to the scholars Michael Moon and my colleague Meredith McGill, a fountain of knowledge about the American nineteenth century. The librarians at the Library of Congress are devoted advocates for readers, and thoughtful guides to the treasures they preserve. The online Walt Whitman Archive, based at the University of Iowa, is a vast, brilliantly designed and organized resource.

My deep thanks to the editors whose requests for essays helped to shape this project, especially Sigrid Rausing and John Freeman, Ted Genoways, David Groff, Alex Dmitrov, and Bradford Morrow. Mesa Refuge in Point Reyes Station offered the exact environment needed to advance this project, and Tyler Meier and his staff at the University of Arizona later provided me with a necessary hermit's cave in which to complete it. I'm also deeply grateful to my friends Luis Caicedo, Michael Rogers, and John Daly Bruning for the gift of their remarkable Hudson Valley Cornell box of a house at crucial moments in my life and the life of this book.

Bill Clegg has been my friend and agent for more than twenty years now. He may be the most perceptive reader I know; this book would never have become itself without his critical insight and fundamental sympathy. Like my editor Jill Bialosky, he is one of poetry's true champions in our time. It's my very good fortune to work with them, as it is to have friends willing to read this book in earlier versions; both Paul Lisicky and Marie Howe brought their deep feeling intelligence to the text, and spurred me on.

Thanks too to Michael Taeckens for wonderful positive energy, to Drew Weitman for her kind and necessary persistence, to Janet McDonald for brilliant diligence, and to Carolyn Williams, Adam Fitzgerald, and Jason Schneiderman for love and support.

This book is for Ethan Fairbank.